Reflections of the Mole

A *Mole's-eye* view
of
Reality TV's smartest show!

By

Bill McDaniel, MD
Rear Admiral/USN/retired

Reflections of The Mole

An Intellect Publishing Book

Copyright 2007 by William James McDaniel

ISBN: 0-9729761-2-4

Cover design and artwork by Julie Sokolosky

All rights reserved
This book, or parts thereof, may not be reproduced in any form without permission. The scanning, uploading, and distribution of the book via the Internet or via any other means, including storage in any form of informational or retrieval system without the express written consent of the publisher, except for newspaper, magazine or other reviewers who wish to quite brief passages in connection with a review, is illegal and punishable by law. Your support of authors' rights is encouraged and appreciated.

First edition: November 2007

Intellect Publishing
P.O. Box 8219
Kirkland, WA 98034
www.IntellectPublishing.com
for enquiries:
info@IntellectPublishing.com

www.TheMoleBook.com

Printed in Canada

Acknowledgements

Geez. I think I have to go all the way back to grade school, or even before that, to properly thank folks who were responsible for my being on this TV show, thus being able to write this book. My sisters, who taught me the value of being able to divert suspicion away from myself in times of stress...toward them. Usually unsuccessful, but the attempts were made and clearly aided me in being able to eventually carry out this task. Playing cowboys and Indians as a kid with my friends...getting shot and pretending to be dead...only to rise up again and enter the fray. What a valuable trait to possess in doing this show! Learning the fine art of projecting abject terror and screaming in apparent severe pain when facing corporeal punishment at the hands of my parents...even when I was totally guilty of the infraction and had yet to actually get any real physical punishment. This was further wonderful training that stood me in good stead during the making of "The Mole II."

As I went along through life, I learned to wrestle...not that wrestling was of particular value to me during this quest. I just wanted to mention it; after all, wrestling paid my way through college at Oklahoma State. I think the intense sweating I had to do to pull weight made this physiological process somewhat easier to achieve for me than for the average person, thus allowing me to sweat on cue during the executions, which fooled at least one person on the show.

Having thousands of Navy and Marine Corps friends during my 32 years in the Navy taught me the phenomenal value of teamwork and friendship...traits that I had to consciously avoid to be a successful Mole. I think that just knowing how to accomplish teamwork so well from these incredible folks enabled me to develop the ability to do the opposite during my 13 week tenure as the Mole. I found this to be a formidable task, but finally fell back on my Dad's strong advice: "Son, no matter what the job is, do it to the best of your ability." So, while being the Mole and going against all that I had learned was difficult for me initially, knowing that this was indeed my job allowed me to apply this same philosophy to it…with some success.

As to the book itself, without my close friends (and I think they are, in spite of the fact that I jacked most of them around royally), the other players on "The Mole II," this book would not have happened. They played the game well…well, maybe not all that well, inasmuch as few until the final two figured out who was doing evil to them! But, they did come to play the game, and truly understood that it wasn't really life; it was a lark.

My most lovely wife, Shirley, has been my true honest broker and strongest supporter. Without her, and the fact that she chided me into applying for the show in the first place, it would not have happened."

Phil Jennings, author (*Train Wreck in a Small Town, Nam-A-Rama,* and *Goodbye, Mexico)* and friend of 47 years, also carefully read the book and made numerous helpful suggestions to its betterment. Phil is an outstanding award-winning author; while I wrote this book, I don't claim author status. Therefore I definitely listened to him!

Finally, John O'Melveny Woods, friend and publisher. John and his lovely fiancé Judy Bishop contributed immeasurably by encouraging me to continue writing, critiquing my efforts, designing the cover and lay-out of the book, and actually pushing it to printing. I cannot thank them enough for their support.

Bill McDaniel, MD

Reflections of the Mole

Reflections of The Mole

I

The Concept

A disclaimer is needed before I start this narrative. I make no attempt to accurately quote everyone to the word; this is not a photograph of our show, but an interpretative painting! Most quotes are as I remember them; while the meaning should be accurate, the exact wording might not be. Furthermore, when I indicate what others might have been thinking in situations, or how they might have reacted, I did not quiz them to determine if I was correct or not. After all, time changes everything, and their memories might be no better than mine anyway!

Perfecting the fine art of spreading innocent havoc and generally confusing the issue - that is a Mole's job! That was....**my** job! I had somehow managed, after a lifetime of honorable work and 32 years of service in our magnificent Navy, to become a competitor on one of the premier reality shows on television. Not only had I become a competitor, but I had been chosen to play the role of the spoiler, destined to make the other players' lives hell for 13 weeks of television! The Navy, I might add, did not prepare me for this role.

Inasmuch as you are reading this, you are most likely one of the people who watched "The Mole II" on ABC, and understand what I'm talking about. If on the other hand you aren't all that familiar about how this show works, let me try to explain. I have talked to many people who tuned in for a week or so, and switched to another show...usually "The American Idol," season one. "American Idol" was straight forward, fun, easy to understand. Just listen and enjoy. If you missed a week, you could pick right up. "The Mole," on the other hand, while fun as

Reflections of The Mole

well, required more involvement and fairly constant attention in order to really understand. (I say this from an adult viewpoint; I've talked with many 5-12 year olds who had absolutely no difficulty in understanding what was going on. They have more experience in playing convoluted games, I expect.)

Here is the general concept...as I understood it! There is a $1,000,000 pot to begin with, and the players are competing against each other for that money, with only one ultimate winner. They survive week-to-week by trying to identify the Mole on a weekly quiz, with the person scoring the lowest (or in event of a tie being the slowest to finish the quiz) being eliminated. The Mole's job is to remain unrecognized as such, while causing the players to lose games, with each loss subtracting money from the initial pot.

In our season there were 14 players on the show. As noted, it is an elimination show, with one person being 'executed' each week, until the only people left standing are the winner and the Mole. The Mole, if any good at all, has managed to subtly sabotage enough games that the producers save sufficient reserves to survive and produce another show later. If the Mole is no good at sabotage, the ultimate winner *could* get the entire possible pot of $1,000,000, (and the producers get the shaft for picking such a stupid person to play the Mole). The show lasts 13 weeks, always, regardless of whether or not someone might have managed to figure out who the Mole is...unless it is canceled by the network for low ratings or nudity or something. (Actually, I suppose nudity increases the ratings!) A quiz is given to all players each week...including the Mole... and every question is about the Mole. The questions are derived from questionnaires that we all had to fill out in applying for the show, our games, and our daily activities; thus we all know the scope of the information we have to find out about each other. (Is the Mole married? What kind of car does the Mole drive? Etc.) The person who gets the most answers wrong is **executed**, but usually given a reprieve and just allowed to go home…unless, of course, they were *really* obnoxious, in which case...

This process repeats itself weekly until the only people left are the two finalists and the Mole. A final 20 question quiz is given all three (inasmuch as the TV audience, and perhaps the finalists, are not quite sure who the Mole is yet), and the finalist who gets the most answers right is declared the winner of the total money won in the games (something less than $1,000,000, unless the Mole is really inept). After the winner is determined, the identity of the Mole is finally revealed, and that is the first time that anyone definitely knows who the Mole is. Simple enough?

Let me add some minor complications. We played 27 games over 13 weeks of television…plus a few little money makers that weren't really games. Each was worth from $10,000 to $100,000. As I have noted, the Mole's job is to sabotage selected games so that the described task was either not finished successfully, or not completed in the time limit allowed. Therefore, the money that might have accrued from winning is forever lost from the $1,000,000 pot that existed on the first day of play. The Mole, if good, manages to do this while not appearing to deliberately do it. Unless, of course, the Mole decides to be *very obvious* with his or her sabotage as a different kind of strategy. When someone *very obviously* sabotages a game, making everyone notice, the others tend to say to themselves, "Ah, that person is just *pretending* to be the Mole to throw us off. So we don't think they are really the Mole." Maybe. Of course, there is *always* the chance that the Mole is just clumsy and poor at subtly messing up a game. It is a judgment call for the other players. Is that saboteur the actual Mole, or someone pretending to be the Mole? Again, see, simple!

How does one become a Mole? Other than the obvious way those little creatures become one, of course. We all applied

Reflections of The Mole

for a show called, "The Mole II." As we went through the screening process to get selected, the producers selected one of us to be the Mole, but *who* was selected for that role was not known to any of the other players. We all knew one of us was to be selected; that was a basic part of the game. I was that person, hopefully unknown by anyone else.

So, all I had to do as the Mole was keep a low profile, spread uncertainty among the other players, while sometimes pretending to *be* the Mole (a favorite ploy among all the better players), but keep from doing something dumb (like being caught talking privately with the producers) that would definitively prove to any of the others that I was indeed the Mole. And, sabotage games occasionally to lose more money and save those producers from bankruptcy.

I'll start with my favorite day of subterfuge. We were only 4 days into filming. Anderson Cooper, the host, had gathered us together in a Swiss village square in Scoul, Switzerland, and tasked us with selecting 3 people, "two who have good taste in clothing, and one with no taste whatsoever." I easily fit the latter description and thus volunteered, my ploy being to assume some control over the damage to be done that day. Dorothy and Elavia tentatively volunteered as well, having good taste in abundance. (More on all the players in a while.) We were taken to an isolated yard and shown 10 ridiculous outfits, some a little outside the bounds of decent wear in public places. We then selected one of those outrageous costumes for each of the other players to wear. Donned thusly, they had to hike the length of this moderately sized Swiss village, find the train station, remain in said attire during a train ride completely across Switzerland, and make a final trek through downtown St. Moritz and into the lobby of a 5 star hotel. The costumes included: a bikini men's swim suit (clearly intended for Patrick, a city manager from New Jersey who demonstrated an unexpected streak of exhibitionism and the joy of being unfettered around a group of good looking women), a woman's corset and girdle (I suggested Al, a warehouse foreman from Long Island, whom I assume...without justification...did not ordinarily wear such things), a pink negligee (Bribs, a Texas A&M grad; no thought had to be given there), a bunny outfit, complete with big floppy ears (Darwin, a lawyer from New York City; it just looked like another day in the office), a woman's swimsuit vaguely suited for a hooker (Heather, a Texas girl who looked like the outfit suited her...very uncomfortably), a cow costume, complete with bell (Rob, who with his blonde spiky hair looked sort of...cute in that get up), and various other Tyrolian outfits for the other women, all somewhat more appropriate to the mountains of Switzerland. (Actually Rob's cow outfit fit in well, too.) Lisa's spangled dress with boa did not seem totally appropriate for an Assistant US Attorney, but did suit her real avocation, that of a beer seller in Comiskey Park.

Dorothy (a bass guitar player in an alternative rock band in New York City, and who worked hard at living up to her Chinese ancestry by being totally inscrutable at all times), Elavia (a public relations person who was the most suspicious acting person ever on almost *any* show), and I had turned down the chance to double the $20,000 to be made that day. All we would have had to do was wear sheer paper diapers, bibs, and pacifiers on the same journey. I was emphatic that no self-respecting Admiral would dare wear such an outfit! The girls were not too thrilled at traversing Switzerland with most body parts on view, so they backed my decision. (Both were into the mode of never quite telling the others any more truth than absolutely necessary, and each claimed later to have made the decision to not wear the diapers, reducing the suspicion I might have incurred from the others if I had been noted as the only reticent one.) Once the outfits were selected and donned, the players were instructed to find their way to the railway station for a 4:35 PM train to St. Moritz; if all players were not on board, *no* money would be earned that day. All were present and accounted for by about 3:00 PM, except for one couple, Bribs (a graphic designer) and Ali (a recent Navy nurse who was now thinking of trying acting as a career).

Lisa and I were delegated to find the errant twosome, truants that they were. We set off to search the city, with me being ever vigilant for opportunities to screw the game up and lose more money, or at least confuse everyone. As noted, all 13 players had to be on the 4:35 PM train en route to Zurich, or the pot would lose a potential $40,000. Everyone was concerned about the possibility of Bribs and Ali being offered an exemption from being eliminated (executed) in the next quiz, just for deliberately missing the train and thus costing the pot the money that would have been earned by the day's activities. Elavia had capitalized on a similar offer for the first execution. No one at any time wanted anyone else to get an exemption, thus increasing the chances of all the others for being executed. The only person you wanted to have an exemption, desperately, was yourself!

As Lisa and I began our search, I initially started wandering off in the wrong direction, deviating from the course we all had taken when coming through town. I'm elderly, after all, and can't reliably be expected to remember where I am at any given moment. Lisa, however, was quick to point out to me that we were going the wrong way, and to persist in that diversion might have caused her to harbor suspicions about my motives. As an Assistant US Attorney, she is used to ferreting out and exposing big time criminals, which description the Mole certainly matched in everyone's eyes. (Events of the next week were certain to make her look back on my wandering ways with suspicion, and with deep regret that she had not given them more thought!) So, off we went, retracing our steps.

While I looked fairly normal, due to my righteous refusal to wear a sheer diaper, Lisa did not, having to wear the dress picked by the three of us…for her exclusively. However, she did not look nearly as odd as did Bribs when we saw him and Ali standing in the middle of a street outside of a bar. Bribs was standing casually in the street in his pink negligee, looking totally relaxed. (I have never actually been to Texas A&M, you understand, but they must be very secure in their sexual identification there, because Bribs wasn't bothered by his attire in the least!) Ali was in a much cuter outfit, looking great.

Lisa: "Where have you two been?! Everyone has been at the train station for a couple of hours, and the train is due to leave in 45 minutes. They are getting frantic...and cold!" (Especially Patrick, in his Speedo briefs.)

Bribs and Ali replied, "We ducked into the bar to go to the bathroom and get directions to the train station (about 5 minutes away), and some of the locals bought us some drinks." (I never did get any assurance as to which of the two the men in the bar were most interested in.)

Bribs went on, "Heck, this might be the only time I get to Switzerland; we have plenty of time, and I'm not going to pass up the opportunity to enjoy this experience to the fullest! If I had any money, we would have another round."

Before Lisa could turn and lead us back to the train station, I said, "Shoot, we have 45 minutes before the train; I've got some money. We have time for one more round!" As noted before, Lisa doubles on the weekends as a beer salesman in the stands at Comiskey Park in Chicago; she does enjoy her beer. After only a brief fight with her conscience (because, after all, the others were standing shivering in the cold at the station, deeply concerned as to whether or not we would be able to find and return Bribs and Ali), Lisa agreed. "One quick round!"

Back into the bar we ventured, where Bribs and Ali had already achieved a status of sorts. The locals gave us a rousing cheer and ogled one of the two. Bribs winked and they all cheered again. The bartender came over, knowing that Bribs had no pockets, and no obvious place to carry his money...at least, none that he would accept bills from. I pulled out some Swiss francs and bought a round, and we all chatted with great animation. Bribs and Ali were high with excitement; after all, they had already received lots of attention and were enjoying themselves thoroughly. Lisa again brought up the fact that the others were standing in the cold at the station, worried sick. She explained to the two truants that the others were afraid that Bribs and Ali might have been offered an exemption to miss the train, thus costing the group all the money they had been trying to earn by wearing such outlandish costumes across Switzerland on a train (causing deep confusion among the normally staid Swiss, and reaffirming their opinion of the Americans as a deeply disturbed people). Ali was a little offended by the group thinking she might accept an exemption (she would have, of course, if one had been offered), and voiced some indignation. It took minimal effort on my part to subtly encourage her to play that up a little to pay them back, an idea she immediately adopted as her own.

Meanwhile, time was passing. Unseen by the others, I signaled the bartender for another round. When he came over with the beers, we all exclaimed, "We don't have time for this! We need to get to the station!" Having said that, we were confronted with the reality of 4 cold beers sitting in front of us. Consulting our watches, we all agreed that if we just drank quickly, we could make it to the train station with whole minutes to spare, so we did. I chose not to signal for a 3rd round; one of the other 3 might have asked the bartender why he kept bringing more rounds to us.

We dashed out after sucking down that good German beer and made our way the few blocks to the station. There, above us on the platform as we came up the walk, were 9 angry folk. "Where have you all been?! The train is due to leave in about 3 minutes!"

Ali put her hands on her very shapely hips, stared up at the assembled players, and announced, "I'm sorry to tell you that

Bribs and I have been offered an exemption to miss the train. The only reason we came to tell you this was because Bill and Lisa found us and made us come back!" (I enjoy being a hero.)

The group was incredulous. Darwin, looking ever so lawyerly in his bunny costume (if you, like I do, think that lawyers are terribly funny and somewhat demented anyway), tore off the head and ears in disgust and turned away, just as Bribs and Ali started laughing and shouted, "You're taking this too seriously! We're just trying to psych you out!" We then boarded, just as the train was slowly pulling out. (We were later fined $2000 for Darwin's partial disrobing. Darn the luck. I hated that.)

Then came a scene I will always revere. Al, a foreman from a warehouse on Long Island, was standing in his girdle and corset, nose to nose with a negligee-clad Bribs, arguing and shouting about Brib's actions, while Darwin had a look of infinite disgust on his bunny-eared head. Meanwhile, the train was going about 80 mph across Switzerland, slowing down for towns where incredulous townsmen stared into the coach at this most ridiculous scene. It was priceless. Myra (in her cute Swiss costume), Patrick (in his bikini swimsuit), and I (in my normal, very innocent looking street clothes) sat back in a corner laughing at the spectacle. It was truly a unique sight!

The day ended with us arriving in St. Moritz, where we had to make our way from the train station to a 5 star hotel, still dressed in mufti. En route, Dorothy apparently got ill and had difficulty walking up the hill to the hotel. Content with my efforts thus far to sabotage the group's financial and psychological well-being, I assisted her up the hill and thus assured that we would arrive at the hotel under the time limit allowed. No sense in being hoggish with my sabotaging efforts, after all. Someone might get suspicious! (Part of the game strategy, however, was to point out to the others that Dorothy was...perhaps...trying to delay us past the time allowed, thus costing all the money accrued that day. You must never pass up an opportunity to cast suspicion elsewhere, especially when you know that person is not the Mole!)

I do wish the cameras had focused on the expressions of the residents of the hotel as we entered the lobby, however. It is very hard to get the unflappable Swiss to react to anything, but there were numerous raised eyebrows and small smiles around the lobby as we made our entrance. Sort of the American equivalent of them shouting, "Who the hell are you crazy folks, anyway?!" (Striving to prevent more stories of 'ugly Americans,' Myra and I chatted in German, loudly, as we entered. After all, European countries are accustomed to being invaded by weirdly dressed Germans.)

We were all ushered to our rooms and given strict orders not touch the mini-bars. Man, it had been a tough day of sabotage! Besides that, the beers we had consumed at the bar earlier in the day had definitely passed on through. So, Bribs and I looked at each other and said, "What the hell?! Are they going to kick us off the show?" Besides that, I knew if we were caught it would only be a $10,000 fine or so, and it surely wasn't coming out of my pocket! So, we opened the mini-bar, took several beers out, and a pile of Swiss francs in. A fair exchange by any measure.

As I sat there looking out the window at the beautiful lake below us, and the glacier covered mountains opposite us, I started musing. How did I wind up here? After all, I'm a country boy from Oklahoma who eventually was lucky enough to make it through medical school and a residency. Then, off to the Navy, Viet Nam, and a career, where again I was exceedingly lucky and made the rank of Rear Admiral. (For those of you who don't know, and that is most of you, there are 4 ranks of being an Admiral. Both one and two star Admirals are Rear Admirals. No Freudian or snide remarks, please. Three star Admirals are Vice Admirals, and 4 stars are simply Admirals. We are all called

Admiral when addressed, but those in the know definitely know how many stars each of us have!)

Here's how I got started.

II

Background

The events in this narrative are true, as best I remember. Some I don't remember at all, so I have to go only on hearsay. Most of them were events I observed, or was part of, but may be colored by the fact that they were events recorded in a very young mind, and might just possibly be not the truth as an outside observer might interpret it. If you read this carefully, and give it some thought, you will see the seeds that led, many years later, to the producers recognizing me as an ideal mole...and that almost ended my marriage!

February 26, 1943. A world at war. I was unaware. I was lying on a small bed on a farm near Muskogee, Oklahoma; actually, I'm not sure what position I was in, inasmuch as I was still inside my mother's womb. I was trying to get out; I had two sisters who needed supervision. I was a big kid, and my Mom wasn't. So, it was one heck of a trip! The old country doc, Dr. Kupka, was patiently urging Mom to push. Mom was a country woman, mother of 3 already (one sister had died), and the oldest of 12. She had married at age 14, and when I tried to come along, she was only 24. She was a tough lady, and, believe me, she was pushing! In retrospect, I was probably too big to have been born, and should have just stayed in place. However, I somehow was squeezed out after she had been in labor for a long, long time. Sort of like play dough. My head was molded in a very elongated fashion, and my sisters noted that there was a definite point on top. I think I remember their critique. At that moment I was probably 4 or 5 inches taller than the average country kid—a condition I would never get to repeat again. My sisters wanted to paint the top of my head black like our dog's nose, and name me after him. They did the latter. Had they been aware of moles, I expect that moment would have defined my later life. But, I was named after Bill the Dog, not Bill the Mole. The doctor looked closely at my deformed head, and informed my mother that it was unlikely that I would ever be normal. My sisters and Mom have since repeatedly noted that he was an unusually smart doctor.

In spite of that tight beginning, I managed to progress somewhat normally, I suspect. Inasmuch as my folks had only raised three girls, they were not sure what 'normal' for a boy was, which probably prevented me from being required to get lots of psychological help early on. (Actually, that's not so. My Dad did not have the money for that kind of help, and did not believe in it, anyway. His opinion was that there are few psychological disorders that will not respond to loving parents, hard work, and an occasional guiding thump on the butt. Looking back, I might have preferred the occasional therapy session, myself. Might have prevented the role I found myself playing in Switzerland!)

I remember growing up on the farm when quite small, though how young I was when I initially became aware of being me, I'm not sure. I'm convinced, however, that I was older than was appreciated. I vaguely remember wearing diapers. I did not like them; not that I liked anything better, I just liked having no clothes on at all. (That changed when I got to Switzerland, or shortly before then.) Mom progressed me rather rapidly to shorts; if you have to wash anyway, shorts are easier than diapers. And more manly! I did not like shorts, either, and at the earliest opportunity each day would divest myself of them. We had a hog pond about 100 yards from the house, and I would throw the shorts in the pond when they were dirty, which was seldom more than a few minutes from the time Mom put them on me. Mom had little trouble with fishing them out, inasmuch as I could not throw them over about 14 inches from the edge. While

I considered myself almost a full fledged man, there were still some problems with execution of certain tasks.

When I was around 18 months old or so I had already started extensive explorations of the farm, forays which were to continue all of my life. (Eventually leading to this place in Switzerland, where I was definitely in an odd place!) However, my parents were not assured that I was quite mature enough to go wandering about the place by myself, in spite of my gender and manliness. Besides that, for some reason I walked in my sleep as a very young person. (I expect it was to get away from the girls; they surely talked a lot, even then, when I would have preferred to have been the one talking, if I only had a vocabulary.) One night Mom awakened to find my bed unoccupied, and they emptied the house to find me. I was finally located, sleeping soundly under the truck. So, they decided to build a fence around the yard. It started out as a hog wire fence, about 4 feet high, some 2 feet above my head. That was no challenge at all. I could be over it from a standing start about as quickly as if I had just walked over to the other side. Dad took down that fence and built a considerably larger one, about 6 feet tall. I could still climb up it, but took the easy route down by simply getting to the top, leaning over, and falling down the far side. Those multiple landings on my head might have been harbingers of my later life as a Mole, indicating a determination to achieve my goals, regardless of the stupidity involved in getting there. Finally, my folks realized that short of razor wire and severe electrical shocks, I was going to travel! The fences came down, and I continued my perambulations.

My Dad was a quiet man, hard working, who loved his family fiercely. However, he stated again and again that he could not tolerate "a spoiled boy!" Spoiled girls, fine. That was the way of nature. Boys? Nope. No spoiling. So, from some quite early age Dad and Mom were kept busy trying not to spoil me. I think I averaged 2 spankings a day for about 12 years. I was proud of that, because I knew that only receiving 2 spankings per day meant that I had gotten away with lots of things! Even as a youth in dirty shorts I was quite proud of my abilities to cast suspicion elsewhere for my ill begotten deeds.

Quite early on I decided that as a boy, I should not take orders from a girl. I don't remember this as a *conscious* decision, you understand, but it clearly was a basic tenet in my young life. My sisters, Ruth and Gertha, were 8 and 4 years older than me, respectively. Both felt that they should be able to tell me to do....something. Anything! They were real old, and I wasn't. (That situation still exists, come to think of it.) I simply did not take to it. That resulted in fights throughout our childhood. More on that later.

All through those early years, pre-five or so, my memories of life on the farm are sort of blurred, due, no doubt, to the severe beatings about the head and shoulders I received from my sisters. I'm quite sure all that I remember is not so, but, to my mind, it was. So, it is. (Convincing myself and others that things that may not be actually true...but which I fervently believed.... were indeed to became a talent that would directly lead to my role in Switzerland, I do believe.) We did not have much money; in fact, we were downright poor, though I was unaware of it during those years. After all, we lived on a farm. We grew most of our food, both plant and animal. I did not know about the animal part for a long time. It was somewhat disconcerting raising cows and pigs as pets, only to have them suddenly disappear. "They must have jumped the fence." I thought we must have had the most athletic livestock in history, or Dad just couldn't build a fence worth a darn. Maybe he built fences with holes. I helped him a lot, and never observed a hole big enough for something to escape through. However, our animals disappeared, one by one, and we somehow always had meat on the table. It took me years to figure out a possible connection, and longer for my folks to admit it. They were, after all, guilty of pet cannibalism, not a proud admission to make even to an adult son. I still eat bacon voraciously, but manage to do it with occasional pangs of guilt. I'm only glad our dog population remained stable throughout my childhood.

The animals I was aware that we ate, and for which I was thankful, were chickens. Mean things. Those of you who have not had the opportunity to be around chickens on the loose might doubt this. If so, you are mistaken. We had a rooster that seemed to hate me, and in fact, stalked me. I was scared of him, and would avoid him when possible. Even our dogs, Rain and Bill, were afraid of that rooster. (My name is Bill, by the way, and as noted, Bill the dog predated me by several years. I was proud to be his namesake, though he was faster, and, according to my sisters, smarter.) One day I was headed across the yard, and must have transgressed on the rooster's territory. He flew at me, sinking his feet and claws into my chest, and started flogging and pecking. If you don't understand flogging, it is the rooster hanging on tightly and flapping his wings vigorously, beating the devil out of me! I was screaming bloody murder, and suddenly the rooster was gone. Dad had grabbed the rooster by the head and had torn him off me. Then, with a motion of his arm like he was cranking an old-fashioned car, he effected a separation of the rooster's head from his body. That rooster still ran around the yard trying to find me, or perhaps some chicken, trying to have one last sit-to before he found himself dead. That was one tough rooster, but he tasted great! I never mastered the art of popping the head off a chicken; I think that is a dying art—no pun intended. Anyway, I knew that when those chickens disappeared from the chicken coop they would soon appear on our table, because my sisters and I had to pull the feathers off them after they were dead and had been dipped in hot water. I have always liked chickens—fried.

Our chicken house had an interesting history. It was the first building built on the farm, after Dad had bought it in 1941.

Mom, Dad, Ruth and Gertha lived in the chicken house while they were building the house I was born in. (I always told my older sisters that while they got to live in a chicken house, Dad thought enough of me to build a regular house!) I don't know if they had chickens then or not, though I expect that they did not let that rooster live with them. I know that a snake almost ate one of my sisters in that chicken house during that time; probably thought she was a big chicken egg. I could have told that snake his meal would have been unsatisfactory; he would just have gotten indigestion.

When I was 3 or 4 years old, something was getting into the chicken house every couple of nights and eating the eggs and an occasional chicken. Dad was not the kind of farmer to take that lightly, and went about trying to find out what was doing this. One night when he was asleep, he was awakened by the sound of the chickens obviously in a state of agitation. He grabbed his 12 gauge double-barreled shotgun and ran out to the chicken house. The door to the house was a regular sized door, but had a square hole cut into the bottom big enough for chickens to go in and out of. Dad did not want to let whatever was in the house out, so bent over with his flashlight and gun stuck through the hole, trying to see the offending animal. Now, this was winter, and Dad wore those old red long-handled underwear with a flap on the bottom. The flap was seldom buttoned, inasmuch as red underwear was not worn around polite company anyway, and when the flap needed to be unbuttoned, it needed to be unbuttoned fast! So, it was open—which turned out to be critical in this instance. As he bent over, gun and flashlight both pointed through the door, Bill (the dog) sauntered up, curious as to what was going on. He was a big German Shepard. Inasmuch as he could not see in the door that Dad had blocked, he did the next most obvious thing; he stuck his very cold nose where dogs tend to do—on Dad's butt. Dad jumped, yelled, and discharged both barrels of the shotgun. The fox in the hen house wasn't harmed;

Reflections of The Mole

in fact, it darted out under the cover of a storm of flying chicken feathers, and wasn't seen again. Dead chickens everywhere, as well as scrambled eggs. Dad was a quiet man, and did not say a word; we just picked feathers off the chickens, and ate well for a long time. For some time after that Dad buttoned his flap, however. (In later years, Dad denied that this had happened. One of us became forgetful, I do believe. I sincerely hope it happened, though if it didn't, it is a good enough story to warrant being the truth, so I will maintain that it happened as written.)

So, this was my beginning, and might begin to explain how I found myself sitting in a hotel room in Switzerland many years later, sipping illegal beers with Bribs, contemplating my next act of deception.

III

Getting There

After a great career in the Navy, working initially as an orthopedic surgeon, then becoming an Admiral and working on large staffs and as a hospital administrator, I finally retired from that good life on 1 January 1997. For several years I kicked around, not working full time, instead drifting into a role as a 'consultant.' I wasn't even sure exactly was a consultant was, frankly! Depends on who you ask, I guess. But, it seemed to me that a consultant could be hired as a temporary expert on a project, at exorbitant daily fees, but was a person whose advice could be followed or ignored at the will of the person doing the hiring. All the while the hiring person could be shown as "doing something!" While not really having to do anything. So, not really understanding what a consultant was, I figured I knew a lot about many things, and might qualify. So, I became one, and have been ignored and well paid since that time.

Upon retiring from the Navy, I chose not to go to work full time because Dave Shultz, former world and Olympic wrestling champion, and a friend, was shot to death by John duPont. Dave was only 34, was at the top of his game, and was universally liked and revered by all who knew him. Then, in an instant, an idiot snuffed out that flame, leaving Nancy, his wife, and two children. Dave really could have gone on to do most anything he desired. He was a hero throughout the world of wrestling, both here and abroad. He would certainly have made another Olympic team, and I could see him as a senior...and a most ethical and respected...future figure in national and international amateur wrestling. And this idiot killed him? Why? Because he was there. He didn't get to watch his children

Reflections of The Mole

grow up, teach them wrestling, and grow old and content with Nancy. I sat in disbelief watching this play out on television, and decided at that moment in time I was going to stop working full time and partake of those things I had always wanted to do. Dave didn't get to. Therefore I did so, somewhat to my wife's and family's distress, I think. (And, frankly, in retrospect, somewhat to mine, unfortunately. I think I had lots to offer, and chose not to offer it. I liked leading, and was good at it. I should have sought another position from whence to lead.)

However, be that as it may, I became a consultant and starting doing some things in life I really wanted to do, like hiking the 2174 mile Appalachian Trail that stretches along the top (and I do meant the top!) of the Appalachian Chain from Springer Mountain, Georgia, to Mt. Katahdin, Maine. Well, at least I started the AT! After only 130 miles or so, I realized that one of my feet was ideally suited for being a consultant, but not so suited for walking. So, I got off the trail and had a friendly orthopedic surgeon reconfigure my foot into walking, vice sitting, mode. (This was a procedure that I had actually done many times on folks, though I usually reconfigured the offending foot for shorter walks. I'm not sure what my friend, Dr. Marty Deafenbaugh, had to add to my foot to allow me to walk thousands of miles, and don't want to know. The operating room personnel asked me if I would like for them to position mirrors so that I could observe the bloody butchering of my extremity? Are you nuts?! I didn't even look that closely when I used to do it to others! All I wanted were drugs and an immediate awakening knowing my bodily parts had been zipped closed and that nothing that was supposed to be on the inside was still hanging out!)

I finally got back on the trail a couple of years later, having had my days of leisure interrupted by consulting forays several times during those years. I'm not really going to go into the initial 1300 mile walk, except to say that Bill Bryson made the trail sound entirely too easy. It was one of the toughest things, mentally and physically, that I have ever done. However, after only a few weeks of devastating depression and suicidal ideation...and hypothermia and starvation and terminal dirtiness, only to mention a few positives...I finally got in the best shape of my life and hiked on. (The dirtiness is the easiest aspect to get used to. Heavy sweating while carrying a 50 pound pack, going up and down steep mountains, and then being unable to wash up at the end of the day, mainly because if you take a bath in the only stream around all the other hikers will pummel you to death, and all the fish downstream will die of some horrible toxic death...the resultant stench soon smells quite normal to the stinkee. I watched for several days once as six turkey buzzards, who love dead things like I love ice cream, circled lazily above me as I walked, always keeping pace with me. What were they doing? Finally, someone explained to me that they had a great sense of smell, and most likely I just confused them. They were unaccustomed to something that smelled as bad as I did continuing to move, and were just waiting for me to lie down and be as dead as I smelled. I took care after that to not take naps in the open.)

During the times I was not hiking my wife and I would watch minimal television. I have never been a big TV fan; I like to 'do' rather than watch someone else 'do.' However, my wife became a fan of a couple of the original reality shows, "Real World" and "Road Rules," and watched them late at night for years. I would idly watch over her shoulder, but couldn't get too engrossed in the former because it was too much like growing up with 4 sisters and raising 3 daughters. Been there, done that, and while I would not object to again being the youth involved, would prefer not to do that again, if possible. So, watching Lindsay (whom I met once in Aspen), Trish, Pauline, Abrahms, Daniel, and others attempt to grow up and exposing all those embarrassing aspects of themselves while growing out of them did not especially appeal to me, the challenges the "Road Rules" contestants faced did appeal to me. OK, I understand that they were as immature as all people that age are, groping to find themselves (at least this is the reason I used to give my dates), but they *did things*. They weren't just...emoting. (While I understand that emoting is a young person specialty, and the person who gets the most folks involved in their particular emoting is declared the winner, I still think the rest of us should not have to undergo it a second time. My own emoting was embarrassing enough.) Anyway, I would observe the crazy things the contestants would do, and repeatedly stated (many times, my wife notes) that if there were ever a "Road Rules for Seniors," I would like to do it.

So, on about 1 March 2001, my wife called me to the television one fateful day. ABC was advertising for participants on its second season of "The Mole." Now, we had watched the first season, and enjoyed it thoroughly. While never guessing the identity of the first mole, Kathryn Price, a female lawyer from Chicago, I loved several things about the show. (Who would have guessed that a lawyer...from Chicago...could be sneaky, underhanded, and back-stabbing? Just went against the grain, somehow.) I loved the fact, first, that personality and competence were not automatic disqualifiers. You could not be voted off because no one liked you. I noted that at least one of the contestants on the first "Mole" show benefited from that exclusion! If you were too gifted physically, you were not automatically gone because you represented a threat to the others. (Unlike "Survivor.") Also, unlike "Survivor," being cute and female (both somewhat beyond my capabilities) did not automatically mean you got to stay around for quite a while regardless of other qualifications. "The Mole" actually required thinking and observation...and lots of luck...to stick around until the next week. And, like the other shows, being successful on "The Mole" depended a tremendous amount on your ability to coordinate and cooperate with folks you could not trust for a moment...just like real life! All in all, being on a show where all I had to be from week to week was smarter...or luckier...than only one other person each week appealed to me. I have always felt smarter than at least one person in my group, and if not smarter, at least luckier. So, when ABC advertised for players on its second season, it found in me a somewhat reluctant applicant.

Why reluctant? Well, after downloading the questionnaire from the web site, I found lots of questions I did not know how to answer. 'What's your favorite movie of all time? Favorite book? Favorite song? First girlfriend? (Did she have to like me in return? That would sharply limit the number I had to consider.) First kiss? (Do relatives count? Mom, Grandma, really good looking cousins?) First car? (Did it have to run when I had it?) Most innovative thing I have ever done? (Probably involved some story I made up to get a date in college, but I didn't want to talk about it.) The second most innovative thing? (Geez, she wouldn't fall for it twice!)' Lots of hard questions. After reading them over, I chose not to fill out the questionnaire; shoot, I didn't know the answers! So, my wife, Shirley, answered most of them for me in a manner that might make my application stand out from thousands of others, in her attempt to have me gone for the summer! ("You *should* have read ......, and if you had, you would have liked it and declared it your favorite book." OK.) So, we finally got the application filled out....only to come to the fine print at the end of the questionnaire about doing a 3-5 minute video! I don't do videos! (I actually did not have a flat thing about not doing videos; it's just that doing videos involved innovative thinking and perhaps a talent for acting, neither of which I could lay claim to in abundance.) So, I stuck the answered questionnaire in my suitcase and left for Florida to go kayaking in the Everglades. That was a lot better than doing a video.

Reflections of The Mole

My brother-in-law, Blair, and I kayak for a week every spring break somewhere in Florida. We are never overrun by comely coeds in non-existent bikinis; the alligators and mosquitoes in the Everglades seem to discourage them. That spring break Blair wanted to cut the kayaking a couple of days short...probably because he had hit a bridge with his canoe and broke it in half, sharply limiting his ability to keep up with me. So, we came back to Orlando. On the last possible day that an application to "The Mole" could be postmarked, he suddenly suggested that we make videos for both the next "Survivor" and "The Mole." Not having time enough to worry about having to be innovative inspired me, so I agreed.

Initially we took the kayaks out to a river and tried to make videos, only to find out that a howling wind blowing directly into the mike of a camera makes any words spoken from several feet out in the river...no matter how witty they really were...unintelligible. Clever feats done in a kayak (my 180 degree roll is my specialty) go unrewarded when the only sound on the sound track resembles one of the many Florida hurricanes.

So, with only hours before the post office closed, we returned to town and visited a costume store. I chose a Sherlock Holmes outfit...double cloak, two billed hat (so it could not be determined if the clever detective was coming or going?), large magnifying glass (could Sherlock have been near-sighted?), and large pipe. I tried to light the pipe and almost ended the video attempt immediately. You should not try to light plastic pipes. I sat down on a stump, Blair stuck the video camera in my face, and I B.S.'d for 3 minutes or so. No script and no foreknowledge of what I was going to say. Careful planning always pays dividends.

I talked about growing up on the farm in Oklahoma, stealthily creeping up on unsuspecting birds and squirrels in the early mornings, and watching my older sisters make out in the car when arriving home from their dates...at least until the windows fogged up. I was demonstrating (I think) to the viewers of the video my ability to be sneaky and sleuth about, capabilities I figured one should demonstrate if one wanted to be on a sneaky show like "The Mole." (My sisters did react somewhat negatively when I inadvertently stated in the video that it took me years to realize that one should not attempt to drive with one's feet on the steering wheel, a physical feat I claimed to have observed in my late night forays observing them and their dates. I admitted to them that I might have embellished that part of the video; after all, the windows got foggy so fast that I could not really be sure what I was seeing in the later stages of their dating rituals.) I concluded the video by noting that today I'm a physician, a person who can take a very few facts, lots of assumptions and maybes, and convince others that I emphatically know what I am talking about. No mean feat, that.

We stuck the video in the mail with whole minutes to spare; I included the questionnaire with all of Shirley's answers.

Three weeks later I had returned from the dangerous shores of Florida. (Well, actually I never went to Daytona, but could have.) Shirley and I were sitting relaxing when the phone rang.

"Bill, this is Patti from "The Mole." We liked your video (apparently they had low standards at that point) and would like for you to do another one."

Wow! So began the process of being selected for the show. First came a secrecy vow; immense penalties would accrue immediately if we ever told anyone else that I had heard from the show. (Of course, up until this point we had only told…oh, maybe a thousand close friends and family that I was applying. Suddenly we went silent. "The show? What show? Me, apply for something? I'm retired, and tired. I sit and rock." There remained a slim chance that some of the more suspicious of our friends suspected something, though my family seemed to accept my disclaimers as fact...having to do with the rest of my weird life, I suspect.)

We underwent multiple iterations of phone calls, phone interviews, etc. One of the wilder aspects of all this involved the references I put down on my original application. Now, you like to count as references the most impressive people you know...or, at least I do. Shoot, why know them, otherwise? So, I had put down people like the Navy Surgeon General, the Chief of Naval Operations (who, as the title would imply, runs the Navy), and others of similar stature, never dreaming that they would actually be contacted. What if I had put down my closest friend Colin Powell? (Well, I met him once.) I got a call from the Surgeon General's office, asking if it was OK for the boss to talk to an unnamed company regarding my application? I was quite surprised, but told them that was OK. I actually got a call a day or two later from a somewhat confused Surgeon General. "What the hell are you applying for? That was one of the longest...and the wildest...reference calls I have ever received! They asked me questions about you for a ridiculously long time! I came close to telling them it was all a mistake and I just didn't know you!" I had similar input from the other 4 references on my list, all of whom were regretting giving me their phone numbers by that point.

In addition, the production company ran a security check on me that should be the envy of the CIA. Someone went door-to-door to many of my 50 or so neighbors asking questions about me. "Does he party all the time? Is he in debt? Does he appear to be a deadbeat? Do you ever see his wife, and does she appear bruised at times? Does he work on old cars in his driveway and clutter up the neighborhood? Does he keep cows or other livestock in his home?" I started getting phone calls from my neighbors. "Hey, Bill! Someone from a TV show was here asking wild and wacky questions about you today. Don't worry;

we lied for you! By the way, congratulations on being chosen for "Survivor!"'"

Ah, the wrong show! That's OK. Looking back on my contract, which had a penalty of $10,000,000.00 if I told anyone I was being considered for "The Mole," made me realize that while I couldn't say anything, under penalty of undue financial hardship (assuming that a lifelong bankruptcy could be considered as such), *they* could be as obvious as they chose. The only saving grace was that all my neighbors, along with most of America, did not understand "The Mole," and therefore watched only "Survivor," which is a simple show with complex people. So, since that was the only show they understood, it had to be the one investigating me. Regardless, the investigation was quite impressive. I do applaud the reality shows for their diligence, though I wonder at times how some of the folks I've observed are chosen---if they were the sanest of those screened.

I got a plane ticket in the mail for a flight to Los Angeles, again with an admonition for me to not reveal my destination to anyone for any reason. I told my wife I had to suddenly go to South America on a drug deal, and left. Upon arrival in LA, I was blindfolded at the airport (so much for being unobtrusive and invisible) and led to a waiting car. We drove for a while; I tried to keep track of the turns and guess the direction we were going in, until I realized that I didn't even know where we *started*, so therefore would not know where we ended up, even if I could keep track of a wildly careening car on an LA freeway. All that blind-folded tracking of one's progress sounds a lot easier when you read about it in spy novels.

Once we arrived at the hotel, with blindfold still in place I was led to a room and locked in. My phone was disconnected. I was told not to leave the room for any reason. (I was curious. If I left the room for **no** reason, could I go?) The first thing I was asked to do was fill out a 952 question Minnesota Multiphasic Personality Inventory (MMPI) test. This is a standard test given to try to ferret out personality disorders, and is well known in medical and psychology circles. I've taken it many times, and know all the correct answers, so was not worried. Then began a fascinating series of interviews and games. The producers interviewed us all. I was told that 95 people had been flown in for these trials, though we were never allowed to see or talk to each other. (Knowing the producers, I strongly suspect that the "95" figure was very likely a made-up number; they enjoyed keeping us in the dark as much as possible.) Every time I was taken from the room for an interview, I was blindfolded. It got to the point that I was uncomfortable walking with my eyes open. I would be taken to an empty room and allowed to sit for an hour or so. Was this part of the test? Were my powers of observation being tested? Should I know everything about the room I was in if asked? So, I memorized everything about every room I was left in. How many chairs, where they were located, how many pencils, what the pattern on the walls was…everything! It's astounding how much there is to see in an empty room if you look hard enough. I was never asked anything about those rooms, and was left with a cluttered up brain for days. They were just getting us into position for our interviews and the games they made up on the spur of the moment.

The interviews with the producers were fun. First, they just seemed to want to get to know you, and would ask general questions and let you answer at length. In my first interview with them, I thought there was a chance I could shortcut the entire process.

"Gentlemen, let me tell you something that might disqualify me. I watched last season's show, and there are some things I won't do. I'm a retired Admiral and have a wife and family who have certain expectations of me. (Not a lot, understand, but there are limits.) So, there is a good chance you will ask me to do something that I think might be embarrassing to the Navy or my family. I will not knowingly do that. So, if that invalidates my application to a reality show, you should know now so we can all save some time and effort."

They looked at each other and grinned. "No, Bill, that's not a problem. Why you choose to do...or not do...a challenge just adds to the confusion of the game, and presents no difficulty at all."

So, the interviews proceeded. I found out later that we were all asked, "If we ask you to be the mole and work for us, foregoing any chance for the big money, would you do so?"

We all said sure, except for Myra, the airline pilot for Delta. (She undoubtedly knew Delta was soon to ask their pilots to take a pay cut, and was trying to make up the difference. Too bad; she would have been a great mole!) I was asked why I thought I would make a good mole? I explained that having a background like mine might be one that would not lead someone to assume I was the mole. Physician and Admiral. Plus, I had ready made excuses for any mistakes I might make that would cost the group money. My age and my 'status' as a retired Admiral. (In reality, I thought, 'Why pick me? Last season they had a 28-year-old female attorney. I'm sort of the opposite of that, and in spite of my statements otherwise, I would be the most obvious choice to be the mole.')

On the evening of the third day of interviews I was told I had an emergency phone call. My 81-year-old mother had just undergone emergency exploratory surgery for severe pain, and had been diagnosed with advanced ovarian cancer. I apologized to the producers and asked for an immediate ride to the airport. En route one of the producers asked me if I were declaring myself out of the game; I replied that I was unsure at that point, inasmuch as my Mom has had multiple surgeries and has always bounced back stronger than ever from them. So, they told me I had 72 hours to let them know for sure whether or not I was still a contender.

Reflections of The Mole

I arrived home to find Mom in an ICU in Muskogee, Oklahoma. Mom and Dad (who had died in 1995) had always lived vicariously through my travels, and loved to tell their friends where in the world I was at any given moment. So, after I had walked into the ICU and spent a little time chatting with Mom about her condition (grave), she asked, "Son, do you have any more fun trips planned?"

"Nope, Mom, not really. I had a possibility for one this summer, but have canceled it out." I could see that she was extremely ill, and the doctors I had chatted with had not been encouraging. Their advice was just to take her home, feed her pain meds, and let her die.

"Why have you canceled any trips this summer?" She wanted to know.

"Well, Mom, frankly, you're quite ill. And the trip I had planned was one to the far reaches of China (already getting into the mole mode and lying vigorously), and communications would be very difficult. I probably would not be able to contact you at all." (A true statement, unlike the others.)

"So what?"

"Mom, if you were to die, I wouldn't be able to get back here for the funeral. I could never forgive myself!"

"You goose! If I die, I don't care if you are here or not! I won't know! Besides that, your two older sisters will be here to take care of me."

The conversation lapsed. Later that day I was in the cafeteria, where my two older sisters found me. "What's this about you not taking some fun trip this summer?" I went through the same explanation I had given to Mom.

"You don't think we are capable of taking care of things without you, is that it?" Delivered in the same ominous tone they had used all the time we were growing up, immediately prior to another very physical battle.

Needless to say, shortly thereafter I agreed to take the trip, if offered. There is no fighting successfully with three women. I called the producers and told them I was still available, and returned immediately on their bid to LA.

Back in LA. More extensive interviews. An interview by a psychiatrist who had the results of my MMPI. After a short while, he inquired, "Bill, what is your deepest, darkest secret?"

I laughed. "I'm not sure I have a deep dark secret. **But**, if I did have one, and told you, it would no longer be a secret, now would it?" He laughed.

"Bill, everyone who comes in here like you knows that I work for ABC. I'm not here trying to counsel folks. But you would be surprised at the stories I have heard this week, about some very bad subjects. Child abuse, incest, and the like. Those folks are on the next plane home. We **are not** doing a show about people's mental problems (though some might contest that!), and **do not** want to hear those things aired in some episode on national television!" OK, I'll buy that. I would not want to hear them, either, unless I were watching "Dr. Phil" or "Oprah!"

After having a complete physical exam and signing disclaimers (ABC is not responsible for any pregnancies which might result from participation in this show. Wow! I wanted to do this show more than ever!), I finally returned to Oklahoma to help with my Mother, not knowing if I had made the final 14 or not.

In Oklahoma I found that the doctors involved had been true to their word; they were just giving Mom pain medications and leaving her in the ICU. Now, folks, let me put on my physician hat for a moment. Do **not** stay in any ICU one moment longer than you have to…ever! Not even as a visitor. As intensive as the care is (and there is a good reason it is called 'intensive care unit'), and as helpful as the nurses are (and they are outstanding), an ICU is filled with very, very sick folks. When someone is infected, it is usually a very bad infection, or they would not be in there to begin with. **So,** once the first few days where you truly require 'intensive care' have passed, get the hell out of there! You only stand to be exposed to germs you don't already have, and really, really don't want!

Therefore, upon finding Mom in the ICU...still...I immediately demanded her removal to a ward. I also impressed upon my two older sisters the need for that move. By the end of the day Gertha, my sister who had broken many a broom stick over my head, had cornered the Nurse Administrator of the hospital and with considerable emphasis let her know the need for Mom to have her own room. Believe me when I say that Gertha has *impressed* me many times, and is not to be ignored (though God knows I've tried) when she is in that mood. So, Mom was moved, somewhat to her doctors' surprise.

By this time 10 days had passed since surgery, and she was still on a liquid diet, though she was hungry and had good bowel sounds. In addition, she had not been out of bed. I'm an orthopedic surgeon, and firmly believe that being upright is much better for a patient than being supine! So, my sisters and I started bringing food from the cafeteria, and had advanced her to a normal diet by the time her doctors realized she might not be dying immediately. In addition, late one night I got a very large ward nurse to help me, and we got Mom up in a chair. By the time I flew home two weeks later, she was arguing with her oncologist about whether or not she was going to lose her hair in chemo. She was determined not to do so, and felt it was a matter of will, not medicine. (She was to have her way in this matter ultimately.)

I was not callous enough to return home while Mom was still in the hospital deliberately, by the way. My sisters are good people, but I would have been flailed severely about the head and shoulders had I threatened to leave without good cause. One Friday two weeks after LA I got a phone call. "Congratulations! You have been selected as a participant on "The Mole II," and will be leaving the country for parts unknown within 10 days! Furthermore, if you tell anyone anything at all, you owe us $10,000,000.00." Dummies. If I had that much money I would not be doing the show regardless!

About 2 hours later the phone rang again. On a conference line were the 4 producers. "Bill, congratulations! We've selected you to be the Mole!"

"Thanks…I guess! When do you tell me what to do?"

"Don't worry; we will tell you all when we get to Europe." (The first deception for the Mole, as it turned out. They never did get around to telling me how to do it!)

So, I returned to Oak Harbor, WA, where we lived. There, Shirley and I sat about making up stories that might stand up to casual inspection as to where I was going to be for 7 weeks. I had made a trip to China for a company I worked for the year before, so told that company I was going to hike the last 972 miles of the Appalachian Trail, and would be out of contact for a couple of months. For all others I was on an extended trip to the nether regions of China, where phones had not been invented yet. (You might understand how odd my life has been when everyone accepted my stories at face value, and thought nothing of them.) The hardest part for Shirley was keeping track of who was calling for me while I was gone. She had to ascertain whether or not they were connected to the company I had traveled to China for before answering. Shirley is very truthful, and found this task somewhat daunting and distasteful. However, in the hope that I might win a million dollars, she was willing to do it. (You might have deduced by now that I had decided not to tell her that I had been chosen as the Mole.)

Finally, on the 2nd of June, I waved good-by to my wife and life as I knew it, and boarded an airplane for Zurich, Switzerland.

Should I have stayed home? Well, the answer to that is, most likely. However, having grown up with two older sisters, both of whom who alternatively protect and love me interspaced with kicking my tail to do something worthwhile, it was not as simple as that. They wanted me to leave and 'do my thing.' They had things at home in hand. And, if I didn't leave…there was no other interpretation they would put on it than that I really did not trust them to carry the load for a while.

    Between a rock and a hard place…

IV

Sisters

My sisters. I had lots of leisure time as I was growing up, from about ages 0-10. (I got too busy to just sit around after that; the pressures of being the only male in the family...other than Dad...with oversight duties!) I observed my sisters closely during those early formative years. The oldest was almost like a Mom. Ruth was 8 years older, responsible, helpful. She was perhaps of most help to me when I got to observe her dating strategy, which started when I was about 7 or so. Highly educational! I was young enough to be totally ignored by her and Gertha, and old enough to listen and understand some of what they were talking about. Strategy; my God, they had strategy. (This stood me in good stead in my efforts as the Mole; I'm not claiming to understand girls, but I certainly became a master at irritating them!) I became convinced that there was no such thing as an accident when involvement with the opposite sex was concerned. I felt sorry for the boys who were on the receiving end of those strategy sessions; they simply had no chance. Having grown up and gone through the dating rituals with my friends, I can truly say I have never heard men strategize the way the girls did. They would decide who they wanted to date, and then start laying the groundwork. And, almost invariably, sooner or later that male would show up at the door to take one of my sisters out, never suspecting that his actions had been foreordained long before he knew either of them. He thought he had free will, and had arrived there totally on his own volition. Not a chance!

Ruth started dating an excellent basketball player from a small local school, whom she ultimately married. Every time he would come into the house, one of my other sisters or I would yell "TIMBER!" I have no idea why we did that, but he would turn beet red every time that occurred, and Ruth would threaten us with great bodily harm if we ever did it again. We did it every time. When I was 9 years old, they got married; I could not believe it. I remember participating avidly in the chivaree, a country custom. A night or two before the wedding a group of young, and not so young, folks would gather the two up and take them to a local pond, where they were thrown bodily in, clothes and all. Then, we would go to 'our' town, Haskell, Oklahoma, 7 miles away, and she would have to push him in a wheelbarrow down Main Street. I have no idea how this custom got started, but suspect it had been going on for hundreds of years…or, maybe we just made it up. I don't even know what it means, but it was sure fun to observe and participate in! I became such an enthusiast in these activities before and after weddings that as I grew older, I received fewer and fewer invitations to friends' nuptials.

Back to my two older sisters. I have two younger sisters, also, and while I might have been a major factor in their young lives, they weren't around to give me grief when I was young; that category belonged to Ruth and Gertha, primarily the latter. For, as noted before, Ruth was enough older that she seemed like sort of a Mother. A little scary and too darned big to defy directly! As I have also noted, she was primarily a source of education, primarily about the weaker sex…men.

Gertha. Man, oh man. She was trouble. She wanted someone to be able to boss, and I was the only candidate. Oh, I know, she did have control over Dad, and all the boyfriends who were to enter her life, but she needed someone to *practice* on; none of this indirect manipulation kind of stuff. Direct, snapping the whip, 'you'll do as I say' kind of control. The only problem with that entire program was that I just never developed the knack for obeying. Therefore, conflict. And, I must add one more thing. Gertha was also my biggest supporter, and would come to my defense with a ferocity that would alarm those who might think to do me harm. No one was going to mess with her little brother. I was *her* boy 'toy!'

Gertha and I fought. I mean, we fought physically. From the time I can remember, which was somewhere en utero, I think, we were locked in battle. She would direct me to do something, and I would ignore her. She would start trying to physically push me to the task, and I would physically resist. The battle would commence. Mom despaired over the years, using every wile in her armamentarium to dissuade us from our tussles. And being the oldest of twelve gave Mom lots of material...all to no avail. Gertha always tackled me without external instrumentation until I was 7 and she was 11. One night we were in a wrestling match, and Dad had restrained Mom from interfering. Perhaps if there were a clear victor this epic struggle would finally cease. Gertha had slung me across the living room, and I stood up slowly, shaking my bowling ball head and clearing my eyes. I leaned forward and took off on a dead run at her; she braced herself, anticipating another leg tackle. Instead of that, I just lowered my head and butted her in the stomach in full flight. She crumbled like the 11 year old girl she was! Dead away. Unconscious. Mom screamed, Dad looked alarmed, and I tried to look nonchalant. I wasn't, really. I didn't want to actually *hurt* her! She came around soon, however. I think she was just faking so she could plan her next move...which was soon to be an escalation in the fine art of warfare. She immediately went to external devices, primarily brooms. There are many, many broken broom handles littering the grounds of our little farm today, all courtesy of Gertha's arm and my head. We made quite a successful pair in testing the quality assurance program of the standard broom handle.

By the time I was 10 or so, our fighting days were nearing an end; as I got bigger the only way she could have stopped me was with a deadly implement of some kind, and neither of us wanted that! (Maybe that's true, and maybe not.) However, Mom was still trying to find the combination of punishment/rewards that would give us pause in our pursuit of the perfect annihilation of the other. She whipped us repeatedly. Just added spice to the adventure. She made us kiss each other. We didn't like that, but it wasn't going to stop anything. Time outs, restriction, grounding, sitting in our rooms, not being allowed to bring friends home from school, all to no avail. If we had had television, we would never have seen any because of these restrictions, but the lack thereof resulted in no deprivation from that quarter. Finally, Mom hit upon Dr. Spock, the ultimate authority on kids. He must have an answer, and he did!

One day as we were locked in combat Mom came in and separated us, handing us each a belt.

"Kids, I'm not going to have this any more! From now on when I catch you fighting, instead of me spanking you, you're going to have to spank me!" With that, she turned around and bent over.

Gertha and I looked at each other, wide-eyed. We had never agreed on anything in our life, but suddenly were in complete accord. We backed off from our mama…just to good swinging distance. We then started whaling away on her behind; an opportunity like this might never again become available. And it didn't. Within a few swings Mom realized the stupidity of Dr. Spock, grabbed the belts out of our hands, and proceeded with a sigh once again to spank us. She never again "assumed the position." Darn the luck! Just when Gertha and I had found something we could do together without fighting!

Our last fight came soon after that. We had a younger sister, Nancy, some 4 ½ years younger than me. Nancy looked to both of us for guidance, resulting in a life of confusion for her. She followed us around frequently, much to her peril. She was delightful, inquisitive, bright, and had never known a moment of silence in her life. She could talk more than anyone I had ever heard, and every other utterance was a question. Gertha and I had taken great pride in furnishing answers to every question she had ever asked, regardless of whether or not we had any knowledge of the subject matter. You want an answer? You got an answer.

Nancy looked up to me, I know, but it was not for many years that I finally came to understand the close scrutiny I was under during those times. She thought I had tried to kill her once upon a time, and was carefully watching me to make sure she could duck the next attempt. One rainy day when she was six months old or so, I took her for a ride in my red wagon. As we exited our driveway (about 100 yards from the house) onto the road, her lack of driving ability became apparent when the wagon turned too sharply, dumping her off into a drainage ditch that was quite full of muddy water. I turned and watched her with some interest. Could she swim? (I couldn't, and was justly curious.) Well, apparently she could, configured rather oddly with her butt in the air and her head under water. Was there something I didn't understand here? And, at the same time she could blow bubbles! Man, this is talent galore! I couldn't do either one of those things. I finally grabbed her diaper and pulled her out of the ditch; she might drink all the water and dry the place up. She was still smiling, but most amazing to me was Mom flying down the driveway, picking her up and crying, then picking me up and praising me for saving her life. Saving her life? She was swimming! And, in great danger of drinking all the water. I didn't save her life. Nancy swears today she still remembers that event, and in her memories agrees with my version. Except that she notes that time as being when 'I tried to kill her.' Shoot, I did not. I had tried that on Gertha, and sisters were just too ornery to die.

Back to our last fight. Mom had gone to town to buy groceries for our little soon-to-be-bankrupt country store, leaving

Reflections of The Mole

14 year old Gertha in charge. She loved being in charge, if only someone would cooperate. The inevitable occurred, of course. I refused to do something...whatever...that she wanted me to do. We fought. Nancy watched, chewing on a nail she had picked up. (I said she talked a lot; I never meant she was all that smart!) Nancy was safely out of the way behind me. Gertha was on the other side of the table, and we had resorted to throwing things at each other. Gertha picked up a heavy shoe (probably Dad's) and flung it at my head. I ducked; I'm not stupid, after all! Nancy didn't, and the shoe hit her right in the head. She reflexively swallowed, then said something profound, like, "Uh-oh!" Gertha and I paused momentarily. Uh-oh? What's that all about? Nancy explained to us that she had been chewing on a nail, and when the shoe hit her she had swallowed it. Why had she been chewing on a nail? Why do girls do anything?

Gertha and I went into panic mode. What could we do? Well, precisely nothing, but it certainly served to stop our fighting. Mom came home, we all made a trip to the doctor, and the doctor took an Xray. Yep, there was the nail, all right. Amazing! The doctor told Mom that this, too, would...pass in time. I guess it did; I didn't want to know.

In spite of all of this, or perhaps because of all of this, Gertha and I became the best of friends. She did all my preliminary checking on girls I might like to claim as girlfriends. She ran interference. While I was a pretty tough kid in class, the other guys sure didn't want to run afoul of my sister; while I *might* be bad, she *was* bad!

So, when my two older sisters, one like a Mom, and the other my biggest protagonist and staunchest supporter, told me to take my 'fun trip,' I sighed and left. There are some things just too difficult to fight!

V

Travel to Parts Unknown

Having spread misleading tidbits about my presumed travel to all those who might be interested, Shirley and I paved the way for my unnoticed departure from the States. I left it to Shirley to keep the various non-truths straight as she chatted with relatives and friends over the next couple of months; after all, I was strictly an amateur in these dissimilation efforts. (Although my sisters might beg to differ...)

I received a plane ticket from the producers. Depart Seattle, and head to Zurich, Switzerland, with a return ticket from Rome some 6 ½ weeks later. Where I was to be in the interim neither of us knew. Shirley did have an emergency number in Los Angeles by which she could contact me, but we both agreed that she would not use it, unless under the direst of circumstances. I had made a commitment, ill-advised as it might have been, to remain on the show for the duration. Shirley, of course, still did not realize that I had been selected as the Mole, and thought that with my power of observation for little details, there was an excellent chance I would be home quickly. She had no faith! Or, perhaps she had just lived around me too long and knew me too well...

Shirley asked me what she should do if the worst happened and Mom died. Swallowing hard, and with tremendous guilt, I told her not to call me. If that occurred, it was really too late for me to do anything, anyway. As Mom had explained so eloquently to me, if she was dead, she wouldn't care whether or not I was there or not! I had great faith in Mom's ability to recover from her cancer; she was one of the toughest people I have ever known. Besides that, my two older sisters were in attendance, and had proven to me time and again in my life that they were highly capable. Gullible, maybe, but capable. However, all rationalization aside, I left with a heavy heart and lots of guilt.

I flew away, having no idea what I would do once I arrived in Zurich. In spite of being the Mole, I had not had any further communication with the producers, and had no inkling of what was coming, or where it was going to occur.

I landed in Zurich and looked around while awaiting the arrival of my luggage. I was dressed in Bermudas and a short-sleeved shirt; after all, it was hot at home. I expected that perhaps someone would be there to greet me and guide me along the way. Nothing. Further, I expected my luggage to come down the carousel. That expectation was also for naught. No luggage, no people waiting. After perhaps 45 minutes I made my way to the lost luggage counter to fill out a slip. When the question came up, "Where will you be staying?," I had no clue as to what to put down. Where *would* I be staying? Where could they deliver the luggage, in the unlikely event they found it? I left that blank and told them I would get back to them on that. Maybe.

I went on through customs (an easy task, inasmuch as I was carrying nothing and was barely dressed) and surveyed the crowd waiting in the lobby. Where, oh where, was someone—anyone!—from the show? Wherever they were they were not in my field of view. So, I had to give some consideration to the possibility that this was the first test of the show. Was I supposed to go out of the airport and look for clues? But, this wasn't "The Amazing Race," and I had no idea what the corporate flag of Gonzo Productions (Scott Stone, Owner and Producer) looked like.

I chose to wait. I'm stubborn, and when I have absolutely no idea what to do in a situation, am an expert at inaction. Why run in circles? I was already at the point I would have returned to anyway.

Finally, after about 45 minutes in the lobby, a girl rushed up to me.

"Are you Bill?!"

Well, yes, come to think of it, I am.

She thrust a train ticket into my hand and said, "Get down to the train station! You have 5 minutes until the train leaves. And, by the way, you have several train changes; I'm not sure what or where they are. Good luck!"

"My luggage didn't arrive!"

She grabbed my baggage claim ticket and urged me to depart the premises, quickly! (I figured that all 14 of us were probably arriving on the same day, and were taking the same set of trains. Inasmuch as none of us had met each other, they probably were pressing to keep us on separate trains and planes, a formidable task! I did keep my eyes peeled for suspicious looking characters on the trip, and saw many! It's surprising how devious looking folks can be if you assume they are. However, none of them turned out to be *my* group of deviants.)

I ran down to the train platforms under the Zurich airport and showed my ticket to someone in uniform. (I did not know if they were in the military or worked for the train; after 32 years in the Navy, asking someone in uniform for directions just seemed the thing to do. I'm just glad he was not a recruiter for the Swiss Navy; I could have been manning a rowboat on Lake Zurich for the next several years!) He indicated a train that was slowly pulling out; I rushed over and managed to get aboard, hoping that he wasn't standing back there on the platform giggling at having sent the dumb American off to parts unknown.

Once on the train, I settled in for a long ride…somewhere. The train immediately started slowing down for another stop. I was looking at my ticket, trying to figure out if I was capable of deciphering where I was supposed to be going. After only a brief effort, it was apparent to me that I didn't have the foggiest idea where I was trying to get to, nor how to get there. So, I asked a gentleman sitting across from me if he knew when I changed trains to accommodate the ticket in my hand. He glanced at it as the train came to a brief halt, only moments from the airport, and advised, "You should get off here." Here?! What do you mean, "Here!" I just got on this train!

However, having asked the question and received the answer, I hopped off. After all, it wasn't that I had to haul all my luggage about. It was just me. I stood on the platform watching as the train departed. Now what?

I found another uniformed person who looked considerably smarter than the first person in uniform I had queried, and showed him my ticket. "Yes, that is right. Take the next train coming there, please."

So, within 5 minutes of boarding my first train in Switzerland, I was now on my second. Again I showed my ticket to a fellow passenger, all the while looking about trying to find some other simpleton looking as confused as I was. There was no one else of that description on this train; they all looked knowledgeable and competent, leading me to the correct assumption that none of my fellow players were aboard this particular train. My new guide told me to remain aboard this train for about 30 minutes, then to change trains at some unintelligible and unpronounceable station, where I would board a train for about 3 hours. Luckily, my confusion registered with him, and he laughingly reassured me that he would tell me when to depart the train, which he proceeded to do.

Ah, now my 3rd train, upon which I was due to relax for 3 hours. I liked that. For at least 3 hours I would know approximately where I was, and not have to risk getting lost without my luggage again.

At this point I had the opportunity to sit and reflect seriously for a while. What the devil was I doing? Leaving a maybe dying mother, my wife unaware of what part of the world I was in, not too long after departing naval service of 32 years, no full time job? Did I think this stint on television would lead to something? Maybe, but doubtful. Plus, I am the Mole. What does that mean? For the first time I really considered that.

My job, should I choose to take it (which I had already done), was to be sneaky, not a team player, encourage dissention in the other players, lie and obfuscate when possible. Could I do that? Wouldn't I be so obvious that my mere presence would be enough to ensure that not only my fellow players, but the viewing audience (assuming this show ever got aired after I finished screwing it up totally) would be painfully aware that I was the Mole as soon as my face was seen? How could they not know? How could I keep from revealing myself at the first opportunity? How in the world did I allow myself to get in this pickle to begin with?!

VI

Preparing for the Role

All of my life I have been able to focus single-mindedly on whatever I was doing at any given time, which was a trait my father had as well. I grew up on a small farm in Oklahoma, having no money except what I could earn picking cotton and doing odd jobs. For a child in the 40's and 50's a 120 acre farm was not a place to lay in extra money!

Dad's advice on working your way through life was quite simple. "No matter what job you are given to do, do it the best way you possibly can, and if you do that, take no crap from anyone about your work." The only way to do a job the best way you know how is to pay close attention to it! (This also worked well over my many years as a motorcycle rider, and my patients probably appreciated my efforts in their behalf as a surgeon, also.)

I applied that principle of doing the best I could through a series of somewhat odd jobs en route to becoming a physician. I did every job a farm can produce, and some of them were not my favorite ways to make a living! I hope to never again milk a cow at 6:00 AM on a cold winter morning, with the cow's manure-frozen tail whacking me alongside my head sporadically while I worked, and all too frequently having the cow step in my pail of milk just as I finished milking. When I was especially frustrated during those moments, I would draw back and hit the cow as hard as I could. The cow seldom noted the blow, but my frozen hand almost always felt like it had just been violently torn off! Milking cows and picking cotton. Two jobs that I would rather never have to do again. (And, I seriously doubt that I will!)

Bill McDaniel, MD

I was a bartender for a couple of years, a night manager of a motel, and worked at every non-skilled job that pipelining could yield. However, I finally became a doctor, and shortly after that joined the Navy, where I volunteered to go to Viet Nam. After all, that was where the action was, and I was a physician with the Marines, as safe a billet as it was possible to get in hostile territory. After that I went to a residency, became an orthopedic surgeon, and eventually worked my way up to getting to go to the National War College at Fort McNair in Washington, DC. A wonderful life.

I really enjoyed my years with the Navy. Everything was teamwork. While you did not have to like your fellow workers, usually it worked out that you did, because you were working together toward a common goal. That goal might be to keep fellow Marines alive in Viet Nam, or just to do the best job you could in seeing as many patients as possible in a Naval Hospital. I was proud of the fact that we practiced the finest quality of medicine anywhere, as is substantiated yearly by multiple nationally evaluating authorities such as the Joint Commission of Accreditation of Hospitals. We were all proud of that. We functioned as a team—both at work and at play--and were happy that most folks appreciated it.

Eventually I was given command of a hospital, then a second one. I was a Navy Captain, a rank I was most proud to attain. I found that I really, truly enjoyed working with people, and having people work for me, because I could help them toward a common goal…providing the best care possible for our patients, while at the same time enjoying themselves as much as possible, and growing, always growing, professionally. (And growing personally; I found that the Certified Navy Twill that Navy uniforms were constructed from would shrink over the years, thus requiring me to buy slightly larger clothes with each promotion.) I also found another capability within me, one that took some encouraging and mentoring from some shipmates in the Navy who were a little wiser than me. One of these was a Command Master Chief, the senior enlisted man at my first command. Master Chief Sam Grant. He mentored me in not only helping my folks realize their potential, but in recognizing those personnel who were….ill placed in the Navy! My tendency initially was to give a second chance, then a third. He taught me that, in fact, there were a significant number of folks who would continue to take advantage of every chance given to them, and would never get around to actually doing their jobs. They were wasters. Wasters of the Navy's time and efforts, as well as my own. Once identified, the best thing we could do for the Navy, and for the morale of everyone else in the Navy, was to enable those personnel to become civilians as quickly as possible. In truth, most of them would continue to be wasters…of their lives, ultimately. However, by removing them from the Navy I greatly improved the quality of life for those of us left *working* in the Navy. Hopefully, some of them found purpose as civilians, though I strongly suspect that many of them remained as big a drag on civilian society as they were on the military. Not my problem. I became very, very skilled at quickly recognizing those disruptions to my life and removing them from my environment! (As I journeyed across Switzerland, I could only hope that that ability to read folks might stand me in good stead in my quest to slowly eliminate them from the game, one by one.)

All in all, I found the concept of teamwork, working toward a common goal, and having common purpose a delightful one.

Perhaps the highpoint of all this teamwork preparation came during the saga of Hurricane Hugo. At that time I was the Commanding Officer of the Naval Hospital in Charleston, SC, my second command. I had decided to retire at the end of that tour, inasmuch as I was now a senior Captain, and had a wonderful job offer as the Chief of Sports Medicine in a little known country in the Far East….Kuwait. I was a delegate for the

United States to the Council of International Military Sports (CISM), and had become good friends with a General in the Kuwait Army, and a member of the royal family, who was a delegate from his country. In addition to my work with the military sports community around the world, I had been one of the United States' Olympic physicians in the 1984 Los Angeles Olympics, so was ready to build on that foundation to depart the Navy (after 24 years) and start making good money.

Then, crossing over Puerto Rico came Hurricane Hugo. Now, most hurricanes look ferocious, but don't really live up to their advance bookings, sort of like most of my dates as a young man. (And theirs as well, I expect.) As Hugo passed through the Caribbean, its projected path, should it choose to remain on a straight line, placed it directly atop Charleston, SC, about 5 days after pounding Puerto Rico. Now, hurricanes do not ordinarily go in a straight line. The pundits and prognosticators pontificated a possible outcome for Hugo. They predicted that its most likely path would be to do a curve up the Eastern seaboard, missing Charleston. However, on Monday morning, the arrow sure looked like it would spear Charleston in a few days.

Now, most old hands in that part of South Carolina (the Low Country) did not believe that those winds would ever muss Charleston's skirts. However, I was born in Oklahoma, and spent my formative years there watching tornadoes regularly tear up places where no one expected them. (In fact, I still have lumps and tiny pieces of glass in my head from one that hit our school in Blackwell when I was 15. Of course, the lumps could be from the brooms my sisters wielded with great accuracy as I was attempting to grow up....)

Part of every military hospital's routine is to run disaster drills twice a year. After all, look at what we train to do all of our professional lives—meet the threat of the ultimate disaster, war. So, we take our training seriously. Therefore, that Monday morning I pulled the staff together in several large 'Captain's calls,' (so named, I guess, because I was the Captain and was calling them to listen to me) and explained to them that we were going to pretend that Hurricane Hugo was going to hit us several days hence. A great drill, and one that would fulfill one of our disaster drill requirements for the year. I told them we would do this as a full up drill, no fudging, no dry labbing. Much to my surgeons' dissatisfaction, all elective surgery was to be cancelled. (Surgeons just love to cut; most of them would probably be just as fulfilled as butchers, were it not for the prestige and money involved.) Patients were to be discharged if at all possible. Pregnant women were encouraged to breath deeply and not get excited, holding those little critters inside for a few extra days. (I think most of them sneered at my pleading, however.)

We worked the hospital, taping all the windows thoroughly. The emergency generators were checked, and fuel tanks topped off. Large containers were brought to several locations on each floor and filled with water. (We later found that when you have 50 or so gallons of water in a large container, it takes lots of effort to pour out of those little outlets on top! Nothing that a siphon hose made of IV tubing can't fix, however.) Food stores were checked and made complete. (The most important food, we found, was coffee. Without coffee people often revert to barbaric behavior.) The large waiting room next to the emergency room was outfitted with 50 temporary stretchers outfitted with IV tubing and supplies, in case of a large influx of injured patients.

We worked as a team preparing for a disaster that we doubted would hit; but, once in the mode, we worked hard at doing it by the book, but more importantly, doing it right. (Those two conditions sometimes do not exist at the same time, as I'm sure you are aware.)

On Wednesday morning the Low Country was under an evacuation notice. Now, we are the Navy, and when possible do not evacuate in conditions such as these. Not to mention that the patients who could not be discharged might be put out by such an action on our part. (Of interest was the fact that we also had a submarine repair facility nearby. While all of the ships that could get under way were steamed out of harm's way early in the week, a couple of submarines could not be easily moved, inasmuch as their engines were sitting on the dock. So, they just moved them out into the middle of the Cooper River and pulled the plug on them, sitting them on the bottom. Interesting to watch, and rather startling, I'm sure, if you were a fishing boat heading up the Cooper and suddenly finding yourself between a couple of conning towers of submarines. I expect several of the fishing boat skippers had rude flashbacks to the days of yore, and prepared to fend off boarders.)

On Wednesday morning I again called my entire staff together. It was apparent by this time that, regardless of conventional meteorologist wisdom (this, my friends, is called an oxymoron), the hurricane had no intention of deviating from its chosen course, which was through downtown Charleston and right over our 10 story facility several miles up the Cooper River. Thus, having prepared all we could, and not having lots of patients in-house, and attempting to convince about 40 women in the last 2 weeks of their pregnancy that I would consider it a personal favor if they would just hold on to things for a while, I announced to my staff that I desired to retain a skeleton staff on board; everyone else should head to parts inland (like Oklahoma) to get out of the path of the storm. Having succinctly and clearly expressed myself, I asked for a show of hands of volunteers who would be willing to stay. Out of about 600-700 personnel present, I counted almost twice that number of hands in the air. I explained what was needed patiently, again, and once more posed my question: "Who is willing to place their lives in unneeded jeopardy, risking life and limb...not to mention cars...by staying through the hurricane?" Again, the same number of hands went into the air.

Reflections of The Mole

I gave up, and suggested that those personnel who had not already sent their families inland should bring them to the hospital. We were at a heady 31 feet above sea level, and likely to survive the hurricane. We hastily began converting a large conference room in the basement to a children's playroom, and I requested that the galley prepare lots of coffee.

On Wednesday afternoon, by the way, I made the rounds of the other 9 major hospitals in Charleston, and offered our facilities to them for the few remaining critical patients in their facilities. Most of them, after all, were down town, about 5 feet above sea level. If the hurricane were to hit at high tide with 145 mile per hour winds, there was an expected 26 foot tidal surge, which would not bode well for those hospitals. They all declined my offer, even when several of the CEO's told me that while it made sense for them to transfer the very critical patients, politically they would really look bad. I empathized with them, but in hindsight I feel the same today as I did then. That was really stupid thinking. (Of interest, I pointed out to one non-physician that his emergency generators were in the *basement* of his hospital, some 10 feet *below* sea level! How did he propose caring for his ventilator patients if his emergency generators were flooded out? (As they eventually were.) He replied that 'his folks' would 'bag' the patients with Ambu bags, manually breathing for the patients until the power came back on. Wow! Man, that is a way to make friends of your patients and staff for life! Squeezing those Ambu bags for longer than 20 minutes or so results in ever-increasing burning pain and cramps in your forearms, ultimately rendering the arms and hands useless for several hours. I asked him if he had ever squeezed an Ambu bag? No, actually, he had not. I did not doubt the truth of his answer. I later chatted with some of his staff tasked to keep those patients breathing for the several hours the generators were flooded out; they were not what you would call happy people.) Several low lying nursing homes, by the way, took me up on my offer, sending nurses and special medications along with all their patients, whom we placed in formerly closed wards. In fact, the advance storm surge flooded out one of the nursing homes late Wednesday evening, fully 18 hours before the hurricane arrived. Shirley and I wound up at the hospital about midnight that night, helping get folks settled in.

Thursday dawned with only light winds and some overcast. However, by noon things were heating up. My staff, their families, and the visiting staff and patients were getting settled in, preparing for the evening's festivities. We set up a control center on the 2nd floor of the hospital, and distributed the few hand held radios we had through the critical areas of the hospital, in case the phones went out. Our control center was manned by several personnel around the clock, keeping track of everything having to do with the storm, including patient numbers, emergency room visits, available beds, etc. I made rounds throughout the facility, saying hello to all, greeting the new comers, and just generally attempting to keep morale high. However, I found that there was little need for that. Everyone was excited, families were settling in, and the smell of wine was in the air in several of the offices I visited…though the presence of wine was actually never noted by me. (One of the lessons learned from our effort was that next time someone should offer me a little wine occasionally!)

One of the problems I noted fairly early on was one I never would have given thought to. In one office I could see crayon markings up to about the five foot point on the walls, in profusion. The kids were bored, and were taking it out on the premises! In addition to that, I noted what appeared to be pooled Pepsi or Coke in the keyboard of a computer or two. I quickly spread the word via our intercom system (still functional at that time) that while our facility might well withstand the coming storm, it might not last through 30 or 40 bored kids! So, I urged parents to take their children to the newly designated playroom in the basement, where we had brought in games from the pediatrics ward. In addition, one of our interns was an excellent guitar picker, and started singing with the kids there. We soon averted further crayon and Coke damage to the rest of the hospital!

While making rounds I ventured with some trepidation onto a ward where we had housed 39 women expecting to deliver within 2 weeks. Inasmuch as we would not be able to get to them at home during (and probably for several days after) the hurricane, we had urged them to come and stay in the hospital for the duration of the event. I received strong support for this suggestion from all their husbands. They were remarkably cheerful, and I again begged them to stay very, very relaxed for the duration of the storm, if at all possible. They all laughed and promised to do their best.

All in all, what I saw during my many rounds made me most proud and happy to be there, and to be the nominal leader of this effort.

We started getting winds in excess of 100 mph before dark. The winds were coming in from the East. The west side of the hospital included our emergency room bay, which had a large loading dock sheltered from the wind. About 50 of us gathered on the dock watching events unfold. After a short while one of the members of my security staff stepped outside, and, not noticing me in the back of the group, announced, "Ladies and gentlemen, it is not safe out here at this time. By order of the Commanding Officer, you must return indoors and get out of the storm!" A sensible suggestion, and while not remembering having actually *given* such an order, I meekly followed the others back in to the safety of the lobby. After all, I had given it, or so I heard.

The night was...memorable. We lost power quite early on, and were on our emergency generators from 5:00 PM. We did not have many patients come in, inasmuch as they could not venture out in the wind. So, we just observed and took care of each other and the patients we had in house.

At about 9:00 PM my phone rang. It was CNN, and they asked if they could interview me. I agreed. They told me it would be a phone interview (no surprise there) and that they had an old file photo of me, which surprised me considerably. I have no idea even today where they got it. By this time the winds were blowing in excess of 130 mph, and we had measured gusts near 200 mph. The hospital was actually swaying enough to be felt on the upper floors. However, at that point we had not lost any windows or exterior doors. I did a 20 minute interview on CNN, reassuring them that things were fine, though noisy. I later heard from several families of personnel who had chosen to stay in the hospital, and they told me that I sounded so relaxed and confident that they went to bed, comforted that their loved ones were not in danger. I'm glad I sounded that way to them, because I surely wasn't feeling that confident!

A staff member's wife was a member of the Naval Investigative Service, and had loaned me a multi-channel radio with which I could communicate with all the city emergency workers. I was hearing things that did not sound good. As the winds picked up to 145 mph (The highest gust we recorded during that time was 237 mph, which tore our wind gauge from the roof!), I heard reports that most of the downtown hospitals were essentially out of action completely, with generators flooded out. Also, a hospital only a couple of miles from us was supposedly hit by a tornado and all the windows blown out, along with furnishings. I was asked by the police if I could send some ambulances to the latter facility; I really did not want to do this, unless absolutely necessary. Driving in winds of that magnitude was inviting disaster. So, I did what the police should have done. I just picked up my phone and called the CEO's private number. He answered immediately, and told me everyone was safe in the inner corridors, and he needed no immediate help.

Reflections of The Mole

I received another very odd phone call; the police dispatcher (only about 200 yards up the street from us) called and asked if I could get an ambulance to a shelter in Hollywood, SC, about 20+ miles away. (This was about 2:00 AM, and the 'eye' of the hurricane had just passed, leaving behind winds even stronger than we had experienced already.) I asked her if they could get police cars out to the shelter, and she said the streets were blocked. I patiently pointed out to her that we were only a short distance away from her, and if they could not get there, neither could we. She then asked if I could get one of my OB/GYN docs to call the shelter there and tell the non-medical personnel there how to do a C-section on a woman in labor; her physician had told her that because of a prior section she would always have to have one. Sure enough, she had gone to a shelter where there was not a single doctor or nurse, nor a paramedic. Nor a policeman or a fireman. Not even any midwives! I listened to her request with an understandable degree of consternation. This woman had watched too many episodes of ER! So, I told her we would be happy to work with the shelter via phone and take the problem off her hands. I then woke up my chief of OB/GYN, who had managed to fall asleep quite soundly in the middle of a howling hurricane, and laid the problem in his lap. (With his guidance…or without it, I suppose…she delivered a healthy baby without having to suffer a C-section by the local lawyer.)

It was a fascinating night, and a wonderful and scary one as well. At about 2:00 AM we lost part of our roof, and the 10th floor ICU, filled with ventilator patients, began receiving more rain than was desired. I rallied a large work crew of volunteers, and we ran up the 10 flights of stairs (only then did we realize that we did not have an elevator on the emergency generator circuit) and proceeded to mop and wet-vacuum several inches of water up from the floor, while others attempted to patch some of the ceiling to keep the rain out. The 10th floor was swaying back and forth like the deck of a ship, and the IV bags were swinging to and fro, the end of the arcs being almost parallel to the floor. I did not know how much movement a 10 story building could withstand before it lost integrity (i.e., broke apart and fell down in a heap), and had no desire to find the breaking point that night. Luckily, we did not reach that state of affairs!

At about this time also I received notice that both the large front entryway to the hospital and the rear entryway had blown in, though the interior doors from the entryways held firm. (I received this news from a LT George Gabb, who calmly called me in the command center. "Skipper, I'm here in total darkness...except for the occasional sparks from electrical wires...under the information desk. It's raining and blowing pretty hard here, so I think I will abandon this desk and come up stairs, if you approve!" I did approve.)

Morning dawned. Trees were down everywhere, part of the roof was gone, and gravel from the flat roof had literally destroyed approximately 100 cars in the parking lot. My 10 ambulances, while all in running condition (and being put immediately to use) all were missing their windows. We had no running water, though we had plenty of pre-positioned drinking water in the building. However, without running water we could not flush the many toilets! One of my nurses looked out and pointed to a large ceremonial fountain in front of the building. She said, "There's all the water we need to flush all the toilets for several days, assuming we don't mind hauling it in." Great idea, and one that worked. The water came back on line within 24 hours, though it was not drinkable for a week or so.

I walked about the hospital, exhausted, watching patients and staff and families perform way above and beyond, something they had done all night. The galley fixed a simple, but hot, breakfast, and served plenty of hot coffee. Teamwork. Shipmates. I could not have been more proud, and don't think I was ever any prouder in my 32 years of the Navy than I was of those folks. So, I went behind the wet and destroyed information desk, found the microphone that allowed me to address the hospital personnel throughout the facility, and told them how proud I was of them and their efforts. I expect that I went overboard a little, but excused it to having been up for 48 straight hours, and having just gone through an incredible ordeal with some incredible people.

I used the PA system fairly frequently in the normal course of events, discussing problems and congratulating folks on jobs especially well done, and always received comments from the personnel afterwards as I made rounds. On this morning I laid down the microphone and felt a trifle embarrassed; I might have been a little more emotional than I should have been, but it was a heady moment! So, I walked wearily up to the 10th floor for about the 20th time since the storm began and started making rounds. Everyone was friendly and happy, looking out the windows at the devastation outside. However, no one commented on my early morning chat. No one. I had opened myself up, poured my feelings out, and no one had noticed! Or, they were so embarrassed for me that they did not want to comment. What a downer after an otherwise exhausting, but emotional and wonderful, event. I went on down to each succeeding floor, talking with personnel and patients, kidding with them, and seeing that everyone was thrilled that we had survived without injuries; in fact, we had done great! But, still, everyone was too embarrassed for me to even make reference to my emotional outburst. I really was feeling lower and lower, and was thinking that it was a good thing that retirement was coming soon; my comments must have been so emotional that they would be hard to live down. Time to move on to a place where I wasn't remembered so well!

Then, I arrived on the 6th floor and stepped into the ward housing the 39 very, very pregnant women, all of whom were still happily pregnant that morning. They started whistling and cheering, and all hopped up and started clapping, gathering around me, with many of them crying happily. I was dazed. Maybe their hormones were so screwed up that they were the only ones not embarrassed by my earlier emotional oration? No, as it turned out, the overhead system was down, and the only ward in the entire hospital to hear my soliloquy was that ward. And they loved it!

Charleston did not return to normal for a long time. However, the Naval Hospital never shut its doors, and throughout that long weekend saw all comers (about 1000 of them), both civilian and military, inasmuch as we were the only truly functional hospital in town. We were also one of the few places in town where hot coffee was available at all times, and many emergency workers took advantage of our hospitality. Most staff and their families lived in the hospital for several days, until the streets were cleared of trees and their homes made habitable again. However, they all pitched in and worked, doing everything from sweeping and mopping to cleaning up glass and relieving other personnel in patient care. We were all exhausted and happy, and working as a team, doing what we were trained to do. Meet the crisis, face the emergency, and emerge victorious.

I was selected for Admiral by the selection board 6 weeks later, postponing forever my proposed stint at working and making lots of money in the generally unknown country of Kuwait, where I had intended going to work after retirement.

My Navy experiences defined teamwork, and leadership, and was what I had trained to do all my professional life. I was good at it and proud of it. And it was the antithesis of what I was being asked to do as the Mole!

VII

Can I Do This?

And, it was the antithesis of what I was being asked to do as the Mole!

I kept this thought in my head as the train wandered across the Swiss mountains. Eventually we slowed to a stop at an outdoor platform somewhere high in the mountains, and a helpful Swiss person informed me that this was where I needed to switch to the final train to my destination, Scoul, Switzerland.

I stepped off the train onto the platform, clad in my Bermudas, short sleeved shirt, and sandals, sans luggage…into a driving snowstorm. This was smart! It was the second of June, for crying out loud! It's not supposed to be snowing on my shivering minimally clad body! Luckily, I had to wait for the next train for only the length of time required to become just slightly hypothermic. I hopped aboard as soon as it stopped, not sure if it was really the correct train, but registering the fact that it was heated. Enough said. It was my train.

Only short minutes later I alighted onto another train platform. 'Scoul,' the sign said. I was here, wherever 'here' was. I absolutely was not sure, but was fairly confident that I had arrived at the destination printed on my ticket, after virtually no instructions on how to get there. Move over, "Amazing Race!" I *can* find my way, though cold and shaking.

A vehicle with 'Gonzo Productions' on the side sat in the small parking lot, motor running. I saw a shadowy arm wave at me, but no one stepped out into the snow, impressing me with someone's basic common sense. I was cold enough for both of us.

I rushed over, hopped in, and explained that my luggage was still…somewhere else. The girl driving told me that several of the others (Ah! I knew there were more!) were also missing luggage, and it would be retrieved soon. We drove a short distance through the snowstorm, arriving at a small hotel. I was escorted quickly through the lobby and into a room, from where I was told never to emerge until someone came to fetch me. (That's what they said. "Fetch me." I worried that I had been abducted onto an English show without knowing it, not a real stretch for a show as complex as "The Mole.")

"Are you hungry?" Well, there had been neither time nor opportunity to eat in Zurich, and certainly not on the multiple trains between there and here, wherever here was. And, frankly, I was so concerned with the prospect of being the 'Mole' that I was…surprisingly hungry.

"Sure, I could use something to eat. Can you include a beer or two?"

"Not a problem; someone will bring it up to you soon." And they did.

Meanwhile, I was sitting in a room, with instructions to not even open my curtains! I ignored that warning and opened the curtains widely, watching the snow fall and getting an occasional glimpse of the mountains surrounding us. Incredibly beautiful! And, while I had been informed that during the upcoming game we were not to be allowed to watch TV, read papers, call anyone, read any current magazines, and neither communicate nor receive communications of any form from anyone other than each other and the producers, I wasn't quite sure if the game had really started yet, so turned on the television. Darn the luck, but all broadcasts were in a foreign language, and here I was an American. Who would have guessed?! However, French Clay Court Tennis Championships were on, and I didn't need commentary in English to enjoy the action. Nor French.

So, I settled in with a couple of sandwiches and some good Swiss beer, only to be interrupted almost immediately.

"You need to fill out these biography questionnaires." In front of me were about 20 pages of questions, and upon scanning them I found that they were mostly repeats of the questions Shirley had answered for me several weeks before. What had she put down? Was this a test? If I did not match her answers would I have to head out into the snowstorm and find my way home? I had no idea what most of her answers had been! After all, she is the literary one, and had put down the answers she thought they would like to see to make my application stand out. She obviously had been right, because here I was. Now, I was being forced to think up answers on my own! Would the producers accept as my favorite book not, as Shirley might have put down, "The Three Faces of Eve," but instead be satisfied with just the centerfold of Eve? (These questions and answers were the basis of many of the questions asked on the quizzes over the next 6 weeks, and the producers had obviously taken the answers Shirley had provided initially and applied them thereto. Luckily, I got to proof read each quiz and its answers prior to everyone being tested, and replaced the erroneous answers with the answers I had given to the others as we questioned each other. It did confuse the producers, however. "Are you *sure* that is the answer? We had something different in our paperwork.")

"Yep, I'm sure; I've grown a lot during the taping of this show, changing my outlook on life." Right.

Then came about 36 hours of boredom. I was visited several times a day by various Gonzo employees, including several times by Patti Stone, who was to be our "den mother." She and her friend Debbie Wier were responsible for the care and feeding of the inmates, as well as keeping us on schedule and happy. I was given ample beer and repeatedly counseled to never look out the window and keep the curtains shut, and *certainly* never to leave the room. As soon as she would leave I would open the curtains widely and gaze out on the mountains again. On the morning of the second day the sun came out on the snow, and by late afternoon only patches remained. I would lean out cautiously looking back and forth, attempting to see someone. Anyone! However, I never caught a glimpse of any of the other players. During this time I really expected the producers to sneak into my room and brief me, but that never happened. I found out much later that no one on the set other than the producers knew who the Mole was (not even Anderson Cooper), and they did not want to reveal that fact to anyone, so dared not come to any room. However, their absence did not improve my frame of mind in the least. How could I carry this off?

Meanwhile, having way too much time to think, I developed further (and well deserved) guilt feelings about Mom. What in the world was I doing here?! I was literally unable to sleep either of the nights I was waiting in that room, and my guilt and apprehension grew exponentially as I sat. Not only was I a bad son, but there was no chance in hell that I could carry this off successfully! I was to find out that there were 85 crew members, 4 producers, 14 players, 2 alternates, and 7 large truck loads of sound and lighting equipment in this entourage, and I was about to screw up so royally that all involved would lose their jobs! I lay awake at night envisioning all the ways catastrophe could happen, and there were many. All my fault, with the possible exception of an avalanche.

My luggage did eventually show up. I luckily had several books in it. I would like to report that I had carried along the unabridged Bible and perhaps "War and Peace," but I actually carried along several current mystery and science fiction books. I had seen the movies, and knew how both of the former books ended.

Finally, early on 4 June, there was a knock on my door well before sunrise. "Put on this blindfold and don't say anything." I did all of this without commenting on it, which

Reflections of The Mole

seemed to fit the conditions given. Shortly someone came into the room and took my elbow. "Come with me, and step up and down when I tell you." Made lots of sense to me, inasmuch as I could see nothing.

We went outside the hotel, where I was maneuvered into a van in which sat multiple other bodies. No whispering, no noise. The van started up, and we ascended sharply from the hotel for 30 minutes or so, then were escorted from the van and led to what felt like a rocky wall. "Everyone, sit or lean on the wall, but don't lean back; it's a long way down." Got it. Don't lean back. I was aware of considerable shuffling and movement around me as the other players abruptly leaned forward, but no one talked.

Suddenly a hand gripped my elbow and I was walked quite a distance away. (I found out later that we all were led away, one by one, and one of the producers would ask if we were doing OK.) In my case, a voice whispered, "Try to sabotage the first game. If you are selected as a leader, and we think you will be because of your background, try to choose teams for the various tasks that might fail." End of instruction. I didn't even know who was talking to me! It could be one of the other players, trying already to figure out who the Mole was. I didn't know.

We were soon led up a steep hill, then into an old, drafty stone building. We stood around quite a while, and someone said, "If you have to go to the bathroom, hold your hand up, please." Apparently several folks did so, because I could hear considerable movement. I was so concerned with trying to figure out how to sabotage a game which I knew nothing about that going to the bathroom never occurred to me. How could I plan when I had no idea what was going to happen?

We were then led, one by one, into a large room and seated close to each other. I could feel someone on my right, but the chair to my left was empty. A familiar voice, "Do we have everyone?" I *knew* that voice. Anderson Cooper! An answer from one of the producers, "No, we're still missing one. He's having problems in the bathroom."

Finally, someone sat down on my left. "Here he is."

The games then began. Anderson Cooper: "Everyone! Remove your masks!" Let the games begin! "No talking!"

I looked around, casually, trying to appear nonchalant and not obviously stare at everyone else, all of whom were inspecting each other as closely as I was attempting to appear not to do. I noted that the fellow on my left who had entered late was a tall fellow with a small goatee. He whispered, "Sorry I'm late; travel really upsets my stomach. I've had a nervous stomach ever since we arrived."

Anderson: "I said **no talking**!" Anderson was steely eyed, not grinning. Looking grim. To my right sat Myra, a 46 year old airlines pilot from San Diego. She had the biggest grin there, eyes flashing as she looked happily about.

Anderson had each of us stand and introduce ourselves, giving a very brief bio of who we were. He had us do this several times, actually, the only time this was to occur during the taping of the show. It was, after all, a 'reality' show, and there were to be no retakes. We weren't actors, and retakes would likely just confuse us! However, the sound and light technicians were trying to calibrate their equipment, so on this initial effort we all got to introduce ourselves 3 or 4 times.

We were then told to select two leaders. Ali, a former Navy nurse, immediately nominated me. "He's a real Admiral!" Everyone seemed OK with that. I had done a quick survey of the people there, and would have liked for one of the women to be the other leader. I figured that the two leaders would be working together, and thought I might have a better chance of influencing one of them rather than one of the guys. (My initial preference was Lisa, an Assistant US Attorney from Chicago. After a couple of days association with her, I realized that if Lisa had indeed been selected, I would have had no chance at all of swaying her about anything!) However, one of the others nominated Darwin, a 30 year old bald headed black lawyer from New York City, and he was immediately accepted.

Anderson told us, "You have 5 minutes after I finish speaking to go to the next room, where you will find your luggage. You will find Mole bags with your names on them. Pack those bags with all the items you want from your luggage for your time in Europe. You will not see the remaining luggage again until you leave the show!" Wow! I thought I had packed my bag sparingly as it was, and now I had to pare away half of that again!

"Leaders, you have those 5 minutes to get to know the other 12, and are then going to pick teams for the games coming up today based on your extensive knowledge of the capabilities of your fellow players." He delivered this is a deadpan voice, not cracking a smile. Anderson was good at that, not cracking a smile. I determined at that moment that I did not want him looking at me, if I could prevent it. I felt enough pressure as it was. Besides that, I had not managed to sleep since arriving in Europe!

He finished speaking, and we all rushed into the next room. I hastily piled as many clothes and books as possible into my Mole bag, all the while talking and listening to as many of my fellow players as I could.

"Time's up! Everyone outside. Darwin and Bill, come with me." We followed Anderson outside into a beautiful Swiss day, and found ourselves outside a 1000 year old castle high in the mountains. Anderson explained the three games we were to pick teams for. The first was to be a bike ride down a steep hill where the rider would retrieve a crossbow arrow, then puff his way back up, where he had to calm down, then be allowed three tries to shoot the arrow into the bull's eye of a target. If he missed, he had to ride back and do the entire task over again.

While I had not had time to get to know the others very much, Rob, a magician, had told me in the brief time that we chatted that he tried "never to go outside." He did video training films, and described himself as "totally non-physical." However, he was only 22, and when Darwin said, "What about Rob? You talked to him. I think he's young enough that he could do the bike ride."

"Sure, why not?" We then picked two others, but I was content with picking Rob. I could always use the excuse that I really did not get to chat with him enough to get to know him. If I had been picking the *best* team for this event, my other selection would have been either Patrick, who appeared very fit, or Lisa, who is a competitor of renown! For my purposes, however, Rob would do.

For the second game, the 'Rope/Pulse' game, we had to pick 4 players to go up and walk on a rope strung 20 feet off the ground between two trees, holding on to a rope 6 or 7 feet above their head. They were to wear a pulse monitor, and if their pulse went over 135 had to stop in place until it went back below that. Again, they had a time limit. I didn't really care who else did that, but wanted two people specifically, Al and Myra. I knew Al had been having problems with traveling, and had spent the morning in the bathroom. He should be a little dehydrated, and that combined with the altitude should drive his pulse way up. Myra was short, about 5 feet tall. I figured she might have trouble reaching the rope above her, although as an airline pilot I doubted that the height would be a significant barrier to her success. Again, the logical choice for this game would have been Elavia, a yoga practitioner. During my brief (and confusing) chat with her I had gleaned that she practiced yoga daily. She likely could have been excellent in pulse control; I certainly did not want her to do this event!

The final game was to jump from a 250 foot bridge, swinging on a 100 foot rope. I didn't care who did that, inasmuch as we were not putting any money on that game. I did mention that Patrick was game for anything, and certainly was a natural for this. (We were to pick 2 of the three games to bet on, and I felt that I had managed to stack the deck well enough on the first two.) However, both Darwin and I wanted to jump off that bridge, and immediately began bugging Anderson and the producers to let us do that with the others.

Darwin and I went with Anderson to the top of a little hill to watch the first game. Anderson cautioned us to not talk to the other players during the day; after all, they did not know what was riding on each game, and he did not want us giving that data to them. The bike game began, with $40,000 riding on it. Bribs and Bob were the first two riders, and, as expected, had little difficulty doing the tasks. Plenty of time left. Then came Rob. He rode *down* hill fairly well, though he was pretty wobbly. I became a little concerned that he might crash going down and hurt himself. But, he made it down and retrieved the arrows OK. Now came the part of my calculated deception that should pay off! He started back up the hill, and almost immediately became nauseated and got off the bike, pushing it slowly while dry heaving vigorously. Inasmuch as Darwin and I were the team leaders, and it did not interfere with my strategy and would add to my stature as a team player, we ran to the edge of the hill and started urging him on, cheering loudly.

"I **told** you, no talking to the other players!" We jumped back from an apparently angry Anderson Cooper. He was in our faces, and both Darwin and I reacted somewhat negatively. Actually, Darwin got pissed,. I was just startled, and irritated, inasmuch as I had already determined that I needed to stay in the background where Anderson was concerned. Let him make friends, or not, with the others. I just wanted him to forget that I was there!

Much to my surprise and chagrin, Rob finally crested the hill, leaning over the bike and heaving mightily, but he was there.

He picked up the crossbow and took aim, fatigued, arms wavering about wildly. I looked on, smiling. He could never do it! And, if he missed three times, he had to go back down the mountain and get another arrow. The money was as good as mine! Arms wavering, stomach heaving, eyes bleary, Rob tried to hold the crossbow in position, closed both eyes, and shot...right in the bull's eye! I couldn't believe it, and neither could Rob. (Much later, I asked him if it thought it odd that we had selected him to do the bike ride, inasmuch as he had told me he never rode bikes. He replied that he just never thought about it. He was so happy at having completed the task he never paused to think if there might have been a reason he was chosen. Too bad. That's the nature of this show; you have to think about every possible thing if you are to survive. Rob didn't.)

Toward the end of the bike portion of the day, Darwin suddenly proposed that we form a coalition together. I casually replied, "Sure," and he reached across to shake hands on it. We shook, and that was the last we ever discussed this partnership.

I was to find out over the course of the next several weeks that Darwin firmly believed in having a coalition with everyone, including the cameramen and Anderson Cooper, if possible. His motto was: "No information is worthless; all information is suspect." I guess he figured that if he formed a coalition with everyone, someone might be of benefit to him...somehow. I'm certainly not sure how! In actuality, I had no desire to have a coalition with anyone. I wanted free reign on my abilities to subtly screw the games up, and did not need any other worries!

The second game went pretty much as I had planned. Myra, Lisa, and Heather made it across the rope with ease, much to my surprise. Myra did have to stand on tiptoes to reach the upper rope, but seemed unconcerned. Their pulse actually *dropped* as they crossed it! However, again, Al met all my expectations. His pulse shot to above 135 quickly, and he had to

Reflections of The Mole

stop advancing. He became upset, which amplified his problem. Minutes passed, and Myra, a former physician's assistant, yelled up, "Massage your carotid! It'll slow your pulse!"

Helpfully, I yelled, "Or, you'll faint!" Just trying to be of assistance, mind you.

Finally, with only 2 or 3 minutes left in the hour they had been given, he managed to inch his way across! Darn! I was such a lousy Mole! I couldn't even sabotage a dollar's worth that first day!

Along came the bridge jump, with Darwin and me bugging the producers to be allowed to jump. They kept laughing at us, but finally explained that due to insurance considerations, there was no chance we were to be allowed to do so. We watched, irritated (as well as being a disappointed failure as a Mole on my part), as Patrick boldly jumped. Then, Dorothy, scared but defiant. Ali came next, and was rather calm and smiling serenely as she leaped into space, looking up at the top of her arc and smiling and waving at Darwin and me. Then came Katie, the school teacher from New Hampshire. Panicked, crying profusely, she finally overcame her fear and leaped off. She cried copious amounts of tears until she was pulled back up on the bridge, whereupon the tears immediately shut off. The river below was spilling over its banks by that time, however. That girl could cry!

Finally, Elavia. None of us had even figured out what her name was by this time. In fact, several names that were somewhat similar to her name were proposed, but silently rejected by her. Incredibly mysterious looking, never looking directly at you, but always cutting her eyes up at you from another angle. Not talkative. Remote. Anderson pulled her off to one side and chatted with her. Finally, she came back to the group and announced that she was not going to jump; she had been offered an exemption if she would skip the jump, and had taken it. That meant she could not be kicked off the show at the first execution. Luckily for the group (and unlucky for me), there was no money riding on everyone jumping, so the group walked away with $60,000 that day. I was truly a parody of a Mole, and could feel the producers sighing heavily and regretting not picking someone else. Anyone else!

Now, I knew that I was going to be briefed as we went along about all upcoming games, somehow, and knew that I was going to have to do something that Admirals almost never have to do: think, carefully, before I talked! Every time. No quick answers or observations. I had decided to put that into practice immediately, and had done so all day. Darwin, quick witted and quicker with his tongue, dashed off observations and speculations about who the Mole might be all day, proposing alliances, pushing, theorizing. Every time he asked me something, or at times when I was expected to respond, I would always pause for a couple of seconds and think about my answer. Was it going to give anything away? I would finally answer his questions and observations, but ever so hesitantly and slowly. At the end of the day, I felt confident that I had not given myself away, even while conceding to myself that it really should not be a concern; if I continued to do as poorly as I had started, it didn't make any difference who knew I was the Mole! (I did not realize then what effect my hesitation in answering might have on Darwin; I can only *dream* that I could have that much foresight!)

Toward the end of the day, before Darwin and I joined the others, I casually mentioned to him that maybe we should have put Elavia on the ropes because of her yoga background, and perhaps Patrick could have done a better job than Rob had, inasmuch as Patrick was a competitive rider. I did this strictly to make Darwin pause a little and think, perhaps wondering why I had just now brought those facts up. However, inasmuch as we had won $60,000 already, Darwin ignored my statements, dismissing them with a "Whatever." I was to speculate many times over the upcoming weeks about a lawyer's theoretical ability to digest facts and come up with reasonable conclusions. Darwin seemed to defy that premise. Of course, he would be the first to state that: 1. He does not like being a lawyer, and, 2. He works corporate law anyway, and logic is not necessarily a valued part of their thinking processes. (My words, of course. Darwin might not really say this…or he might.)

Thus, the first day's games ended, and we were piled in several vans and driven into the gathering darkness, heading up a steep mountainside on a small dirt road. We finally came to a halt about ¼ mile from a cabin lit up on the slope, and were dropped off and told that we were to head toward the lights. We did so, arriving at a cabin with a couple of large bunk rooms, a kitchen, a small dining room, and several crew members milling about, building fires inside and out and cooking.

A word about the crew. They were told in our presence that if they ever attempted to talk to one of us, or responded to an approach by one of us and had a general conversation outside of strict, need-to-know directions regarding the various games, they would be fired on the spot. We were a little disbelieving of this heavy-handed approach, but the producers assured us that they were serious. One of the problems with these reality shows where the people are eliminated one by one seems to be that the crew developed their favorite players, and the fear was that either intentionally or by accident they might give away a bit of information that would allow a player to stay in the game. The producers were really paranoid about that, and thus the rule. You talk, you walk.

As we settled into the cabin, claiming bunks, getting plates of food, sipping some wine or beer, we noticed the Mole from the first season, Kathryn. She was off to the side, writing. I immediately went over to her.

"Hello! You're Kathryn, aren't you?!" She looked up at me, said nothing, and got up and left the room. So much for my charm! We saw her frequently during the coming weeks, but she never talked with us. (There was the small matter of the danger of being fired which might have had a dampening effect, I suppose. Or, maybe she just didn't like us!)

We all immediately started quizzing each other, attempting to elicit as much information as possible about each other. We had all filled out the same bio information, and knew from the first show that the answers to that information comprised most of the questions asked during the upcoming quizzes. And, while only one of us was the Mole, none of us (with the possible exception of me) knew who that one was. Therefore, we all had to learn everything, and I mean everything, about each other. A favorite gambit for the first few days was to suddenly turn to one of the others, only inches away from their face, and demand, "**Are you the Mole**!?" Somehow, the reaction of the person being asked was supposed to be significant. I'm not sure how. Some folks even started answering, "Sure! I thought you'd never ask!" That game became old, quickly, however, and only Patrick persisted in it till his end. Darwin pointed out to the group that I was just the opposite of Kathryn, and was therefore the most likely to be the Mole.

I replied to that, "Darwin, your logic is perfect. Now, think about it. Would the producers pick the most likely one of us to be the Mole? The answer is, probably not. Therefore, if you apply more logic to it, I am not only *not* the most likely, but in fact the *least* likely person to be the Mole!" Several of the others agreed with that logic. I then continued, "Therefore, as the *least* likely person here to be chosen as the Mole, there is an excellent chance I am, indeed, the Mole." Silence for a moment.

"Screw this! Let's talk about something else!" Darwin had a disgusted look on his face. This game requires the most convoluted logic...and lots of luck.

This went on for hours. I was exhausted, inasmuch as I still had not managed to fall asleep in Europe. Also, as the other men will attest to, when I'm tired or have drunk too much, I snore, *loudly*. So, sometime after midnight I decided to try to sleep in the dining room on a couch, in an attempt not to eventually disrupt the sleep of the others. I was not successful at falling asleep, so picked up a cold beer and stepped outside. I had to come to grips with my paranoia about possibly ruining the show, as well as figure out how I was going to communicate with these folks from a distant generation. It was tough! They seemed to know all about each other, and I was definitely the odd man out in my mind. Even Patrick, with teenagers at home, knew what they were talking about. And Myra? She might have been 46, but was definitely a teen-ager at heart and in spirit. She had no problem communicating at all. What could I do? Perhaps I could subtly appear to undermine the producers' authority when I got the chance. This might serve to both let the others identify with me a little, and give them another indication that perhaps I really wasn't the Mole…so long as I did not go overboard with my rebelling attitude. Too much rebellion might be suspicious, also. Shoot, what am I saying?! Anything might be suspicious! I just wasn't sure what was and was not!

I was to find out later that back inside, the quizzing of each other continued heatedly. People were writing down information in their journals furiously. The journals had been on a table when we arrived, and we were told to pick one. Everyone was suspicious about who picked which number, and great care was taken by all to record which number belonged to whom, and in what order people had picked their books. There seemed to be some feeling that the Mole would have a particular number. I waited until only one journal was left to grab it, thus taking myself out of consideration…but not really, as the Mole might deliberately wait until the last journal was left. Or not. As I said, significance can be read into any action if you are paranoid, and we all were.

After I had left the room, something happened. I'm not sure exactly what it was, but the stories differ. According to Bob, he called out to Darwin, "D! How about Bill? You were with him all day, and clearly know him better than any of us. Could he be the Mole?"

Darwin laughed, "Are you kidding? Old Bill is not only getting long in the tooth, he is *really* slow mentally. It takes him forever to answer a question!" (Thus the previously mentioned, and totally unintended, side effect of my deliberate answers to Darwin. I couldn't have done better if I had planned it! Darwin vehemently denies these...exact...words, but others say they heard them; regardless, it was a gift to me! And, if D. is right and the others are wrong, and he didn't say this...he should have. Makes for a better story line. And, let's face it. Darwin...somehow...convinced almost everyone else that I couldn't be the Mole. He is a persuasive...and probably a pretty good, lawyer!)

Inadvertently Darwin and I had formed an unwitting alliance, with me as the principal benefactor. Having nothing to go on about each other, we all were willing to accept observations initially about others from someone who sounded like they knew what they were talking about, and Darwin was the most positive minded person you could find. He *never* doubted himself, and therefore most others didn't really doubt him, either. In fact, his total confidence made him a very likely candidate to be the Mole. With one exception, briefly, from that moment on I was not a consideration by the others to be the Mole. If I had known that then, I would have felt lots better!

After only a couple of hours sleep, we were herded outside and down to a beautiful meadow, where again we were allowed to spend the day in a relatively free fashion, with no one but cameramen about, and few of them. We explored the surrounding hills, played soccer, and watched Rob as he performed magic card tricks for the incredibly tame cows milling about the meadow. A nice day, and again one intended to allow us to get to know each other as quickly as possible. The journals were always in clear evidence, of course, with most folks writing furiously in them. There were several exceptions, however. Myra and Rob did not write much in their journals, and while I made a minimal effort, shoot, I was the Mole! Why should I put all that useless information about everyone else down in my journal?

The second night we were taken to another castle and allowed to check in. We were each assigned roommates, and ultimately virtually all the men and all the women had roomed with everyone of the same sex. (For awhile there was speculation about the clause in the ABC contract about them not being responsible for any pregnancy resulting from the show, but there was no opportunity for such acts, and little inclination.)

I was in my room, alone, when there was a knock on the door. I opened it to find all four producers of the show standing there. They entered. I don't know to this day how they got to my room unseen, nor where my roommate was at the time, but in retrospect I knew they must have been extremely worried to have taken such a chance.

"Bill, how are you doing? You really acted exhausted last night and today, and just don't seem like yourself. Is anything wrong?"

"Guys, I have to admit that these days have been very, very hard on me. I can't get over my guilt about leaving Mom behind in the hospital, and haven't slept since we arrived here. I am exhausted. And, I'm paranoid. I sit here seeing every possible way I could screw this show up!"

"Well, do you think you are going to hack it? We **have** to know prior to the quiz tomorrow night. We do have alternates along, and could replace you prior to that quiz without disruption to the show. **But**! You've got to level with us. Are you going to be able to do this?"

"Gentlemen, the last thing I want to do is ruin the show. Let me try to sleep tonight, and if it's OK with you, we can make a final determination tomorrow."

"Fine. Tomorrow we will be interviewing each of you for an hour and a half, and the rest will remain in their rooms. You should be able to rest up all day if you need to." (This last bit of foreknowledge almost did me in a few hours later.)

After we had settled in, about midnight the den mothers knocked on all the doors and told us to get dressed and meet down in the lobby. We all had green shoulder bags that had been issued to us, and some of us carried quite a bit of our personal gear in those bags when we left the hotel…luckily for us, as it turned out.

We were all seated in a bus and headed across the mountains. Soon, in the distance we could see what appeared to be a bonfire, and we pulled up short of it, disembarked, and walked to a bluff looking down on a large fire. Hanging above it was a cargo net holding some bags, too far away to identify.

Anderson announced, "OK, listen up! You've all been quizzing each other non-stop for 48 hours now. You should know everything about each other by this time. I need you to select the 4 fellow players, immediately, who you think have elicited the most information about all of you, and whom you trust to answer any questions about each of you correctly. Keep in mind that if you inadvertently select the Mole as one of the four, that person could screw the game up and cost you lots of money…and much more."

We all looked around and picked 4 to answer questions. Ali, Dorothy, Katie, and Patrick.

One of them…or all of them…would surely screw up and look suspicious to the others! I needed the reassurance of someone else looking like the Mole, inasmuch as I felt like it was stamped clearly for all to see on my forehead. I carefully refrained from looking smart, which was an unnecessary precaution after Darwin's observations about me the previous evening. The four smart ones were taken down below us so that we could not clue them to the answers.

Anderson then announced, "OK, you've made your selections. Again, I must caution you that if you have selected the Mole as part of this group, it might cost you more than money. Because! If you look closely (as he handed us binoculars) at the bags in that cargo net suspended over that fire, you will see *your* bags containing all the possessions you left behind in your rooms. Look carefully."

Katie grabbed the binoculars. "Those **are** our bags! My God!" Quite a few of the others voiced similar concerns.

The questions, absolutely impossible to get right, followed. After each wrong answer, the crane lowered the cargo net partway down. The group gasped with each move, and tears started flowing.

Heather cried, "My Bible is in that bag! It's a family keepsake, and I always have it with me!"

Lisa noted that her 2 carat (soon to be as valuable as 2…carrots) earrings were in hers, and several of us helpfully pointed out to her that diamonds won't burn, and we might be able to find them in the ashes after they had cooled. She did not seem mollified. Katie was crying hysterically. "Meadow Muffin, Meadow Muffin! My cow is in my bag!" We all looked at each other in some confusion. The bags just did not seem that roomy. With some exasperation she explained that Meadow Muffin was a stuffed cow that she had owned all her life, and never left behind. Well, she seemed like a good hearted girl; maybe Meadow Muffin would just get to heaven a little sooner than she would.

Questions asked, answers wrong, bags lowered. Then they really burned. Now, I knew nothing about this. While I was the Mole, I was not told more than I had to know so that I could react naturally. So, I did. "Bull! I don't believe it! There's no way they burned all of our clothes! The producers aren't that dumb...I guess." (My first attempt to badmouth the producers.)

"But, you saw the bags! Those were our bags! They had our names on them!"

"Right, they had our names on them. I wonder how much it costs ABC to have duplicate bags made up?!"

"That seems awfully suspicious, Bill! You don't seem concerned at all."

"Well, folks, I'm really not that concerned. I absolutely don't believe they will burn our bags. Period! But! If they *did* happen to burn my clothes, I've got to tell you that I'm not emotionally involved with my clothes. I figure anything they buy me to replace them will be better than I brought."

We filed back to the bus, glumly, and climbed on. By this time it was 2:00 AM, and it was dark on the bus. Myra sat down in front of me and noted, "Man, I'm pooped! I wonder if we are going to go like this every night."

I responded, violating the one rule I had strictly made to myself the day before. "Ah, we'll have plenty of time to rest tomorrow while we all get interviews." Oops! I didn't say that!

Myra immediately picked up on the slip. "How do you know that?" She turned around in her seat and looked in the dark back at me. If it had been light I would have been done for. I could feel the color rising in my face as I realized what I had just said.

"Ahh. Patti mentioned it on the way back to the bus a while ago." Right. As if Myra was going to buy that one!

At that moment Patti stood up. "May I have your attention! Tomorrow is quiz day. That means that each of you will undergo a 90 minute interview on camera, and the rest of you will remain in your rooms all day, until the quiz tomorrow night. So, don't worry about not getting much sleep the last couple of nights. You'll be able to sleep as much as you want tomorrow."

I sat, disbelieving. I could not believe that Patti had just, totally by accident, confirmed the story I had made up to tell Myra. Myra sat back and relaxed, dozing immediately, and never gave another thought to my slip. (Until months later as she kicked herself repeatedly when we discussed it.)

Back to the hotel we went, climbing wearily into bed. I still had not slept in Switzerland, and now was faced with the pressure of trying to decide if I could really do this! And, I still was lying there in the dark, sweating, thinking of what might be, thinking of Mom, one of the toughest people I have ever known. Could she survive this? Should I be here playing games?

VIII

Mom

Mom was made of strong stuff; somewhat stronger than most people, and certainly stronger than all us kids as we were growing up!

She was the oldest of 12 children, and along with her twin brothers one year younger than she, terrorized the other kids and the teachers at the school they went to with their antics and practical jokes. They weren't bad; just very, very active, and very smart. And, probably bored. Regardless, teachers dreaded teaching at that one-room school house, and were justified in their dread!

When Mom was 14, Dad came a'visiting. He was 24, the oldest of 14 kids, and a quiet, religious man. He was actually doing church census, and although Mom had been in a Sunday school class he had taught a couple of years earlier, he did not remember her. He had just returned from spending a year working in Franklin Delano Roosevelt's CCC camps, building railroads and highways.

Mom and her brothers weren't sure of Dad's intentions, inasmuch as my Grandmother was actually closer in age to Dad; she was 32. So, they did what any red-blooded brood of hyperactive and mischievous kids in those days would do; they threw rocks at Dad's horse and made it run away with him. (Dad's story is that Mom just wanted to meet him and this was the only way she could get his attention.)

Now, as the oldest of 12 kids (some of whom had not been born yet), Mom was ready to quit being the "mom" to them, and I think she saw in my quiet Dad a way out. Regardless, they were soon married. And, while the age difference (14 and 24)

Reflections of The Mole

seems rather extreme, Mom shouldn't be faulted too much for choosing Dad. He certainly had no choice in the matter; she knew what she wanted. In fact, she was seldom unsure of what she wanted in her entire life! Dad always said the best way to get a good wife was to marry her young and raise her right. I suspect that in Mom he got considerably more than he bargained for!

They settled into their wonderful "digs;" actually, a tent. They lived in a 12 X 15' tent for the first year of their marriage, and Mom says it was the best year of her life. (Of course, at age 14 she was probably still in the "playing house" mode, and this was just another chapter…without all her younger siblings to supervise.)

15 months after marriage my oldest sister Ruth was born, followed closely by Cleta and Gertha. I'm sure Dad was despairing; nothing but women! He must have changed things up somewhat then, and 4 years after Gertha I came along. Pointy-headed and funny looking, but a male being, by damn!

We had a tiny farm in Oklahoma, as noted before; this was a place guaranteed to ensure that one remain penniless! So when I was about 7 Dad started driving trucks on the pipeline, traveling all over the country. Mom was perfectly capable of running things on the farm and in the small country store we tried to run for a while, before finding out that it too was designed to suck the last cent out of unsuspecting owners.

During the next several years we would leave on sudden trips to see Dad, wherever he might be. Mom's technique was simple. She would get out a road atlas of the US, take a ruler, and draw a straight line from our farm to wherever Dad was. Then, she would attempt to stick as closely as possible to that line while driving. If a highway was going that way, fine. Otherwise, a gravel road, a dirt path, or anything semi-navigable in a 1946 Chevy without air conditioning. We saw some interesting country, met some wonderful people, and got lost innumerable times. However, Mom always managed to extricate us from whichever national monument we had become lost in, and those trips will always stand out in my mind as representing her irrepressible spirit.

Our life paralleled our road trips…adventuresome, somewhat confused, but eventually we found our way, and one way or another Mom was usually at the center of things. She had multiple major surgeries in her lifetime. A ruptured gall bladder, an aortic aneurysm repair, a quadruple bypass, a swallowed a toothpick with a resultant bowel perforation, and multiple surgeries later for cancer. And, she just bounced back stronger each time, often to our distress. We would not have minded if she had just slowed down a little bit occasionally! Each surgery just served to speed her up that much more.

Mom loved my travels; making Admiral was OK, but inasmuch as she had never been around the military, didn't mean as much to her as my living all over the world. She was always quizzing me about the people around the planet, and eagerly awaiting my next trip so she could talk with her friends about it.

So, here I was, headed off into parts unknown (to both of us) again. She would rather take a chance on living through her cancer and being able to regale her friends with my latest travels than have me remain behind to see if she survived. After all, while she was 81 at that time, she denied being "old," and was rather disdainful of all the things "old folks" seemed to resort to. If immortality were a state of mind, she would be with us forever.

IX

Decision Time

Ah, the morning of our first quiz. Someone would be going home tonight...and it might be the Mole!

I awakened to the sound of my door opening. The producers and cameramen all had passkeys. One of the prices you pay for the potential of being recognizable by the entire country is a total lack of privacy. We would awaken most mornings, pull back the covers...and see three cameramen---or women---standing there with a large camera pointed our way. I'm not sure what they expected to see; maybe just one of the perks of the profession is getting to observe folks with bad morning breath and uncombed hair peering blearily out of their beds and looking...well, like folks with uncombed hair and bad breath. (Wow! I want to be a cameraman!)

In walked four producers. They looked worried. Long faces, no smiles. Where was my roommate? I don't know. (He was doing the first interview of the day, it turned out.)

"Bill, how are you this morning? Any better? Can you hang in here, or do we need to call one of the alternates?" They looked very serious and concerned, as only men with their fortunes and reputations riding on the backs of a guilt-ridden Mole can look.

I gazed at each in turn, stretched, and said, "Fellows, I'm fine! I just got a great night's sleep, and feel wonderful! Bring on the games! Excuse me for a moment; my teeth are in need of a morning brushing." With that, I hopped up and went into the bathroom, firmly closing the door behind me. It's hard to have a serious conversation with producers in the morning when you have a full bladder.

I emerged a few minutes later, and the amassed producers looked no happier. In fact, they now looked frankly worried, and a little perplexed.

"Bill, yesterday you were a wreck! You had bags under your eyes so big we couldn't even airbrush them out in editing. What happened last night? Did you stay in your room? Why are you suddenly so chipper?" They were looking at each other uneasily. Was I out of contact with reality suddenly? Had I broken under the pressure? Should they lose all faith in the military? Was I dangerous? After all, I'm a big boy, and even though Darwin felt like I was rather long in the tooth, if unleashed I could be dangerous for those exceedingly few moments until I ran out of energy.

"Guys, I'm not sure how to tell you this without sounding…oh, like I believe in aliens or the cookie monster or something. Last night when we got back in from the most delightful bonfire ("And, tell me, honestly. Those weren't really our bags you burned, were they?" They didn't answer.), I lay down with some severe reservations, and thought about quitting and letting you put someone more stable in my slot. But! Suddenly I felt a warm feeling, and felt the presence of my Mom. Not the real, physical presence, but just the…essence of her. Really! I don't believe…much…in the occult, but that Mom presence told me, "Son, I'm fine. I just want you to relax and enjoy yourself. Don't worry about me." I smiled, rolled over, and did not awaken until you all came in a few minutes ago."

I looked at them, smiling. They looked at me, unsmiling. They looked at each other, then me, then elsewhere. No comment.

Finally, "Your Mom's….essence?"

"I don't know what it was, fellows! Shoot, probably just a great defense mechanism I have built in. I don't care. I feel fine."

"Ah….Okay. We'll…be back." They turned and left the room, not daring to look back at me. Probably afraid of turning to stone, or seeing a miasmic mist rising from my skull or something.

A few minutes later there was another knock on the door. In walked Dr. Geoff White, the distinguished psychologist assigned to us for the duration. You would never believe it from watching most television reality shows, but they do strive to keep crazy folks from appearing on them. Homicide and suicide are apt subjects for dramas and comedies, but not reality shows. So, we had our own psychologist to talk us out of our depression, and to identify which of our split personalities should be in evidence at any given moment.

"Bill! How are things?" Right, a social visit!

"Geoff, I'm doing fine. How's the family?"

He frowned. The "family" was not on the agenda. I expect that if I had done something really odd, like don my underwear on my head or the like, he would have just turned around and quietly closed the door as he exited.

"Bill, the producers just told me an interesting story. Can you tell me what happened?"

While I wait for the men in the white coats?

I again went through my story. Geoff, unlike the producers, understood defense mechanisms, and immediately grabbed on the idea. "So, you think your mind just came up with a good rationalization for your remaining here, is that right? And, you didn't…*really*…see your mother last night?"

I pondered, briefly. Actually, I thought I had…*really*…felt my mother's presence. However, it looked apparent to me that that line of thinking would not be a particularly fruitful line to pursue. "You've got it right, Geoff. The occult is something Rod Serling investigates for television. My Mom is 6000 miles away, and did not fly here last night."

He smiled, and relaxed. "Bill, I'll tell you honestly. The producers are really concerned (*about their investment going down the tube...or the booby hatch*) about you, and asked me to come in and evaluate you. Your story...worried them. But! I think you're fine, and just have a great defense mechanism!" I thought talking in psychological terms might get him on my side. "I'll tell them that we can continue with the show as originally planned."

So, the show went on. I really was feeling fine, and still think my mother found a way to reassure me!

I did note that the producers looked rather oddly at me for a few more days, and were careful never to be alone with me. Well, actually, they were careful never to be alone with any of us...but especially me.

X

Let the Games Begin!

Now I was back to simply being paranoid that I was going to ruin the show for everyone else. I'm not an actor. I don't belong to SAG. Why didn't they pick one of the lawyers, Darwin or Lisa? They were trained to do this stuff. In fact, lawyers probably should do all these reality shows. Most of them involve backdoor dealing, deception, moderate amounts of treachery and backstabbing, and it would keep a large number of lawyers off the streets and out of courtrooms!

That day of our first execution was interesting, entertaining, restful (for me, at least; I could not be executed), and informative. We all had to stay in our respective rooms all day, except when we were taken in for interviews. For the interview, I sat down on a stool in a room with several cameramen present, and the producer, Clay, sitting off to one side near the principal camera. I was supposed to answer his questions by rephrasing the question, then giving my answer, inasmuch as his questions could not be heard on camera. I.e., Clay: "What have you found most interesting about the show thus far?" I could not just answer something like, "The tame cattle in the meadow." I had to rephrase his question. "You know, what I have found most interesting during the brief time we have been here has been...." While this technique became somewhat second nature by the time we had finished filming, the immediate tendency was to just answer the question, especially in instances where he asked a question easy to answer and hard to rephrase. In the beginning, I had many instances of first answering his question, then apologizing and rephrasing so that I included the question as an observation. I think there is a game in all of this. Sit around with a group of friends and ask each other questions. When a person answers a question without repeating the essence of the question, they are eliminated. I'll bet most folks are out within 2 questions!

So it was little wonder that the interviews went an hour and a half. A large part of that time was spent in trying to restate what had already been stated. One of the interesting questions asked that first day was, "In one word, what is your initial reaction to your fellow players?" One word?

Ali: Cute

Bribs: Likable

Heather: Texasgirl (Say it fast, one word. They let that go.)

Darwin: Angry (Not sure why; he just impressed me as having a lot of hidden anger. Maybe he didn't like being a lawyer.)

Rob: Amazing (Although Rob really resented being billed as a magician, inasmuch as he runs a video training company, he could do magic with cards and coins. As carefully as we all watched, we could never catch the tricks as he did them.)

Bob: Cocky (Actually, he was just confident, with big teeth.)

Elavia: Mysterious (I'll bet everyone answered either this, or "Sneaky.")

Patrick: Player (He clearly came to play the game his way, more so than anyone else. Within a few days I would have added "Irritating." Patrick just chose to play differently than others. He would have been first voted off in "Survivor.")

Dorothy: Inscrutable (She worked at that Chinese inscrutability thing, and was quite successful. Later, I would have said, "Brilliant.")

Al: Earnest (Al came to play and win, and wanted everyone else to do the same, and follow all the rules.)

Reflections of The Mole

Myra: Delightful (Big smile, mother to Katie...Thank you, thank you, thank you!)

Katie: Emotional (I do mean...emotional! I've never seen so many tears out of one body. She should have looked like a prune from the dehydration.)

Lisa: Analytical (After all, she is a lawyer, and a beer salesman. I suspect she keeps the latter job for respectability.)

Bill: Scared! (They didn't really ask me about me; I just thought you might be counting and be confused when there was one missing.)

At the end of the interview session, Clay explained to me (and the others), "OK, each week we will do one of these interviews, and this will be the one chance you have during the week to speak frankly with me, off mike and off camera. If something is really bothering you and you don't want it on national television, you will have 5 minutes in private with me at the end of each interview to get it off your chest."

Sure enough, at the end of the interview Clay led me out of the room, shut my mike off, and we walked openly into the middle of a small field. Instead of me getting to vent, however, Clay quickly said, "OK, here are the 10 questions we are going to ask tonight. Look them over and see if the answers match what you may have told all the others." I have explained that we quizzed each other constantly about our backgrounds, families, education, first cars, etc., inasmuch as we knew that those answers would be on the tests...but the only correct answers were those that related to the Mole. We were told that we could not lie about any of our bio history, though we were free to lie about anything we observed on the show if we chose to do so. So, each week, while pretending to tell Clay some imagined transgression I did not want repeated on national television, I would quickly read the questions and correct any misinformation they might have included. After all, as I have noted before, they had obtained much of their information from those initial questionnaires we had filled in when we applied. And, inasmuch as Shirley had provided some of my information, and I did not know what she had put down in many cases, I occasionally changed answers that they were sure were right. "Are you sure!? That's what we had down." Me: "As I have said earlier, I've grown emotionally since arriving, and my perspective has changed in some cases." (They seemed to accept this, probably thinking all those years in the Navy had left me emotionally stunted somehow.)

In addition to quickly checking the questions and answers for the quizzes, I was briefed on some of the games we would be playing in the next 3 days. All this took place within 5 minutes, inasmuch as I could spend no more time with Clay than the others did. Needless to say, my information on the pending games was sketchy, but from that I was to try to figure out which of the games I wanted to partake in, which to sabotage, and how to sabotage them. In addition, some of the games I definitely did not want to do, and I had to plan my strategy in order to stay *out* of particular games. Finally, some of the games I was not briefed on at all, and was to play those straight....unless a great chance to sabotage one of them came along.

We all met for dinner, chatted, drank a fair amount of wine and beer, milled about smartly, and prepared to take our first quiz. Gut check time! There was one interesting comment made at dinner that we all noted. Anderson was talking with us all about how we could possibly begin to try to figure out who the Mole was, when Bob spoke up. "I'm almost certain I know who the Mole is!" Everyone was flabbergasted! How could Bob have this foreknowledge? I have never got to ask him who he thought it was, but events were to quickly prove that he didn't have a clue.

We were then led into a small room with a cameraman, an ABC lawyer with 2 stop watches, Anderson Cooper, and a laptop computer with the Mole fingerprint on the screen. We were given initial instructions. "This is a timed quiz. Charles here is a lawyer who works exclusively for ABC, and will be the final arbitrator in case of a tie for last. It will be his decision as to who was the slowest amongst those tied for last and will thus be executed. Once you select 'Next' on the initial computer screen, the time will start. There will be 10 questions, and the correct answer to each and every question will be the answer that pertains to the identity of the Mole. The multiple choice answers will include information about all the remaining players. You need to decide on an answer, then select 'Next' to advance the screen. Once the screen is advanced, you cannot go back; your answer is final. When you click the answer to the 10th question, the time will stop. Any questions?"

"Ahhh. How do we know how well we did? Do we ever get our results?"

"You will know you were not the worst on a quiz when someone else is executed. You will never get to see your results, so will never know if you are on to the identity of the Mole, or are just a little less stupid than another player." Anderson had a way with words.

So, we took our first quiz.

I didn't find it that hard, actually. Of course, the fact that I had read all the questions and provided the answers only a few hours before might have had a bearing on my perception of the quiz. I like that method! This was to prove to be the only series of tests I have ever taken whereby I made all perfect scores.

I should point out that we did not get to take that first quiz until about midnight; they were setting up lighting and sound, I suppose. Regardless, we sat and waited, alone. We were not allowed to be together before the quiz. Following the quiz I was taken to a room to find that I had a new roommate for a few hours, Bob, the toothy one. I had never really spoken to Bob much in the few days we had been playing, so it was fun getting to know him. We each quizzed the other about the 10 questions and answers, though neither of us would tell what our answers were. (Well, I certainly wouldn't!) We talked for about 2 hours about our lives, families, jobs, and hopes for the show. The most fervent hope, voiced by almost everyone at one time or another, was not to be first one off the show! A story that we were all familiar with, whether true or not, was that the first person executed in a French version of the show went back to his room and killed himself, from humiliation. Amazing! A Frenchman who felt he was humiliated enough to commit suicide? That's almost an oxymoron. They seem to have managed to humiliate themselves throughout history in one way or another; how could this have been any worse?

Regardless, none of us wanted to be the first off, and only 2 of us were assured of that. Elavia and the Mole, who was me. At least I thought it was me. Elavia was so sneaky I was starting to doubt my role. Could the producers have recruited her when they thought I was having problems? Could I just be another player now? Might I be the first executed because I put my information down as the answers to all the questions? If so, did I have any recourse? Nope, not a bit. And, it certainly would not be beyond the realm of possibility for a reality show to throw in a twist like having *two* moles! (If I ever get to be a producer of this show, I think I might just designate 2 moles, and not tell either of them that there is another mole running about. Hmmmm.)

Shortly before we were rousted from our room to attend the execution, Bob nervously laughed and said, "Bill, if you're the Mole, I'm screwed!" I looked for the screw marks, and sure enough, they were there!

That first execution did not take place until about 3:00 AM! We were all so tired by that time that we were willing to draw straws to see who went home. As we met and milled about for an hour or so before we went into Anderson's Inner Sanctum, we continued to constantly elicit badly needed information from each other about our pasts. Everyone was nervous, edgy, not meeting each other's eyes, except for Patrick, Myra, Lisa, Bribs, and Darwin. They all seemed confident, even cocky. I worked at projecting a worried image. How could I do this? I tried as best as I could to convince myself that I could be executed, and to appear worried. I furrowed my brow, and managed to work up a little sweat. I don't think anyone even noticed, except Myra. She came up to me and we chatted quite a while. We had some marked similarities in our backgrounds. She was an Air Force reservist, daughter of a career Air Force officer. She was a Physician's Assistant in the Air Force, and had been in Desert Storm. She was very involved in the reserves, as was her boyfriend, another Delta pilot. She was fun to talk to, and other than Patrick, was closest to me in age at 46. We went into the execution together and sat together, which we did for the next 6 weeks, until she was executed. Myra has a strong mothering streak in her, probably from her Puerto Rican background. She could see that I was obviously sweating and appeared nervous, and it was painfully obvious that I was sort of the odd man out of this mole crew. I didn't know their songs, movies, heroes, habits, or language. We could barely be considered to be from the same country! So, I think Myra adopted me as a mother hen might adopt a stray chick who didn't fit in. I suspect that from her medical background she was really concerned about how someone my age might stand up under the pressures of the games and executions. I do feel bad about Myra. Months later, when I was revealed as the Mole and we sat drinking some beer and talking, she asked, "How in the world did you manage to make yourself sweat during the executions?! I was so concerned about you!"

    I really did not know how I managed to do that. Somehow it occurred, however. Myra, as I have noted, seems to have been the only one to really observe that, as I will explain shortly.

Anderson delivered the spiel that he always gave, with an evil glint in his eye and a malicious little smile ever present. He was great at making everyone feel insecure. No matter how good your answer might be to a given question, Anderson had a way of saying, "Really....?," that made you seriously doubt your answer. ("Really! My wife's name *is* Shirley. Isn't it?")

He started calling out names, one by one, typing them in on the computer screen, then hitting "Enter." There was always a great, dramatic pause after he hit that key; that must have been the slowest computer in the world! Then, the thumbprint would show up, either green or red. When he called Bob's name, and the red thumbprint appeared, Bob was devastated. He could not believe it, and looked briefly at me as he left. I was the only person Bob had eliminated totally in his deliberations, and at that moment (he said later) he decided I must be the Mole.

There were gasps around the room, but mostly of relief. No one was too sad to see Bob go, or anyone else, so long as it was not them...except maybe Ali. She liked Bob a little. I mean, we all did, a little. But, Ali *liked* Bob a little. Anderson went around the room, randomly, asking people how they felt about Bob leaving. Several people expressed some sadness, with little conviction. Then Al, honest Al, expressed what everyone else was really feeling. "Ah! I'm not sorry to see him go. I didn't know him anyway! Better him than me." So sayeth we all!

Following the execution, as the time now approached 4:00 AM and we were all ready to fall down with exhaustion, Anderson explained another mole show tradition. Confessional. We each were placed, one at a time, in a small room with only a camera on us, with no other people present. We had 12 minutes to...talk about anything we wanted to talk about to the camera. Selected portions of the clips could later be edited into the show. Most of us absolutely would have preferred to have skipped that routine. It always came after an execution, when by and large you were emotionally drained and thankful to just still be on the show. So, people would sing, do tricks, nap, hold imaginary talks with their spouses (my routine), and fantasize about the future show contracts and riches that might result from being on this show, none of which ever happened, of course! All I wanted was something simple; perhaps to host SNL. Nothing out of the realm of reason, of course.

Thus, our first execution ended. Bob's favorite color was blue, by the way.

Now we were 13, a good number. I was still paranoid, convinced that at any moment I would blow it, Clay would look at me in a disgusted manner, Darwin would say, "Why did you give yourself away like that?" Oklahoma State University would write a letter asking that I stop wearing their shirt on the show; they had enough troubles without me adding to them. Just your standard, run-of-the-mill paranoia.

Bill McDaniel, MD

What Was He Thinking?

Bob

When we first started I didn't really suspect anyone based on looks after we took off the blindfolds as far as I remember. However once I met Lisa I had her in my sights as a suspect. I didn't think anyone would ever suspect that the producers would put in another female attorney as the mole.

I figured with her experience at being an attorney, her smarts and her ability to handle pressure and possibly negotiate deals, would make her an excellent candidate for the mole. I remember that she went just before Al on the tightrope walk. I was watching her every move and she seemed to do the task with relative ease and she seemed to be trying to do a good job at succeeding. This would be a perfect time for the mole to come out and look like a strong player and do a good job because it seems that everyone on the first day was instantly suspect if they did anything that might limit the success of the challenge.

After she was on the tightrope Al had stepped up and he was instantly over the allowed heart rate of 100. He kept saying that he didn't feel like his pulse was that fast and he thought something was wrong with the monitor. Before I had gotten onto the show while I was applying I had been reading up on other mole shows that occurred in Europe. I remember specifically they had a similar challenge and the mole in that show had been able to fix the monitor in a way that gave an improper signal. In that case it made the next person lose the challenge b/c of the high pulse. It would be the perfect diversion. The mole being able to make someone else look like they just weren't strong in the challenge or a potential suspect themselves. I thought Lisa was able to mess with the monitor and get Al to look like he had a very high pulse.

I remember speaking to Darwin about it. Darwin and I had a pact, I can't remember the name of what it was always called a coalition maybe, I don't know. Anyway, Darwin wasn't agreeing with my theory. I think Darwin at the time wouldn't have agreed with any theory. He was just out to collect as much info as possible by forming as many groups as he could and keep anyone and everyone off of good theories and off track of the mole. He originally started a coalition with Lisa. I think I was number 2, maybe. He had many, I think six.

    Anyway, after all was said and done and we went to the first execution my strategy was to place an answer to cover everybody on the list. I figured that one or two people would get zero answers right and would be sure to get at least one answer. In this way time wouldn't be a concern. My strategy obviously didn't work as I was eliminated....the producers said it was based on time after the show and that Darwin and I were off by a half second or so.

    After the elimination it was a whirlwind and I had no idea about anyone in the group. Who was the mole, who was telling me the truth, who was lying? I just really had no idea. Darwin was on the list though after my execution. I thought maybe it's a male attorney this time! In reality I had little to go on, with 14 people in the group and a couple days to work with I think it was a bit of a crap shoot. A guessing game at best so I just started looking for signs even after the show.

    I was going to a TV Guide in Los Angeles for an interview about the Mole II as the Mole's first victim. I was sitting in the chair and the assistants were hustling about layering me with makeup when I looked down and saw a time magazine on a table in the room. The title was something to the effect of "The Truth about Darwin" with subtitles on theories of evolution. I laughed and took that as a cosmic road sign of sorts and thought for awhile that Darwin could be the Mole.

    All I can say is that the whole experience was bewildering. To be thrown into the mix with 14 strangers and chase information down for an impending execution exam was a wild experience. I think I may have over analyzed the information that I had gotten and maybe a better strategy would have been to *rely more on gut feelings about people and the situations that were happening.*

As far as an update on what I am doing...after the show I had a really strong desire to start traveling. The mountains in Switzerland were amazing and it was my first trip to Europe so I left a bit enchanted by the place. It took me a couple years but I went back for three weeks. I didn't go to Switzerland; I wanted to save that for a separate trip but I went to Italy, Austria, Germany, and Czech republic over the course of three weeks. It was amazing. Since then I have gotten the travel bug and I've gone to the UK, Costa Rica, Iceland, Mexico City. My next trip will probably be somewhere in South America. The show definitely fueled a strong desire to travel. I think for me much of the excitement came from the fact that we were traveling for the show.

As for work I have been working as a financial consultant as I was during the time of the show. However, I have moved back into Orange County where I also became part owner in my fathers commercial installation business. I purchased a condo in Yorba Linda, North Orange County back in 2002 and everything has been going great. As of now I live in Yorba Linda, CA, work with my father and in my own financial business and try to travel whenever I have the means to do so.

I'm still single, but I do have a serious girlfriend that I have been dating for about nine months. No plans for marriage at the moment and only time will tell :).

XI

Who Are They?

If you are to be a successful player on a show like "The Mole," you had best be able to read your fellow players, and once read, be able to communicate with them.

I have already indicated that had I been playing the game for real, I might have been in trouble. Not that I felt a lack of ability in being able to read people; my professional life has been one that of necessity involved me being able to quickly assess the capabilities and strengths and weaknesses of folks. You don't become a successful leader in the military with multiple commands if you lack people sense. However, for the last 20 years of my Navy experience I was considered a "senior officer." That is, I was the boss. The young people…while perhaps not scared of me, most probably felt that the better part of valor was to avoid me. When the whims of a senior person could control your future, it takes a very self-assured young person to deliberately seek him out. After all, who knew which side of bed he might have arisen from that morning?

So, all in all, while I felt that I might be able to read the folks who had worked for and with me over the years, I had not been close to them, especially in social settings. My daughters were all grown and gone, and the exposure I had had to the current trends in music, arts, and young folks' interests was minimal, and mostly involved me shuddering and seeking exposure to something other than that. I was still stuck in the values, music, and movies of my youth, in the 50's and early 60's. "Rap" was to me what my first grade teacher did to my head when I was being naughty. And, furthermore, that was all I wanted it to be!

So, when I got to meet virtually all the others on "The Mole II," and heard their favorite...oh, everything...I realized we had a sizable gap in our collective experiences! And, it worked the opposite way. Because of my work I have traveled extensively in the world, being in perhaps 60 plus countries in my life. I have lived in Spain, Japan, Okinawa, Viet Nam, and Hawaii, and much of my career as an Admiral involved traveling to various countries, mostly in the Far East. So when we all discussed things about our lives, a necessity when one has to collect biographical information about everyone, my various travels and places I had lived would invariably come up. Of the group of 14 of us, only 3 of us had traveled much: Darwin, Myra, and me. And they had traveled far less than I had. In discussing the answers to many of the questions we threw at each other, when I would mention various places in the world I had been in response to the questions, the reactions were varied. Mostly, they were just uncomprehending. For most, my travels were just an oddity, something to complicate their recording of my history. Interestingly enough, Patrick seemed to take my travels and living experiences personally. I have no idea if this was a real reaction or just part of the way he chose to play the game. "Of *course* Bill has lived there; he probably owns *property* there." "Gee, I can't *believe* it! Someone brought up a country Bill has not lived in."

His reactions were interesting and irritating to me. I ceased talking about my travels, even when asked. I saw no sense in alienating others, if that was to be their reaction.

Unfortunately, we still had to get information from each other, and my travels and career are a large part of who I am. So, one night only a few days into the making of "The Mole," I explained a little to the others.

"Some of you seem to find my answers to your questions somehow offensive." (Actually, no one but Patrick did, but I did not see any sense in specifying that.) "Let me point out something that should be obvious. We all come from different life experiences, and are at different places in those experiences. Being 58 years old, at least double the age of all of you but two, I very likely have had a lot more life experiences than you have had. In addition, I have been career military all of my life. All of my peers have traveled just as much as I have, and many of them far more. To me, to those hundreds of thousands like me, it is normal to have favorite restaurants in other countries, and to be able to speak a smattering of several languages. That's *normal* in my life, and not a source of amazement, and not a reason for…oh, denigrating someone because they happened to have freely moved about the world. So, as you ask your questions, keep this in mind, please."

There was not much response from the group. Mostly, "Ok, fine. The next question is…." Later in the room (I was rooming with Bribs then.), he asked me, curiously, why I felt I had to point out the obvious? They all knew I was older and had had much different experiences than them. I told him about Patrick's reactions, and that I had no desire to alienate the others.

He laughed. "Patrick? He's got problems."

The issue dropped.

Later we discussed the big gap I felt between all the others and myself. Bribs again was not impressed. "Gee, I don't see it. Sure, different music and interests, but we all really like you. We all have parents, and you are sort of like them…but not really. You are playing the game just like we are. We all have to learn about each other, and one of these sneaky bastards is the

Mole. In fact, in might be you and you are just playing me!" He laughed when he said that, but watched me carefully.

One of the things I had not learned to do well yet was to joke about maybe being the Mole. Everyone else did it, apparently easily, and it should have been a normal part of my response to questions. ("The Mole? Good gosh, how did you guess so quickly!? I thought I was doing pretty well!") I really found it hard to even hint at the possibility I was the Mole. Luckily for me, several of the others refused to do so as well, including Al. Al was one of the most outspoken individuals there, and came to play the game as hard as he could. He never pretended to be the Mole, and in fact urged everyone to "play each game as hard as they could, and not to pretend to throw the games. That way, when the Mole starts sabotaging games, we'll know who it is!" Luckily, most people felt that part of their strategy was to try to get the others to seriously entertain the possibility that they might be the Mole, thus throwing everyone's test results off. Several people laughed openly when Al made his suggestion. That took me off the hook. As noted, almost everyone had already decided that I could not be the Mole anyway, and had dropped me from consideration. I was just unaware of that for a while, and sweated and worried, needlessly as it turned out.

Back to Bribs. Once we had completed our cross country jaunt on the train from Scoul, Switzerland to St. Moritz, Switzerland, Bribs and I were roommates for a few nights. We arrived in St. Moritz, where we were reunited with our Mole bags and clothes. Sure enough, they had not burned. I knew they wouldn't do that! Heather got her family Bible back, Lisa her diamond earrings, and, thank God, Katie retrieved her limp, wrung out, stuffed cow, Meadow Muffin. We all got to cease wearing that one pair of underwear we had been washing out nightly for several nights. We moved into our new rooms, with everyone carefully noting in their journals who was roommates, which room everyone was in, and any other inane observations they thought might be included by the sadists on the upcoming quizzes. (Observations included what color clothes everyone wore, color socks, order we arrived at the hotel, where we sat in relation to each other any time we sat down, where Anderson was at any given time, whether or not we had wine for dinner, and which color it was, who had dessert…the list goes on and on, and includes any observations we might care to make about anything around us. We never knew what arcane questions might be asked on a quiz. As you read this, look around you. What if you were suddenly taken out of your house and given a quiz about the room where you spend most of your time, without notice? Quickly, without looking up, what photos or paintings are in the room? Where are they? What book is lying open on the desk? What color is your couch? You see these things daily, and I'll bet you couldn't answer all those questions. However, we all felt we had to! Except me, or course. Why should I record all of that useless information? All I had to remember was where I had been at any given time, and in what order I had been sitting, or standing, and what I had been wearing, what I ate, whether or not I had wine or beer with dinner….geez, I'm getting mentally fatigued even trying to remember that!)

  When we arrived in our room - a very nice one looking out on the lake and across at the glaciers on the mountains - Bribs and I noted the minibar, as I mentioned earlier. Despite Patti and Deb's denial of minibar privileges, we got out some good German beer and placed some Swiss francs in its place. We then settled down in chairs in front of the double doors leading out to the patio, looking at the incredible scene in front of us. Bribs noted, "Bill, let's forget the game for a while. If you're the Mole, I could be screwing myself, but let's just…shoot the bull and enjoy this. I might never get to return here again." So, we did that. For two hours we shared stories about our families, life experiences, Oklahoma vs Texas, and such. It was delightful, and the only time in my 7 weeks in Europe that I ever totally did not play the game. In fact, if you saw the show, you might remember that shot of us sitting, shirtless, looking across at the glaciers, beer bottles in hand. Clearly, the cameramen know we had invaded the mini-bar. I have no idea if the producers knew quickly. And I doubt that the cameramen would tell anyone deliberately. They were a cool group.

Bribs is a hell of a fellow. If I had a son, I could not be more proud if he were to turn out like Bribs. We were...and still are...good friends. He is level headed, and understood fully that this was a most unique experience, but wasn't life. It was just a game and an experience to be savored. Something about our discussion, however, struck a chord in Bribs, and he decided that I could be the Mole, and acted accordingly on the next quiz. Clay, the producer, told me in our brief session after the second quiz that Bribs had answered almost every question with my information. Clay was curious if I had let anything slip. Not that I was aware of, and believe me, I felt I knew when I slipped! It haunted me the few times I did so. However, after the third quiz Clay reported that Bribs did not answer one question with my information! Could Bribs be the Mole? Absolutely. He had the mannerisms, and enjoyed the game. He would have done a super job as the Mole.

At this point in the game we still did not know a lot about each other. Other brief impressions included:

Darwin was very intelligent, made snap decisions, was willing to be argumentative, and had no hair. Could he be the Mole (said the others)? Yep, without a doubt. He has a sharp wit, and needled Katie multiple times about her various phobias and her stuffed cow; however, he was fast to recognize when he had really caused her angst, and would quickly mollify her. He did not really want to be cruel. (Or, did he?) While Darwin was a lawyer, he pointed out that he really did not like being one. I think he would have much preferred being in entertainment.

Reflections of The Mole

Katie wore her emotions on her sleeve, and had already cried more than should be legal on most TV shows. I have never seen a woman who could cry that quickly, that much, over that little! It was hard to imagine her as a teacher; while she was undoubtedly smart, it would seem to me that students would delight in keeping the tears flowing freely. Katie was open, friendly, likable...but sweated...and cried...about everything. Luckily for all of us, we had an ace-in-the-hole: Myra. She adopted Katie, and could shut her tears down rather quickly. Myra's philosophy was simple: "No sweat." If it is over, why sweat it? You can't do anything about it at that point, so worrying and crying simply do no good. So, get on with life. She was able to impart that philosophy on a regular basis in many situations to Katie. I only hope Katie still remembers Myra's valuable teachings! Could Katie be the Mole? We all agreed that if she were that good an actress, she would be doing lots of work on Broadway and would not have time to do this show. Not a chance!

Al and I had been roommates early on, and grew to be good friends. Our backgrounds were very similar. We were both the only boys in families with several girls, both grew up in a poor to moderate background, both were impressed by our fathers with the value of hard work being a cornerstone of life, and both generally laughed a lot and enjoyed life. Al was the only one in the group without a college education, but he was easily as smart as anyone else there, and told the best jokes ever. With his Long Island accent, his jokes were priceless. In addition, he was incredibly quick-witted, and his comebacks were superb. (Once in one of the episodes Anderson chided Al about women's underwear ('G' rated humor, I assure you!), and Al's response was quick: "And you know this how?" Anderson did not try to reply, but just grinned.) Al's standing jabs at Katie about her 'unnatural' jelly phobia kept us in stitches many evenings. Katie had told us early on that anything resembling jelly "terrified" her;

how does that happen? The jelly-like amniotic fluid? Jelly-like baby foods? What?

Unfortunately for Al, we became good enough friends that he just would not seriously consider me as the Mole. One other thing about him. He believed in following the rules, at all times. He had a routine that he would follow before each execution. Not exactly a superstition, but each week he would add little gestures and actions to his routine. (Place a picture of his family in the same pocket for the execution, sit in the same seat, wear the same shirt, etc.) By the time he was executed in the 11th week, he was starting to drive everyone a little batty! Could he be the Mole? Well, maybe. But, his penchant for following the rules exactly seemed to rule against that, and I don't think Al was a serious consideration for the Mole after the first couple of weeks. A super fellow, however.

Patrick was interesting. We did become friends of a distant sort after the show, and chatted several times. However, he came into the game with a definite idea of how it should be played, and was very aggressive and (it seemed to me) felt free to backstab and lie to get ahead. I really think he was anticipating being on "Survivor," and had adopted his strategy accordingly. He did not go out of his way to be friendly, or to make friends. Unfortunately for him, in this particular game you had to have the ability to exchange lots of information with everyone else daily, or you were not going to survive. Information was the key to lasting in the game…unless you happened to know who the Mole was. So his direct, inquisitorial manner, devoid of a soft side, was not one that endeared him to the others. He didn't seem to care. That was the way he chose to play the game. That attitude alienated him to the point that I believe it eventually resulted in his being executed. Could he have been the Mole? Yep, without a doubt. Several of us agreed that if he were the Mole, the last 3 or 4 players would probably commit either homicide or suicide before the time in Europe ended!

Reflections of The Mole

Elavia was an enigma. Totally mysterious, very sparse with sharing information, in the mode of *always* looking and acting suspicious. Would the Mole *always* appear to be the Mole? Well, no one (except me, and I harbored doubts) was sure about that. Constantly looking like the Mole might be the best way to play the role, and one not previously tried. Consequently, having no one else really in their cross hairs as a suspect, most players started putting Elavia's information down on the quizzes fairly early, and continued to do so until she abruptly left in the 6th week of the show, throwing everyone into turmoil. What all the players did not realize until then was that with the exception of Elavia and me, everyone else was getting all 10 answers wrong every week! There were multiple ties for last place, and Charles, the ABC lawyer, was kept busy with his two stop watches determining who amongst all the ties completed the quiz the slowest. No one ever knew who the person just departed had put down, so all continued to think they must be correct, inasmuch as they had put down all answers for Elavia and were surviving. I would have loved to see how the game had gone if she had not taken a bribe and left.

Dorothy was another mysterious person. She actively pretended to appear suspicious as part of her strategy. I realized early on that Dorothy almost never drank anything. I watched, and while her glass was always full when she raised it to her lips, the level seldom went down. She was being very, very careful and observant. As events were to prove, she was an excellent player, and incredibly smart. She also enjoyed playing the fool at times. For some reason we began pretending to wind her up with an imaginary handle in her back, and she would do a wild little uncoordinated dance, much to the amusement of those folks trying to figure out who these people with cameras following them were. Dorothy would bounce about for a while, then run down, slumping forward until someone else went over and wound her up. A definite candidate for the Mole!

Ali was sweet, a nurse who had just departed from the Navy. We had several friends in common. She was liked by all, and before we could figure out if she was capable of being the Mole, she departed, darn it! We lost some definite sex appeal from the show with her departure. (Not that the show *needed* that, you understand. But, *we* enjoyed it!)

Rob was another moderate enigma. Rob came in billed as a magician. As it turned out, that irritated him. He did professional training videos, and wanted to break into some aspect of show business, and the fact that he was constantly identified as a magician did not please him. He was the youngest of the players, at 22, but did not seem that young. He fit in well...much better than I did. And, he was truly a gifted magician! As noted before, he did many tricks only inches from us, and we never did catch him out. In fact, one evening at dinner Anderson asked him to show him one, but warned Rob that he *hated* it when he could not figure out how he was being fooled. The trick Rob did had two parts; after the first part when Anderson could not see how Rob had done what he had done, Anderson suddenly slugged him on the shoulder. "I hate that! How did you do that?" Rob finished the trick, edging away from Anderson as he did so. If Anderson hated being fooled in the middle, he was *really* going to be unhappy at the end! Rob was very young, and being the Mole might be mentally wearing on him, but there was no doubt that with his magic training and inclination, he could fool everyone on multiple levels. So, he had to be considered strongly.

Heather was the beauty of the crew, a Texas girl, as I have noted. She was not bashful, spoke out quickly about whatever was on her mind, and was obviously very intelligent. While her family Bible was very dear to her, as noted early on in the burning bag episode, she was not a goody two shoes. She could get down and dirty if the occasion demanded. In fact, and I suppose it is normal these days, those young folks could devolve into a vocabulary that would have made a sailor blush. (And did so frequently.) It was somewhat paradoxical, but just part of their normal life, I believe. Heather told us early on, and often, that she was almost engaged to Nathan. Heather also came to play the game, and play it hard. Other than Elavia, she and Dorothy were the two who most often pretended to be the Mole. And she would have done well had she been the Mole.

Lisa is an Assistant US Attorney in Chicago, and there is no doubt in my mind that she is excellent at her job. She had to take a leave of absence from that job, and was told that if she did not return within 2 weeks would have to be replaced. Clearly, she was hoping that new hire would take place. Her other job, and her avocation, was as a beer seller at Comiskey Park in Chicago on the weekends. She knew baseball and all the players, and enjoyed talking about it. She was extremely smart, and would bear watching closely. If anyone could ferret me out, I figured she might be the one. One other thing about her: she was a competitor. A fierce one. She plays soccer routinely, and I would not care to be in front of her when she is headed downfield. There was no doubt in her mind that she could compete on an equal basis with a man in most sports, and all the men enjoyed putting her on about this. She could be easily riled! She would have made a marvelous Mole. However, the first Mole had been a 28 year old female lawyer from Chicago. Would they do that twice? Maybe, just maybe.

I have already mentioned Myra. Myra was delightful, my best friend (with Bribs) during the show. (And both remain close friends now.) She was constantly up, always bubbling, enjoying, laughing, watching out for others who might be having problems coping...like Katie. She could have been a perfect Mole, but it was hard to imagine her conniving and deliberately misleading people. Along with Rob, she did not bother to put down all the information in her journal that the rest did. (Later I was to find out that she used her own shorthand to record things in order to keep anyone from ever reading her journal and knowing anything about her suspicions or plans.) She is a good artist, and made artistic drawings in the journal that *apparently* did not include much meaningful information. She befriended Patrick when everyone else was irritated at him, and actively defended him. A delightful person. Could she be the Mole? I doubt that many people thought so. (On the other hand, I expect she would have handled that role with the same good nature and "what the hell" attitude that she demonstrated at all other times.)

The final person directly involved in the making of "The Mole" was Anderson Cooper, son of Gloria Vanderbilt, and a foreign correspondent at age 17 when he traveled to South Africa as a reporter. Anderson had grown up in a penthouse in New York City, and with his somewhat privileged background could have been expected to be a real snob. He was not. He ran the show. He was a hard ass at times, could yell at the players with apparent real anger (some examples later), was sarcastic, cynical, humorous, incisive, biting, and delightful. We came to know him well and appreciate him, even while dodging him on occasion. He clearly had his favorites, and his less favorites. Occasionally he would act the fool, and do it in such unexpected circumstances that he would catch everyone off guard, but get us laughing, causing us to enjoy the show even more. Anderson did not know who the Mole was, I was told. I actively tried to stay out of his line of sight most of the time. Luckily, he seemed to really enjoy ribbing and chatting with Bribs, Darwin, Rob, Al, and Myra, and by and large left the rest of us alone, which was fine with me. Heather, especially, felt that he did not like her, and that he was constantly out to get her. Maybe. More about Anderson as this narrative unfolds. He was voted in an on-line vote as the best host on reality television. I agree with that. Congratulations, CNN! Anderson is a '360' kind of guy, and was a friend to all of us.

Reflections of The Mole

So, that's a summary of what I felt about each of the other competitors at this point in the game. I continued to experience considerable mental anguish in my role as the Mole. Rightly or wrongly, I felt that the entire weight of this multi-million dollar venture rested, none too easily, on my shoulders.

XII

How Not to Play

Once we were settled into the hotel in St. Moritz, we had the chance to get to know each other better. We were to play a game the next day, but it was raining and the producers felt it might be too dangerous. So, we were allowed out for a while to see the city. Always together, of course, with minders and cameras ever present. Everyone was always watching to see if anyone tried to sneak away to meet with the producers. We really did not see much of the sights; we paid too much attention to each other! It is amazing how paranoid and suspicious you can get, even when totally innocent. Which, of course, I wasn't.

During our perambulations about town, several of us spied a cigar store and took our daily allowance into it, where all the men bought cigars. We knew there would be an opportunity at some point to smoke them. That evening following dinner we were told we could visit each others' rooms so we could continue our perpetual quest to try to figure out who the Mole was. I looked earnestly at each person in turn, not really caring who was looking suspicious, but because everyone else was doing it. When in Rome… In truth, everyone looked a little guilty. When you are being viewed closely by 12 other people, it is inevitable that you are going to be somewhat uneasy, and that can look like guilt. Or so I hoped. Being *observed* so closely made everyone uncomfortable enough to become a tad fidgety.

We all gathered out on the balcony of one of the rooms, where 6 cigars were lit. The girls were there as well, and eventually almost all of them borrowed a cigar from one or more of the fellows and puffed a little. Togetherness, you know. That scene was not shown on TV, but it was a nice evening. I think that was one of the times we all really enjoyed each other, and there were few questions asked, and even the ever-present journals were not obviously in evidence. (Though I have no doubt Patrick, Lisa, and perhaps Heather were busy memorizing things to write down as soon as they returned to their rooms.) Finally, however, the cigars were smoked, the cigar smoke dissipated, and we all were told to return to our rooms.

That night, as recorded on TV, Lisa and Dorothy managed to get Darwin and Katie to illegally come to their room, thus gaining exemptions for themselves during the next execution. While Darwin reacted with mild chagrin (he knew he had been caught, and accepted it only slightly grudgingly), Katie blew up. She stormed about on camera, and much more that wasn't shown. Anderson looked a little unsure about her actions; after all, it *was* a game! When we all met down stairs and were told about the events, and the fact that two more exemptions were given, Katie again blew up. Rob spoke what everyone was thinking. "Why did you leave your rooms? You knew it was illegal, and knew something was probably up. Why are you blaming someone else for your actions?" It was a game, and they got gamed!

We also played the Las Vegas game during that evolution, and Lisa, Katie, Rob, and Darwin looked great in their evening attire. However, they quickly lost $20,000 of the already accrued money pot, while managing to look somewhat suspicious through their ineptness. It wasn't a lack of effort; just a lack of knowledge on how to bet in some cases, and having the cards run against them during a long stretch. I regarded it as a cheap lesson. While the money we were playing for and with was real money, and was on the table, it was not really *our* money. Oh, it was to be somebody's in the group, but that was far enough off that it was not real to anyone. I just smiled and watched. No pressure on me; I really didn't care if we won or not. I had no desire to play in that game…though the tuxedo would have been nice to dress up in! I might note that Anderson was in a tux, also, and looked like he had been born in one. In fact, I suspect he might have been.

We returned to the hotel to a very, very nice dinner. I have not mentioned much about food. This was not "Survivor." We were not on starvation rations. In fact, every meal...including breakfast...had multiple courses. The restaurants were 4 and 5 star restaurants; the owners knew cameras would be present, and the meal possibly on television. Therefore, they all attempted to outdo the last place we ate. This was nice, but at least in my case was a disaster for my weight. I gained several pounds in the time we spent in Europe. I work out avidly in my normal life. We were taken to a gym twice during our stay in Europe, and work as I might, I could not undo seven weeks of pasta in just two workouts.

The dinner that night was to be somewhat special. I have mentioned that we seemed to enjoy wine and beer...a lot. The first season's players on "The Mole" were an abstentious crew; i.e., only one of them drank at all. I expect Anderson felt like a lush with his one glass of wine with dinner when dining with them. We did not want him to feel depraved, nor deprived, and managed to make him feel better about himself. All of us liked wine, though 5 of us really preferred beer. (Myra, Lisa, Katie, Bribs, and me.) That night in St. Moritz we had our usual bottles of wine scattered about the table as we ate, and several of us ordered liter mugs of beer. Dinner went on...and on...and on. Anderson kept telling the waiters to bring more beer and wine, and he finally stood up with a proclamation, delivered somewhat blearily and with a tad of a slur in his voice. "I would like to announce that you all have set the record for this and all future mole crews in alcohol consumption at one meal. We have just finished off 14 bottles of wine and about 35 liters of beer!"

Cheers erupted, and there was a call for more drinks to celebrate our victory, dubious though it was. Anderson hastily put a stop to those suggestions. "No! No! No! I've got to be sober for the camera tomorrow, and you all have to be prepared for your next execution!" That served to sober everyone up…slightly.

What really served to sober us up was when the several hundreds of pounds of lights erected by the camera crew over the table suddenly came crashing down just before we left the table. Luckily, no one had passed out on the table, and even more luckily, all the wine and beer glasses were empty. It would have been truly irritating to have lost good wine and beer just at the end of the evening. It did make for an impressive end to a fun evening, and was one of several scenes that would have made great drama on television…though drunks seldom are as funny and as witty as we think!

The next day we were faced with our second round of hour and a half interviews, as well as our second test and the second execution. After my interview with Clay the producer, I quickly went over the questions for the next night's quiz, and again provided my answers, vice my wife's answers. Clay briefed me on the upcoming games, and told me that in the next day's rappelling game everyone was going to look suspicious, and I was to stay out of it if possible. No sense in inviting attention.

That evening we were tested, again, and the stress level ratcheted up. It was interesting to watch folks. No one wanted to be executed, no one wanted to go home, and everyone became jittery. When we had finished with the quiz, we were paired up and sent to different rooms to wait for a few hours until they could set up for the execution. My roommate for the wait was Ali.

Ali and I had some background in common, as I have noted. We talked about our mutual friends, the Navy, and the game. She was delightful, and I would be sorry to see her leave, because, leave she did! She was the Mole's second victim. (I actually had a pang when I would hear Anderson say "another victim of the Mole!" People were really victims of themselves, not me! I didn't do it!)

Later I was to find out that Bribs had been approached by Darwin after the second quiz to form an alliance. When he asked Bribs who he had put down for the Mole, Bribs replied, "Bill." Darwin was incredulous, and informed Bribs that he was absolutely certain that I wasn't the Mole, and the only reason Bribs was still around was probably because Ali was even dumber...and slower...than he was. Bribs was swayed, much to his eventual dismay, proving that actually he *was* dumber than Ali. She had no clue as to who the Mole was, and was thus executed. Bribs? He had me pegged, and believed a lawyer. Go figure.

A note about dumbness here. In fact, all of the competitors were quite intelligent. The problem was that none of them had the slightest clue about who the Mole was, and taking the quizzes was almost like taking tests written in, say, the Urdu language. While Bribs accidentally decided I was the Mole, it really did not do him any good, inasmuch as he was dumb enough to believe Darwin and immediately switched to someone else. OK, you say, if no one knows who the Mole is, why not just rush through the quiz in 30 seconds or so, insuring that someone else is slower than you were. That might work, but the producers built in some gimme questions. There were always 2 or 3 questions on every quiz that everyone should get right. I.e., "What color socks did the Mole wear in yesterday's competition?" Well, all of us but one wore white socks, and unless you are really sure about that one...and there was absolutely no way you could be...you had to play the odds and answer 'White.' One question right. Another similar question was, "Did the Mole eat dessert at dinner last night?" Well, we all ate dessert...except Myra. She doesn't eat dessert. (And still she smiles, and has such a sunny disposition! I didn't notice her smoking funny cigarettes, nor popping pills. How does she do that?) Again, unless you were convinced Myra was definitely the Mole (and if you were, you *were* too dumb to continue playing), you had to answer, "Yes," the Mole ate dessert last night.

The bottom line was that you just could not rapidly finish the quiz in 30 seconds or so, putting down random letters as your answers to all questions. You had to read the questions, at least, and *quickly* randomly select an answer for those majority of the questions that were specific about the Mole. "Which college did the Mole attend?" *Since you have no idea who the Mole is, don't waste time on it! Just select an answer right now!* But you must get those 2 or 3 questions right that are give-away questions.

So intelligence had little to do with who was executed in the first half of the episodes or so. If you did all the above *just so*, and got all the answers right that you should get right, and hurried…someone else should be the slowest. That someone got executed. IQ had little to nothing to do with it!

So, Bob and Ali, rest easy. You are certainly no dumber, and probably smarter, than many of the other players. You're both still cute, though Ali's cuter! (My wife thinks Bob is cuter!)

What Was She Thinking?

Ali

Ali can still be seen on television. She is now a reporter for the CBS and Fox affiliates in Jacksonville, Florida. Shortly after returning from the Mole II, she went back to school to earn her Masters in Broadcast Journalism from Northwestern's Medill School of Journalism. She covers health and medical news as much as she can.

But she still can't believe, day one, she ruled Bill out as the Mole!

XIII

It's Chilly in Here!

Following Ali's departure, the group settled down to business. After all, everyone realized that the first couple of folks who departed were just victims of bad luck. It could have been any of us. Almost any of us.

During my interview on the execution day, Clay told me that at breakfast the following morning we would be exchanging journals. There was to be another major game played, but he told me to play it straight, so I was told no details about it. However, the alarming point was the journal exchange!

People treated their journals with great secrecy. It was understood that they were not to be violated; you would never read someone else's journal. (Unless, of course they left it out and open in a public place; we were, after all, starved for new reading material...) The reason we all agreed that we would not read each other's journal was the fact that we roomed together. While you *could* carry your journal into the shower with you, there were certain drawbacks inherent in such an action! The journals were the one place we could write anything we cared to write, and most people—with the prior noted exceptions—used them to write down all the biographical information on the others, and to actively explore in a systematic manner who their current Mole suspects were, and why, as well as who they had eliminated as a suspect. The journals explained *how* people were thinking. As I have indicated, you needed a strategy to survive in this game. *Perhaps* you needed a strategy. The journals had not been exchanged during the first season of "The Mole," which should have been everyone's major indication that that rule might be broken in the second season. However, no one suspected that, including me.

I went back to my room after my interview and sat down with my blank journal. I attempted to write a page or two on my "strategy," and realized upon reading what I had written that all it did was make me really look suspicious. I casually went into the bathroom and got a small knife out of my kit and carefully cut those pages out and flushed them away. But, I had to have something written in the journal, or it would be a real clue to whoever got it that I might have a reason not to worry about recording any information in it! I sweated over the journal for a while, and to provide some filler picked up one of the hotel information brochures, written in English and German, and started recording translations of words and phrases in the back of the journal. Bribs was sitting over in a chair reading and asked me what I was doing? I told him that I was just brushing up on my German; after all, the group depended somewhat on Myra and me to provide translation in some instances. He grunted and went back to his book.

I finally hit upon a scheme. I started writing a letter to my wife, and made it somewhat personal. The letter went on for 5 or 6 pages, and in it I recorded multiple strategies I might be using, and listed my suspects for the Mole, as well as observations on those I had ruled out. But, most of all, I deliberately made the letter *personal*, telling her how much I felt like the odd man out in this group of young people, and how I did not see how I could compete with them. I missed her. I was destined to lose early, and felt incredibly fortunate in managing to not get executed in the first two weeks. And so on and so on. It was a love letter with vague strategies included. If the book were looked at closely, it would be immediately apparent that I had little biographical information recorded, though I did vaguely include some in the body of the letter. It was the best I could do on short notice, and I only hoped it would be enough to get me by and not reveal to the person receiving it that I was a good candidate to indeed be the Mole. I worked on this for about 2 or 3 hours while Bribs read. He did comment a time or two about how much effort I was putting into my translation efforts, but did not dwell on it. He mused over this months later, again mentally kicking himself for not being more suspicious and observant.

The next morning we all met for breakfast. Anderson was his usual moderately caustic self, making wry and funny comments, deriding us a little for not accruing more money, and gigging Katie about Meadow Muffin. She over-reacted to everything about that stuffed cow, which seemed to delight Anderson. He announced that he was looking for an opportunity to steal Meadow Muffin and hold it for ransom as a way the group might be able to make more money.

As breakfast ended, Anderson looked around. "Myra, pick a number!" We all looked a little confused, a normal look for us. Myra immediately said "Four!"

Anderson then directed, "OK, everyone pass your journal four people to the left."

There was a general look of shock around the table. Our journals? Our priceless, strategy-laden, personal journals? Patrick, who had written in his journal virtually non-stop since we had received them, said, "Do we get them back?" There was a pleading tone in his voice, but he was voicing the thoughts of everyone at the table, including me.

Anderson smiled his smile, which did not really appear to contain humor at this point, and said, "No. The journal you receive from the 4th person on your right is your new journal. Congratulations!" Again, consternation registered around the table, but especially on the faces of those who had *really* recorded all their thoughts and strategies in their tome. Patrick, Katie, Lisa, Heather. They appeared to be most shocked.

Patrick persisted. "Can we ask the person who receives our journal to let us borrow it to record some things out of it?"

Reflections of The Mole

Anderson nodded. "That's between you and that person. But, again, let me make this clear. The journal you are giving up *is no longer your journal!* If the person who receives it wants to be nice and let you look at it, that is their choice. But, *you* have no right to it! And, since it is not your journal, you are not allowed to do anything to it other than read and record out of it." This was to prove an important point within a few days.

We passed the journals. I received Heather's, which was a wealth of information. Heather had carefully recorded every bit of biographical material from everyone in a very systematic manner. I was really thankful at this point that I had not bothered doing so in mine. Why do it if Heather was going to do it for me? She had also recorded the names of those she had suspected might be the Mole, and while I was not eliminated, I was way down the list behind Elavia, Dorothy, Bribs, Darwin, and one or two others. She had eliminated the same few people I had eliminated. (Well, actually, I had eliminated *everybody*. But, to keep the game interesting for myself, I tried to rationally figure out who I would have eliminated had I not been the Mole. Katie and Al. Probably Rob and Patrick. Everyone else was fair game.)

Lisa received my journal, and I was not to hear her thoughts on it until the dinner preceding our next execution. I could only hope I had not gone to the top of her suspect list. She is, after all, used to ferreting out the bad guys. Was I one?

Of the others, the two notable cases were Katie and Elavia. Katie received Patrick's journal, and immediately he accosted her and asked if he might borrow it back to copy some material. Katie made the rash statement, "Why don't we all promise not to read what the person wrote in their journal?" Right! Even Katie did not believe she had suggested that. Patrick did, however, frequently remind her of her statement, while fervently hoping she would feel too guilty to read his entries. Fat chance!

Elavia was told by the recipient some of what was in Katie's journal, and approached Katie. "Is it true that you called someone (me) a bitch in your journal?"

Katie was circumspect. She had, but did not want to admit it out loud. As I have noted before, Katie wore her emotions on her sleeves, and held little back. When Elavia had chosen to accept an exemption in the first game, in an event where they had both supposedly been participating (jumping from the bridge), Katie was furious. Not only had Elavia possibly cost them money (not true, as it turned out, inasmuch as Darwin and I had put money on the other two games played that day, but not the bridge jump), but Katie had been terrified of heights and had jumped anyway. And, Elavia had made it all for nothing! (Actually, Katie was never more proud of herself than she was immediately after being pulled back on the bridge and realizing that she was still alive. The prospect of dying had put somewhat of a damper on her exuberance for a while.) So, relations between Elavia and Katie were not real close for the remainder of the game. Again, this controversy between the two came back to haunt everyone several weeks later.

After breakfast and the journal switch was over, Anderson introduced a minor game whereby Myra was designated as the person who had to go find a fountain in the city and retrieve some information in a specified time; she succeeded, and we added $10,000 to the pot. Following her successful mission Anderson then told us that due to her success, we could select one person in the group who **could not** receive an exemption during the next execution. Sort of a "who do you want to screw next" kind of prize. There was some shuffling, and Darwin proposed Dorothy. After all, she and Lisa had both received exemptions for the preceding execution, and it was logical that one of them…or Elavia…should not be eligible for an exemption at this point. The vote was quickly taken, and was 11-1 for Darwin's proposal. Dorothy, obviously, was not overly happy with that suggestion and outcome! Me? Shoot, I didn't care. Anyone. Regardless, someone would be going home…and it wouldn't be me!

Later that day we all convened for explanations of the upcoming games. While we sat around chatting, Rob challenged me. "Bill, I've been watching you the last two executions. You don't seem all that worried. Is there a reason for that? Do you, for instance, know that you can't be executed?"

The others looked at me. These kinds of challenges were routine as everyone tried to determine who might be the most untrustworthy of all.

"Rob, let me explain something to you. We've chatted before about the differences between you all and me in our lives. Let me explain to you some of the things that have worried me in the past. When I am operating on a patient and the anesthesiologist tells me that the patient's blood pressure is dropping and we might have a problem, I get worried. When I was in Viet Nam heading into Da Nang in a helicopter (on a beer run, but it sort of decreased the gravitas of the story to add that) and it was shot full of holes, with both pilots shot in the legs, I was actually *quite* worried." (Actually, I was concerned that I might not get to do another beer run, but again, no sense in adding that.) "And, when I was the Commanding Officer of the Naval Hospital in Charleston, South Carolina in the middle of Hurricane Hugo, and the building was swaying back and forth visibly, threatening to come down on the 1200 folks in it, I was *seriously* worried. We, on the other hand, are on an all expense paid trip to Europe, staying in 5 star hotels, preparing to be on national television, and the worst that can happen to me is that I have to go home early. Honestly, that doesn't worry me much." (Again, I was really *not* worried, so I was being truthful.)

The group seemed to think about that for a moment—except for Patrick, who rolled his eyes—and accepted my statement, dismissing Rob's observations. They had already mostly made their minds up about me, and this confirmed their thoughts. After all, among other things I was talking about a war that had happened long before they were born! That was just another indication that Darwin was right; I *was* long in the tooth!

That night the producers suddenly came to each room and told us we could all congregate in one of the rooms for an hour or so, in a continuing effort to get to know each other, especially in the aftermath of our journal exchange. The 12 of us congregated, with the producer and several cameramen, along with a large tub of cold beer and wine. We all picked our beverage of choice and settled in for another challenging time of quizzing and accusing each other of molish inclinations. Clay, the producer, sat and watched us for a while. Patrick was still noticeably upset about losing his journal, and again appealed to folks to "not read what someone else had written" in their journal. Not a chance of that in the world! Clearly, the person who had bared his soul more than anyone in writing had been Patrick, and he was understandably upset about the exchange. Katie, wisely, kept her own counsel and promised nothing. She was deliberately vague about her intentions. None of the rest of us were, however!

Clay suddenly spoke up. "Listen up! You all have already lost 2 people to the Mole. When are you going to realize that one of you is deliberately sabotaging the efforts of the rest of you, and is intent on getting *all* of you out of the game? When will you understand that one of you works for me, and is not to be trusted?! You all are entirely too relaxed about this; you need to find this sneaky bastard!"

I swallowed hard, and was hopeful that no one was looking at me. I felt…exposed and guilty. We did all like each other, with a few minor exceptions, and there did not appear to be any…oh, hatred for this person known as the Mole. The players looked around at each other, with Patrick reacting positively to Clay's announcement. After all, that was his game plan all along, it seemed. No prisoners, no friends. Just opponents and someone else to attack.

Darwin suddenly spoke up. "Clay, that's BS. Sure, we all know one of us is the Mole; that's the game. The Mole's job is to cause problems and prevent the rest of us from making money, and everyone else's job is to try to figure out who the Mole is and keep on adding money to the pot. We understood that coming in. What is the sense in hating everyone and trusting no one? It's a game; we know it's a game. And, without the Mole, there is no game!" Darwin smiled suddenly, and Clay just threw his hands in the air. He gave up. Everyone else smiled and went back to quizzing each other. Patrick looked disappointed.

I think both Patrick and Clay had patterned their proposed game play on the first season of "The Mole." In that season there seemed to be much more diversity in personalities; i.e., several of the players apparently very obviously did not care for each other, and voiced that feeling frequently. As the season wore on, the animosities seemed to deepen, and I expect that added a spark the producers liked. After all, having a bunch of players who like each other and don't fight much might be boring. And, perhaps our show might have generated more interest if there had been more friction. If Patrick had managed to stay around longer, there is a chance we could have seen some rather violent outbursts on camera. But however much that might have made 'good' television, it was not to be. We liked each other, even when we could not trust each other. (In the intervening years I have talked to a lot of people about our show. Those who watched almost uniformly told me that what they really liked about it was that there were not obvious animosities and back-stabbings. Strategy, planning, subterfuge, yep. But few personal attacks.)

The next day we all piled in our vans and drove out into the beautiful mountains surrounding St. Moritz. A note about driving. The players drove the vans, with only players in them. There was always a camera mounted on the windshield, and we were miked, so anything we said could be ultimately added to the footage of the show. We traded off the driving duties...at least, we did so for the first few weeks. More about that later.

We arrived in a meadow with a sizable stream rushing by, and glaciers hanging over our heads from the slopes above us. We were given wet suits and told to strip to our swim suits (which we had been told to wear) and find wet suits and booties that would fit. My problem was than I'm basically an XXL, and the largest wet suits were L, or maybe a tiny XL. I managed to squeeze into one, but was totally unable to zip the front of the top up. Finally Bribs and Darwin got on either side of me and held the two sides together while I zipped up. I felt like a stuffed sausage, and rather suspect I looked like one as well!

We all trooped over to the outflow from a glacial pond, looking for all the world like a bunch of seals...not the flatteringly human kind of SEALS. There we found a log about 12 inches in diameter and about 15 feet long, stretching from bank to bank across a stream flowing from the pond. It was an idyllic scene, beautiful...and very, very cold. That water should have been a skating rink; I don't know how they kept it from freezing. We all tested it gingerly, recoiling immediately. None of us wanted to go there.

Anderson stepped out and greeted us, dressed in khakis and a short sleeved shirt; after all, it was warm if you were not contemplating going in the water. "Players, pick a leader." Immediately Al was selected. He had impressed everyone with his honesty and his refusal to pretend. He was there to win all the money, and few had any suspicion whatsoever that he might be the Mole. Of the other players who might logically be picked as a leader, all were on most suspect lists, and no one wanted to put the possible Mole in a position of power.

Anderson then smiled, evilly, and invited us to look across the stream at two oncoming giants. There came a man, "John," dressed as a woodsman, who was considerably larger than me. In addition, the woman with him, "Jane," was well over six feet tall and had muscles comparable to the biggest of us. We all looked at each other, with some players like Dorothy and Katie looking rather wan. Poor Dorothy. She was extremely near sighted and could not wear her glasses in this competition. All she could see of the two were distant shapes, and in this case they just looked like two more mountains. Katie, on the other hand, could see perfectly well, but just wished she couldn't.

The game was simple. We were to use well padded pugil sticks to walk out on the log and engage one of these two in a fight until someone was knocked into the frigid stream. For each player who managed to make it across the stream $5000 was added to the pot. Al's job was to choose who would meet either Jane or John, and had to be careful to select wisely to maximize the amount of money we might win. He did the predictable, throwing most of the girls at John, expecting that most of them would be knocked off the log by either John or Jane, and most of the men fought Jane. His strategy worked pretty well, and we wound up with 6 of us managing to cross the log, while the other 5 shivered violently in their *wet* wet suits on the far side of the stream. The ones who managed to cross over included Bribs, Darwin, Lisa, Myra, and me. Dorothy tentatively tried to cross the log, and was gently shoved in by John. Katie shouted defiance and showed lots of spunk, but became just as wet as Dorothy, though she did manage to get one solid swing at John. Heather, who had been a gymnast in high school, and whose specialty was the balance beam, needed a narrower log to tread. This one was obviously too wide for her balance beam memory, and she fell off headlong into the water when the wind from Jane's stick wafted by her. No blow need be landed. Suspicious? Perhaps. Rob fought Jane as well, but other than some loud threatening noises, never really threatened. He sounded great and projected violence of a severe nature, but needed a large gun to complete the picture. Without one he was treated to a wet dunking with great immediacy. Finally, Patrick was quickly dispatched as well.

So, we had won $25,000. Then Anderson told us the next phase. Al was again to pick which of us was to meet one of the others on the log, the fight continuing until only one of us was left. Then, Al was to fight that last one, with the winner getting an exemption.

Now, I have mentioned before the value of exemptions. Exemptions were everything. Everyone wanted one, and no one wanted anyone else to have one. Every exemption granted significantly increased the odds of one of the remaining players being executed that week. So, exemptions were truly a double edged sword, and most players would have given almost anything for one. The winner getting an exemption was a big thing, both ways.

We started our battles on the log, and I realized that I should not have too much trouble with most of the players. Since wrestling at Oklahoma State, I have remained in fairly good shape...occasionally. While at 58 years old my stamina might be suspect, I was not being asked to do a strenuous aerobic sport. I was being tasked with balancing on a rather wide log and pushing other people into the water. That didn't seem too daunting a task!

Al selected Darwin and Bribs first, and Darwin pushed Bribs into the water. Lawyers 1, Texas Aggies 0. I then was tasked with Myra and Lisa in turn, and refused to swing my pugil stick at them; my sisters and daughters, as well as my wife, would have given me lots of grief if I had swung at a girl. Myra wisely fell into the water quickly; you don't become a Delta pilot by being stupid! Lisa was interesting. She is, as I have noted before, highly competitive, and feels that she can compete against men on an equal basis. It's a nice thought, though inaccurate in some cases...and this case. She came out on the log to beat me, and I went out to simply push her off the log. I won, but she was enraged, primarily, I suspect, because I did not challenge her by squaring off and swinging sticks with her. I just pushed her off the log. As she entered the water, she screamed, "Asshole!" I did not hear that on the televised version of the episode, however. Finally, Darwin. Darwin is in good shape, and is fit, but I outweighed him by 60 pounds or so. He certainly could have won a foot race, or an endurance challenge…maybe. He realized that to beat me he had to do something unexpected, so when we started our advance on the log, he abandoned any caution and ran across the log at me. He bounced off into the water. 'Whether the rock hits the glass, or the glass hits the rock, it's highly likely that the glass is going to come off second best in either case.'

That left Al. I was feeling pretty good. Although I had been on the log 6 or 7 times, I was certainly not tired. And, I had my strategy. All I had to do was get close enough to use my size and push him off the log, as I had done the others. Al had been watching closely, however. On our first foray onto the log, Al started swinging as soon as he could, while I advanced toward him. We both lost our balance at the same time and went into the water, requiring a rematch. Man, that water was cold! On the rematch Al developed a new strategy, while I chose to stick to my tried and true direct physical assault. While he was still quite a way across the log, I advanced slowly, really paying little attention to him; he was too far away to reach anyway. As I raised a foot to advance, he slid his hands to one end of his pugil stick and swung hard at me, catching me in midstride, totally surprising me. Shoot, I wanted to get close enough to shove him physically, and here he was thinking! That was almost cheating; you don't think at this game! His strategy worked. I teetered, wobbled, and again fell into the water, with Al the very happy winner, and the recipient of a badly desirous exemption! (Since then I have been challenged by many people. "You let Al win that last match deliberately, didn't you?" Nope, I didn't. However, if I had known what was coming, I might have!)

Anderson gathered us around him, most of us cold and wet and shivering rather violently, and not a few of us changing to an interesting hue of blue. "Congratulations to you all! The pot is now richer by $25,000, and Al, you cannot be executed in the next execution!" Everyone looked at each other; all that meant was that their chance of execution had just risen by about 10%.

Anderson continued, "And Al, you get a second perk. You get to pick a second person to receive an exemption, but cannot reveal who you have picked until dinner tomorrow night, right before the quiz. Think carefully, and be prepared to tell us how you selected the person to receive it." Anderson looked at each of us in turn, and laughed. "Now you all get to practice the fine art of sucking up to Al!"

There was a stunned silence in the meadow. Cold, blue lips and numb hands were forgotten. Two exemptions? The chances of being executed just went up another 10%!

However, I immediately saw a chance to sew confusion. When Al had been told he could select a second person, he looked at me. I had won far more matches on the log than anyone else, and Al and I were good friends. I knew he would likely select me; I had worked harder than anyone (little work that it was, I admit), and he was a fair person. Furthermore, he had deliberately set me up to have the most matches possible before he had to meet me, in order to attempt to tire me out, and felt a little guilty. I was fairly sure he was going to pick me for the exemption. So, I immediately approached him, out of hearing of everyone else.

"Al, I want to talk with you, please." He looked at me, somewhat surprised. I'm sure he was expecting me to plead with him that I was the logical person to select, but he was surprised that I would do that. "Al, if you are going to select me, I don't want the exemption. I'm very serious about this. **I do not want an exemption for losing!** I've been an athlete all my life, and when I have won a match in a sport, it's because I won it. I've never 'won' a match after actually losing it, and have no desire to start now. I'll win exemptions soon, most likely, and want to wait until I win to get one. **Not this way!** Pick one of the women; they had no chance anyway."

Now, while all of that may be true, if I were really playing the game I would have most definitely accepted the exemption. However, the reasoning I used was just logical enough to be believable, and would certainly confuse the issue. In the first place, truly, I didn't need the exemption, but they didn't know that. What I saw was an opportunity to really get inside the heads of everyone else. Refusing an exemption on principles? Nah, never happen! No one would do that!

Al walked away, looking troubled. He believed me somewhat, but was confused by my actions. What was I doing, and why? Was it as transparent as it appeared, or was I just protesting, yet hoping he would select me anyway? After all, it was his choice, not mine. He had some serious thinking to do.

As we started to leave the banks of the glacial pond, I noticed that Anderson had taken his mike off, and was chatting amiably with some of the crew. I hastily approached Clay. "Clay, it's a darned shame that Anderson is so….dry!"

Clay grinned. "Yes, isn't it?"

I needed no further encouragement. I grabbed Darwin and Lisa and we headed for Anderson. He saw us coming and realized he was in trouble, but there was no place to run. Darwin and Lisa would have been content to just take him to the edge of the pond and push him toward the water, getting him a little wet in the process. On the other hand, I had other motives. Instead of merely pushing, I bodily picked him up and jumped as far out in the pond as possible; after all, I still had my wet suit on. He didn't. He came up sputtering and blowing, trying to catch his breath, and looked at me cautiously. He wasn't sure what else I had up my sleeve. Meanwhile, the others stood on the bank laughing, somewhat startled by my aggressive jump into the water. We exited and all went to change clothes, Anderson shivering more and more as he walked. He is a little guy with little body fat, after all. He should not go swimming in ice water, and probably never really knew that fact before. I just helped further his education.

I wanted Anderson to avoid me, frankly. I was still feeling tremendous pressure, and was still feeling like I could blow the game with one false move, and felt always on the verge of making that move! I just did not need the pressure of Anderson, with his wit and his steely eyes watching me closely. Let him hang with the others!

We were taken to a local spa to swim in warmer water, relax and sip some beer, and to utilize the most welcome hot jacuzzi. I was the first out of the dressing room, and there in the middle of the pool, treading water, was a relaxed, smiling, Anderson Cooper. I caught his eye and immediately broke into a run for the edge of the pool, straight at him. He realized my intent as his eyes got considerably bigger, and started furiously dogpaddling toward the far end of the pool. I landed only a couple of feet behind him, propelling him onward with a small wall of water. I really was not aiming for him, but he didn't know that. Another stroke to ensure he avoided me when possible, attempting to lessen the tremendous stress I felt at all times.

The rest of the several hours at the spa were uneventful, with two exceptions. First, Katie was walking down some slippery steps and fell rather badly, catching herself with her hand and landing on her butt. I was right behind her at the time, and quickly checked her over. There is an interesting provision we must sign before being on this show, though. We are not allowed to "render assistance to anyone for a medical problem." I told the producers that if the occasion demanded, I would ignore that provision; I'm an orthopedic surgeon, and just can't turn my back when there is the possibility of a good injury! While Katie did not appear to me to be seriously injured, having only a contusion of the muscles at the base of the thumb, they whisked her off to a local emergency room, and for several weeks thereafter Katie sported a green short arm cast. (Later, while watching the show on television, I noted lots of traffic on Mole web sites when that happened, with speculations that the green cast signified...something. Anything! I thought it actually was a cool move on the producers part to offer no explanation; just more mystery to contemplate!)

The other fun thing to watch was how several of the players drifted over to Al and had quiet, personal chats with him. I don't blame them for that. As discussed before, those exemptions were worth lots, and if someone could strike the correct chord with Al, they might get him to consider them. Knowing Al, I doubted that, however. He would have a good reason for his selection. It was actually a fun day at the spa!

The next day was execution day, a day of boredom, really. However, rooming with Bribs had some unexpected positive sides. Bribs was playing with a deck of cards and came up with a new card game that could be absorbing for two people for hours...especially when there was nothing else to do! We called it...Bribbage. I won't go into the details of the game, but look for it on game shelves everywhere! It was at the interview on this day that Clay told me Bribs had put down almost all of my information on the preceding quiz. As if my paranoia and fear of failing at this simple job weren't at a high enough peak! I could not tell any difference in Bribs' attitude, however.

After all the interviews were over, dinner was served. Anderson sat at the head of the table, as usual, directing conversation, smiling an evil little smile, and watching us closely at all times. He really did appear to be examining us, one by one. Unnerving to someone with a guilty conscience. He usually chose a theme of questions to ask us all at dinner, with cameras rolling; ultimately these questions and their answers were to show up on national television. You would think we would carefully craft our answers, knowing that. But as I have previously explained, we were so used to the cameras...and Anderson's questioning so deft...that we usually could be counted on to give a frank and sometimes revealing answer.

Anderson then came to Al. "Al, who did you select to receive the second exemption, and why?"

Al looked around the table, letting his gaze rest on me for a moment. "Well, my first inclination was to select Bill; after all, he won far more battles on the log than anyone else, and was probably going to be my automatic selection. *However,* Bill approached me immediately after you told us this was going to happen, and told me that he would rather *earn* his exemption, and did not want to be given one. I'm going to honor that request." Al said this last statement with a bit of derision in his voice; he clearly felt that I was up to something, but just did not know what. Also, he might have thought I was really trying to get him to select me. I don't know.

Everyone turned and looked at me with some astonishment on their faces. Darwin and Patrick looked disgusted, and Darwin said, "Right..." (In that night's confessional booth, Darwin was still not buying my explanation, derisively stating, "Bill's just trying to look *honorable.*" Darwin was right in his disbelief, but reached the wrong conclusion. I was just being *molish.*)

Al continued with his analysis of who should get the second exemption. It was an excellent analysis, and a perfect example of reasoned thought. He gave the exemption to Katie, who had entered her match with Big John with a great attitude and a sincere effort to knock him off the log, though she really had no chance at all. An excellent choice, Al! And, again, thanks for not picking me. I would rather *earn* my exemption!

Reflections of The Mole

(If we ever play another game, however, and you get a chance to give me an exemption…..)

Then to the quiz. That night we did something different after the quiz. Instead of retiring to individual rooms (and by this time no one wanted to be in a room with me; after all, my first two after-test roommates had both been executed), we were allowed to sit in the hotel bar for a couple of hours. The den mother, Patti, told us all that the producers would buy us each one beer or a glass of wine. That was OK; we all had money and could buy our own! After several beers or glasses of wine each (mixed drinks for Dorothy), plus cigars all around, we were finally herded into the adjacent chambers for our execution ceremony. By this time we were loose and relaxed, unlike most executions. In fact, we were *so* relaxed we didn't really care who went home! Lisa had pointed out to us that her job as an Assistant US Attorney had ended **that day**, and she hoped it had not all been for nothing!

Anderson again began slowly, agonizingly slowly, entering each of our names into the computer. He got down to the final 4 names: Lisa, Myra, Elavia, and me. Hmmm. I was even starting to sweat it a little bit! Lisa's name was entered, and the red thumbprint came up, much to the astonishment of everyone in the room. Lisa gasped, then stood up and waved good-by to everyone as she picked up her bag and departed. This was the first time we had really been startled by a selection. The first two were considered just blind bad luck. Anyone could have gone those first two weeks. However, by now everyone really understood how to play the game, and Lisa was generally regarded as one of the smartest people in the room. She was systematic, took copious notes, was organized, and understood the necessity for speed. How was it she was executed?

I know how now. Having chatted with her since the show, she told me she was so disarmed by my letter to my wife that she finally completely disregarded me as a potential mole, and so for the first time put none of my information down on the quiz. No matter how fast you are, if you are wrong totally, it's time to go home. And, by the way, we found out later that although Lisa had arrived back in Chicago a couple of days past her deadline, she got her old job back. She is there now, prosecuting the guilty and (hopefully) protecting the innocent, selling beer in Comiskey Park...where she is recognized frequently from the show...and entering Urban Challenge races against the guys. She recently sent all of us her first winning press release. I guess she really *can* compete with the boys! (Just not with a pugil stick.)

What Was She Thinking?

Lisa

My quiz strategy from the beginning was to select the answer that I thought covered the most players. For example, if the quiz question asked whether the Mole drank red or white wine with dinner, and all but one of us drank red wine, I chose red.

For the most part, we knew the correct answers to the quiz questions. After the first quiz, I determined what my score would have been if each person had been the Mole. I would have gotten zero right if Katie were the Mole, so I eliminated her. I would have gotten one right if Bill were the Mole, so I also eliminated him. From that moment forward, I didn't suspect either of them. My academic approach to the quizzes was solidified for me by my gut reaction to both of them — I just didn't think either was the Mole.

Unfortunately, I had no idea who else it could be. I spent a great deal of sequestered time identifying and listing "suspicious" qualities in each player; however, I could not eliminate he possibility that each was trying to act suspicious. I had done the same thing, by placing the same bet on each blackjack hand, and being much more quiet than my ordinary personality.

In the end, my days were numbered. I had eliminated Bill early, and doubt I would have reconsidered my strategy for some time. My two coalition partners, Darwin and Dorothy, also didn't suspect Bill, so collaboration also would not have helped. On a positive note, the Department of Justice had not yet processed the paperwork for me to quit and be a reality show superstar, so I returned to the same desk and caseload I had left two weeks earlier. I don't regret for one second that I played the game. But I am grateful that I was able to return to an even more interesting legal career as a federal prosecutor.

Since the show ended, I have resumed my life in Chicago. I still play soccer and floor hockey, run adventure races and prosecute criminals. After the White Sox won the World Series I stopped selling beer during games and started teaching two law school classes. I also increased my distance running, and qualified for and ran the Boston Marathon in 2006. My life is full.

I have stayed in touch with the other players, some more than others. I think one thing that allowed us to click in the first place was the fact that none of us saw The Mole as a path to superstardom. We wanted an adventure, and we each got it. But none of us was looking to be on the cover of US Weekly. When I last saw Dorothy and e-mailed Darwin, we talked about our lives and the day to day adventures we have had outside the show. In the end, we're interesting people who had one helluva vacation. When we were heading back to the bus after the Burn Bags Burn game, Darwin said, "this is still better than working."

Indeed.

XIV

How to Not Play

The next day we awakened, minus Lisa. Now we were 11, one of us a sneaky, no account Mole who had succeeded in getting rid of one of the sharpest members of the team! Patrick was still smarting visibly about the loss of his journal, but there seemed to be little he could do about it. Or so we thought.

We were told to pack up and get ready to travel. It was time to move on to another country entirely: Italy! There were cheers from the group. We had loved the beauty of Switzerland, but, after all, one of the perks of doing the show was travel, and we all looked forward to the relaxed atmosphere and pasta of Italy.

We knew we had a game to play en route, and Bribs, Darwin, and I took turns saying that we had "overheard" the producers talking about parachuting. The reason for this dissimilation, for no one had really heard such a thing, is that we had found out that Al was deathly afraid of that possibility. He had referred several times to the opening of "The Mole I," where the players had all parachuted down to the desert. He would actually turn white when this was brought up; it was his biggest fear. So, in true competitive fashion, we delighted in bringing up the possibility every chance we could, just to watch Big Al get quiet and white. It was something to do on boring mornings!

We left St. Moritz, and arrived at a gravel trailhead somewhere high in the mountains and off loaded. The players milled about smartly, chatting, while the crew disappeared over the hill and headed down a valley. I knew what game was coming up, a fact that was understandably unknown to the others. My problem was that it involved rappelling, and in conversations about what we enjoyed doing a few days before, I had noted that I had rappelled while serving with the Marines, and looked forward to being able to get back into it some day. Therefore, when the time came to pick a team to rappel, it was possible, if not probable, that I would be selected by the others...and I did not want that. This game was basically an impossible game without experience and practice, and everyone who participated would look suspicious. No sense in my being in it; let confusion reign! (A side note here. Every game we played had been played before by members of the crew. Once a game was dreamed up, it was practiced by the crew and the producer to make sure it was possible. What a gig! I think I want to do that in my next life!)

As we wandered about the mountain top, I feverishly tried to think of a way to ensure I would not be selected when Anderson told us what was coming. I looked around and noted a Port-a-potty a little way away. I immediately headed for it, bent over a little. Once in it, I relaxed...at least as much as one can relax in such a place. It was as clean as such a place can be, which meant that I really did not want to be there. However, I camped out in that Port-a-potty. After maybe 20 minutes I emerged, noting several of the others glancing my way. I did not know whether or not they needed in there, but definitely *did* want them to note my presence. I walked a few feet toward them, suddenly grabbed my belly, and retreated again into the small "house that pleases." Another 10 minutes or so, and again I emerged. I did this several times, until I was sure that everyone was probably vaguely aware that I was spending an inordinate amount of time indisposed. As I joined the group, I mentioned to one of them that the meal last night must have been a tad suspect. I stayed in the background, retreating to the Port-a-potty once or twice more.

Finally Anderson came back over the hill. "Follow me!"

We did so, arriving in a large grassy meadow in a beautiful Swiss valley, with one side of a dam in the near distance. Anderson noted, "I need you to pick 4 people who just like to *hang around*, and one person whom you all trust." Several hands went up; not mine. No one even looked at me. I really don't know if any of the others thought about whether or not I could be a player this time, but if they did, I am sure they could see only disaster on camera if I were to *hang around* too long. I had already demonstrated to my satisfaction that to put me in a situation under stress whereby I could not immediately retreat to a private place could result in television coverage that would be considered...undesirable by some. "Fear Factor" maybe, but not our show.

    Anderson then did something which delighted us all, and resulted in the only time we had to go back and film a sequence a second time. The producers and cameramen were a couple of hundred yards up on the dam. Clay motioned for us to come on up. Anderson turned to us, straight faced, and instructed, "Walk this way." He then proceeded suddenly to launch into some sort of exaggerated swinging "Wizard of Oz" kind of walk; we all looked at each other and followed his instructions, all attempting to mimic his walk. After Clay and the cameramen managed to quit laughing, Clay laughingly told us to please go back and try again. We did so with a more normal cadence this time. Anderson is a most unique kind of host!

    Bribs, Darwin, Elavia, and Heather were chosen as those who liked to *hang around*, and Al as the *trusted one*. Heather was fitted with a helmet and a helmet camera, and the technicians were having trouble fitting the components together. Darwin and I offered lots of verbal assistance, Darwin because he just thought he knew how to do it, and me because I knew it had to be irritating to the on scene producer, Luis. Luis finally got aggravated with our verbal help and kicked us out of the area, gruffly telling us to "let them do their job!" I commented to Darwin that clearly the producers didn't have their act together;

just continuing to establish my position as an anti-establishment kind of fellow!

Most of you reading this probably saw the episode. It really was a no win situation. Each of the 4 had to rappel down the face of the dam, one at a time, forcing themselves to swing back and forth across the concrete, concave structure. They were trying to reach small flags on the dam face; next to those flags were questions about various players; only portions of those questions could only be glimpsed at the very end of a lateral swing. They would then have to try to add in the unread portions and come up with numerical answers. Each player had one question to answer, and the resultant number would be entered as one of the 4 numbers on a combination lock on a chest full of money. The answers involved birthday dates, number of players in various games, etc. You had to have obtained all the information possible on all players, then be able to remember it with immediate recall. (i.e., "What is Brib's birthday minus Rob's birthday?" Easy to calculate, assuming that player had gotten that information and could remember it!) Trying to do so hanging 80 feet or so in the air in an extremely unstable pose made the tasks impossible, truly. Elavia managed to somehow launch herself backward against the dam several times. I'm not sure how she did that, but it certainly looked painful!

Everyone made mistakes. Then Al was given their answers (plus the questions) and had to try to figure out if he had been deliberately lied to, or if the mistakes he found were innocent. Plus, he didn't *know* all the answers. He then had to descend head first, slowly, for about 150 feet until he reached the lock box full of potential winnings, enter the numbers derived from the answers given, and be 100% correct the first time in order to get the lockbox to open. He was unsuccessful, and we all then congregated at the bottom of the dam and looked longingly at the money as Anderson opened the chest with an evil smile. "Enjoy this look; you will never see this money again!"

He slammed the lid down, then started stirring the pot, as he surely enjoyed doing. As I said, everyone looked guilty, and the players who simply were sitting and watching added to the general state of suspicion. Katie and Patrick, especially, pointed fingers at various of the 5 participants. Myra, Rob, and I sat back and added comments of blame sparingly. After all, the others were doing enough castigating of each other! All in all, a good day to be a Mole.

We retreated to the vans and started a long day's drive toward Italy. Soon, all thoughts of the game were put aside...for the moment. It was just exciting entering another country!

This was a drive that resulted in some driver changes, however. As we sped down the autobahns (or whatever those high speed death-defying roads are called in that part of Europe), we had about 7 vehicles in line. Two vans of players, a fancy car with producers and Anderson, and vans and buses of crew. Each vehicle had a walkie-talkie so that we could communicate, and we were all following the lead of some local drivers who theoretically knew where they were going. I was driving one of the vans, following one of the local guides in the left lane. Suddenly he veered sharply to the right across 4 lanes of traffic to an off ramp. I started to follow him, but quickly realized that to do so was to really court disaster; traffic was heavy. I kept going straight while someone else in the van got on the walkie-talkie and told the folks up front to slow down and wait. I got off at the next off ramp, turned around, and caught up with everyone pretty quickly. Luis, the Associate Producer responsible for our safe transport and housing and such, stood beside his car waiting. When I pulled up he removed Bribs from his vehicle and put Myra in his place. (While Bribs had not been part of this episode, he had let out a "Whoopee" some time before and had passed a number of vehicles at somewhere around 100 mph or so.) Luis was a little pale and shaken; he could see this show ending suddenly in a cloud of smoke! We resumed our trip after

Reflections of The Mole

Luis offered a few choice words to the local drivers leading us. We finally arrived in a small Italian town, safely.

Our initial hotel there was interesting. This was a small, elegant, privately owned hotel, and while arrangements had clearly been made for our arrival and stay, the owner was surprised and chagrined at the presence of cameras; or, perhaps it was the fact we were Americans, or just too many of us, or something. Regardless, we moved to another hotel the next morning. I would love to know, someday, why he really did not want us in residence. We were nice, not rowdy, well behaved. Maybe he just did not want to suddenly jump into another tax bracket, inasmuch as we were certainly going to increase his occupancy rate for a week or two! On the other hand, his was a…boring hotel. Great for a family out for a quiet break; we had all the quietness we needed, and more!

Eventually, however, we settled into a large, roomy hotel and moved into our rooms, with new roommates. I don't remember frankly who I was rooming with at that point. Everyone who roomed with me complained about my snoring, and I was becoming self-conscious. This was not helping my sleep in the least!

The next morning we were immediately tasked with another game, but had a game to play before the game, as it turns out. I knew what was coming.

As we loaded into our bus outside the hotel, a lovely young Italian woman came over to us and in broken English explained that she had a flat tire. Could we help her? She had not quite finished her explanation before Patrick had bailed out of the bus, trampling a couple of the other contestants en route. I expect he still lacked a couple of merit badges for Boy Scouts, and was just grabbing an opportunity to acquire them. He grabbed the girl and hugged her and told her that we would be happy to do so. Al, Darwin, Bribs and I proceeded to change her tire, while Patrick entertained her and her equally lovely female companion. Patrick was helpful; he kept them out of our way while we worked. We had a little problem with the jack, so I picked up the back end of the car so the others could remove the flat tire and replace it with the spare. In doing so I left an ass sized dent in the back fender; and that is a pretty good sized dent! Myra and the others scrutinized the entire operation with some snide asides, especially as Patrick decreased the distance between himself and the two Italian women until there was no noticeable separation. We then loaded back onto the bus; everyone felt that probably this was a part of the game, so all details of the two young women were reviewed and shared. Patrick had most of the essential data needed. He did love to play the game!

We soon stopped at a gas station to fill up, where, lo and behold, an elderly woman approached us with the same story! My goodness, coincidences abounded! We went to her aid, (with Patrick resting in the background; he had done too much work in the initial tire change and was fatigued), and successfully changed her bad tire as well. Of course, she *was* at a service station; it is not inconceivable that someone there might have aided her! Incidentally, as we worked on her car someone noted her cell phone in the front seat; marked on the phone pad was the message: "Clay, #XXXXXX." Now, why in the world would this total stranger, this elderly Italian woman, have one of our producer's phone numbers? It did serve to make a suspicious person think.

We went on to the next game, the "Smart Game, Dumb Game." I had been briefed, and was to make sure that I volunteered to be one of the smart players, and to ensure that we got at least two of the 5 puzzles right. Not greedy, but I needed to look like I was a contributing member of this money-hungry group. In that game Dorothy suddenly showed her true brilliant colors. I needn't have worried about getting two of the puzzles right. Dorothy showed quickly that she was a master of letters, numbers, and words…and anything else she chose to do. We wound up getting all five of the puzzles right, much to the surprise and consternation of everyone else. While we did add $50,000 to the pot, we also received 3 exemptions for the next execution. This left only 8 players eligible for execution, and assuming one of them was the Mole, lowered the odds to 1 in 7 that one of the remaining players would be executed. This was not good for overall morale, and there was considerable grumbling about that prospect.

However, events elsewhere were moving that consideration off center focus. Patrick had asked Katie if he could borrow his old journal back, whereupon he had taken it into the bathroom and had torn out several pages, pages that he clearly he felt revealed his hopefully winning strategy, or something. Katie, with her 20/20 teacher's vision, did not miss the gap and the torn page edges when she was given the journal back. She questioned Patrick about it, and he told her that he had asked one of the producers, Luis, and had received permission to tear the pages out. This battle escalated quickly. Patrick, as I have noted before, had chosen to play this game in a manner different from anyone else; and, as I have also noted, might have added an element to the game that it needed to keep the audience's interest at a peak. However needed it might have been, it was simply irritating to all the other players. Patrick was rapidly setting himself up on the outside, looking in. If he were the Mole.... The arguments raged, all about whether or not he legally could do what he had done. I was engaged elsewhere, and heard about these arguments from the others, primarily Bribs. And, frankly, I didn't really care! All I looked forward to was another player going home, and I didn't really care who. My job was to keep the game going with some upheaval, and Patrick was handling part of that tasking for me. Keep it up, Patrick! You're doing great!

The next day was execution day. This time we were all allowed to congregate together while the interviews were conducted, and at lunch matters came to a boil with Patrick. Heated words were exchanged between him and everyone else about how he was playing the game. He tried to explain himself and be conciliatory, with Myra chiming in as his advocate. She was not defending his tearing the pages out, but was rightly pointing out that he was playing the game his way, and no one had really prescribed a "right" way that we should play. To no avail. Tensions were high, and were not abated when Anderson announced a hefty fine against the pot at dinner, secondary to Patrick's defacement of his old journal. Patrick argued forcibly that he had had Luis' permission to do as he had done, but Anderson didn't buy it. (Myra has noted that she was with Patrick when Luis gave his permission, however. Anderson didn't care, inasmuch as he had clearly delineated what could and could not be done to other's journals on the morning we had exchanged them.)

Again we took our test, following which we had many hours to wait before the results were revealed. We were supposed to have the execution outdoors at this most beautiful private villa, but it was raining heavily. Rather than tear down the outdoors set, the producers clearly hoped the flood waters might recede, so we all were herded into a room and told it would be "a while." We passed the time by singing every song anyone could remember, and several that no one knew. It turned out to be a fun evening, but the decision was not made until about midnight to move the execution inside. Therefore, at about 2:00 AM, in a new setting, Patrick was the 4th person executed. Did he throw the quiz? I don't know. He knew he was at odds with many of us, and I doubt that he liked the conflict any more than anyone else did. He said later that he had had two final candidates for the Mole, and had answered all the questions for one of them. He said that if he had survived that round, he would have won the game. Shoot, if he had managed to stick around, everyone else might have gone home before their time anyway!

There was general relief at his leaving, but there was a considerable amount of soul searching as well. It was not really that Patrick was disliked; it was more that he had chosen to play the game in a confrontational manner, and one that made everyone else uncomfortable. All in all, most of us were sorry that he had left with bad feelings. On the other hand, as Al was wont to say, "Better him than me." Someone had to leave, after all!

What was he thinking?

I don't know what Patrick was thinking. He was the only player I was unable to find to add something to this narrative, and perhaps was the one I would most have liked to have had input from. We'll never know. Was his approach planned to alienate, and a deliberate ploy? Was it a deliberate strategy or was he just doing what came naturally to him? I don't know.

XV

Rob the Magician

We got to take a day off before proceeding with our next competitions. Off to Venice! I had never been there, and it is an incredible place. We wandered about the city and eventually congregated in the square to feed the pigeons. Several of us bought corn, lay down in the central square, and spread it over ourselves. Then dozens of pigeons descended and walked across our bodies, busily snacking on their tasty meal. Rob was the funniest, and at one point while he was laughing a pigeon stepped in his mouth; he abruptly ceased laughing and sputtered vigorously for a while. He knew what else that pigeon had been walking in.

Venice is a tourist's haven, as everyone knows, and those tourists watched us with some bemusement. Here we were, 10 people of relatively nondescript appearance, being followed about by cameramen with boom mikes busily recording our every move. Every once in a while a tall red-headed crew member would rush over to one of us and pull our shirt up in the back and work for a while. His job was to make sure our mikes were always functioning properly. That required primarily replacing fresh batteries when needed, and he monitored our conversations at all times…not for content, but for strength of the signal. When he would hear one of us starting to fade out, he would replace that person's battery pack. We had fun with him, occasionally talking in increasingly softer tones, convincing him that our battery pack needed replacing. As I said, we were bored. I also enjoyed bringing my mike up close to my mouth and whispering some obscenity in his ear when he was looking away. He would whip around and try to figure out who was doing that, but never was able to figure it out…at least until the end, when I was the only male left with a mike on! Sound exciting? You're right. It wasn't. But, at the moment….

As noted, tourists looked us over carefully. Many were Americans, and we were under strict orders not to speak to them unless we had to, and never to reveal what we were doing. So, the most common response to their questions was, "We're doing a PBS documentary." That never failed to cause their eyes to glaze over a little as they quickly lost interest in our business. I like PBS documentaries! However, if you ever want to kill someone's interest in you, tell them that. It works.

That night in Venice we ate in a large, crowded restaurant. Again, a long table was prepared for us on one side of the room, extra lights were erected by the lighting crew, and several sound men with boom mikes were stationed around the table. You might ask why we needed boom mikes when we were all wearing individual mikes? A very good question, and I don't have the foggiest idea why that was so. Maybe union rules. I don't know. What that *did* do was focus lots of attention on that table from the rest of the patrons, so that when we entered the restaurant, there were necks aplenty craning to see who we might be. No one knew. Someone came over and asked us. I don't know which of us came up with this, but suddenly the word went out: we were all assistants to the world famous magician, The Great Obscuro. Rob. And, in fact, when he was pointed out to a number of the patrons they felt that they recognized him. The wonderful power of suggestion! (Several asked if his first name was Siegfried? We pointed out the marked absence of tigers when that name was bandied about.)

Rob promptly started acting the part, and visited from table to table doing card and coin tricks. As I have said before, he really was outstanding, and soon succeeded in establishing an admiring audience in the restaurant.

We finished dinner, replete with multiple bottles of good Chianti, and the continued attention of other patrons. Shoot, a world famous magician in their midst? This was something to tell their kids when they got home! When several very nice looking young ladies got interested in Rob and started following him about the producers got nervous. (Rob's own groupies! None of us had any yet...and the odds were not good that we would *ever* get any.) We were attracting entirely too much attention with the antics of The Great Obscuro, and they were afraid some local television or newspaper crew was going to appear, so we were finally ushered out of the place. It was great fun, however, and Rob, youngest of us all, settled comfortably into the role of the star of the event. He was born to the task!

We went the next day to a "grappa" tasting event. Man, that was an event. We tasted liquors that should have been sold at a gasoline station, and which would probably provide way too much octane for my car. Several of us had more than one glass of this most Italian of brews, and regretted it rather quickly. It hurt then and later. No one dared smoke with those fumes in his mouth for fear of the resultant explosion. That stuff could be used as a terrorist event by itself. We all looked fondly back...and forward...to our customary beer and wine with dinner!

Back to the grind, but only after another afternoon's break. I expect the crew was working at setting up the next day's game, so we were given one more day of rest. Not that we needed rest. Rest was all we did between games! I am used to going to the gym daily, playing racquetball and other forms of working out, and this enforced inactivity was wearing on me physically. I have had a tendency to develop bad back problems when I don't stay in top shape, and this lying about and feasting on pasta 3 times a day was not the prescription I needed to remain pain free. Plus, I normally like pasta no more than 3 or 4 times a year. Along with Heather and Bribs, I preferred some good Tex-Mex food, but we had seen nary a Mexican restaurant in Italy. I carried along a roller to work on my abdomen, which I was doing daily. But, it wasn't nearly enough. Only twice in the almost seven weeks in Europe did we convince the producers to let us go to a health club. These reality shows *can* be bad for your health!

One of the aggravating things we did virtually every night was to switch rooms and roommates. We would come in around midnight, usually tired, and would be told we were changing rooms. We would then have to go pack our meager lot of belongings and move down the hall, or at least half of us did. I don't know why we had to do this so often. We were told that there had been complaints that not everyone was getting "exposed" to everyone else. I doubt that was the reason. One of the problems I think the producers had with us was the fact that we all got along, especially since Patrick had left. They were likely trying to stir us up, get some action out of us, some rebellion, something! I was soon to try to gratify those desires, always assuming my interpretation of their line of reasoning had any validity whatsoever, of course.

We were now staying in Vincenza, Italy. I had never heard of Vincenza before that, nor since then. We moved several times in Vincenza, as noted. Upon reflection, I still wonder if the producers were paying our bills. Maybe we were skipping out just ahead of the Italian bill collectors! The next morning it was time for games again, and our routine changed; we were called out of bed at 6:30 AM and told to switch rooms instead of waiting until midnight. At least we weren't tired when doing it; sleepy, yes. I wound up in a 3 man room with an upstairs alcove, which is where I pitched my bag. Sound rises? I didn't remember, but thought my two new roommates (Rob and Al) might be able to ignore my snoring a little easier if I were at least out of sight. Wishful thinking, I expect.

We resumed our games later that morning. Again, I had been briefed on the upcoming games, and was determined to sabotage the next game in some obvious manner. I was tired of not being considered as at least a minimal suspect by the others. I was being given a free pass...free of suspicion, at least...due to my advanced age, or my geriatric ineptness, or perhaps just honoring your elders. Regardless, it was getting plumb embarrassing. I was getting no respect as the Mole, and Elavia was getting all the attention!

Think or Swim. That was the name of the game. 3 of us (Darwin, Bribs, and the master swimmer himself, the Mole) volunteered to tread water. Each in turn would have a one kilo weight added around his neck every 5 minutes until he could no longer stay afloat, whereupon he would drop out (or drown). At that point the second swimmer would start receiving weights, and so on until all three swimmers were moribund on the bottom of the pool or sitting wearily on the side massaging our sore necks.

Meanwhile the competition continued around us. Questions were to be called to 3 runners out in town, communications being done between Katie and the runners by cell phone. The runners (Elavia...good in yoga, bad in running; Rob...a self-described non-athlete; and, Dorothy...who had already proven that physical prowess was not her strong point) had to run, in turn, around town deciphering the answers to Katie's questions. Katie was at the blackboard (she was, after all, a schoolmarm to whom this was just like another day in the classroom) next to our pool and would record their findings faithfully (unless she by chance were the Mole). She was trying to complete a phrase correctly using the information they provided; we weary swimmers were vocal contributors to the suggested answers that might complete that phrase. The timers in this entire ordeal were...us. When one of us had received so much weight around his neck that he could no longer remain afloat, his choice was to either drown, or drop out. If he chose to drop out (by swimming over to the edge of the pool), the next swimmer (who had been treading water all this time) would start assuming the burden of the weights as he treaded water. When all three of us had become so fatigued that we all had quit, the game was over. If the word puzzle had not been solved by then, the money ($30,000) was lost.

Picking my athletic event was critical if I were to cost us the money. There was no task that was absolutely sure of costing victory in the game, but the swimming portion seemed most likely to me. I knew Bribs and Darwin were good swimmers, and Dorothy...while apparently totally physically inept in aerobic exercise of any kind...had stated that she swam daily. She probably would have made a good 3rd swimmer, if winning was our goal. However, when Anderson looked us over and said, "Who is going to swim?" I raised my hand. Dorothy wasn't quick to volunteer for anything, and didn't get a chance to demonstrate her only positive physical fitness capability this time either. Of course, if she had known what she was going to have to do instead of swimming, I'm sure she would have been eagerly thrusting her little (really, *really* little!) hands in the air.

I turned to Darwin and Bribs. "I'm not really a good swimmer, but did manage to swim a mile in my flight suit and treaded water 30 minutes to pass my swimming test." I did not add that I had done all of this sometime early in the previous century. I also did not see cause to point out that while I can swim, slowly, I am truly negatively buoyant, and had a SEAL friend almost cry in frustration (if SEALs cried, of course) when he undertook to teach me the basic fundamentals of feeling comfortable in the water. I'm very comfortable...as long as I can stand up or reach over and get hold of the edge when I want to. And, of course, none of this really mattered, inasmuch as I was going to get in and out of that water as quickly as I could do it without looking totally ridiculous. (Ah, actually I didn't mind looking ridiculous; I just wanted to throw the game any way possible!)

The game started, and I was the first swimmer. I seriously considered getting choked on water and having to quit in the first minute or so, but ego is a strange thing. I just could not do that. I didn't mind looking somewhat ridiculous, but not totally stupid! So, at 5 minutes I received the first weight around my neck, and immediately started really, really pumping my arms, sculling as hard as I could. And my legs. And my body, hair, and eyebrows. I was putting out maximum effort, and Anderson watched with some amazement from the side of the pool, where he was monitoring us and telling us whether or not the answers we called out to Katie were right. I was sculling so hard I was causing small waves to break over the edges of the pool, bouncing Darwin and Bribs about. They were watching me with alarm; they had theorized that I could probably last 30-45 minutes before one them had to take over. "Bill, slow down. Breathe!" Ah, to no avail. At 7 minutes, 28 seconds I sank slowly beneath the waves, smiling blissfully at the underwater cameraman. Just in time I managed to roll my corpulent water-logged body from the pool while Anderson looked on with some bemusement. (I expect he was thinking, "Man, if this fellow is representative of the Navy, I hope we rely more heavily on the Army and Marines in the future!")

Darwin and Bribs then took over, and lasted a long time. However, out in town things were not going well. Both Rob and Elavia retrieved the wrong information on their first forays out, and had to retrace their steps to get additional information. Dorothy left, and simply never showed up again. Dorothy, she of 4 or 5 steps between rest stops, had been tasked with finding a set of stairs about 500 yards long and counting them. She fatigued and developed the dry heaves long before she achieved any portion of her count, and would be there today if the cameraman had not kindly brought her home, long after the event had ended.

Meanwhile, back at the pool, first Darwin, and then Bribs, were truly performing heroically, staying afloat with more and more weight, lasting longer and longer. As an athlete who had not given his all (or even part of his all), I felt for them. They deserved better! By a process of guessing and elimination, they managed to decipher most of the needed answers in spite of not having Dorothy's input. Only Katie's mistake, when she transferred the magnetized letters from the blackboard to the final solution board saved the day (for the Mole). She missed one letter, and no one caught it. (I actually saw it, but, darn the luck, was not allowed to mention it to anyone. Heck fire.) Without that letter, the solution was unfathomable, and first Darwin, then a determined Bribs, slowly sank beneath the waves. We had lost.

One of my goals was to have been an obvious saboteur. Unfortunately for me, most of the others messed up so badly that my efforts went largely unnoticed. Darwin did note, "Ah, Bill. He's just trying to pretend to be the Mole to screw us up." I asked Clay at our next meeting if I could wear a sign proclaiming, "I AM THE MOLE!" He told me it wouldn't matter. No one would believe it.

So, after an afternoon of tremendous effort by all of us, save one, we returned to the hotel and dinner. We went out that evening for our meal and drank considerably more than usual (which meant we drank a lot!). Everyone was depressed. Katie was nearly suicidal at having left that all important "G" on the wrong board. If Myra had not been there counseling her, coaxing her, making her drink lots and lots of beer (well, actually, Katie did that on her own), we would all have been driven even more into depression. I had been successful, and *I* was getting depressed! What a lively crew!

We returned to the hotel about 11:30 PM, exhausted and down. Suddenly Patti and Deb, our den mothers, announced, "OK, everyone has to change rooms." We had changed rooms only that morning! **This** was getting ridiculous! I waited for someone to protest, but no one did. While these were all very strong-minded people, certainly not used to being shoved hither and yon, we had all signed a contract with ABC which clearly stated that they owned us, heart and soul. Everyone had just given up any initiative. Whatever they said, we did.

I suddenly saw an excellent opportunity to inject some...life, or excitement, or perhaps just energy into this group of dispirited players. And, to establish some more credentials as someone working against the producers a little, and who clearly could not be the Mole working closely with them. (Of course, everyone thought that anyway. I was as safe from detection as a Mole could be. Maybe I should have just gone to bed!)

I squared myself in front of one of the cameramen, staring into the lens of his camera. He seemed nonplussed, and started to move out of my way. I grabbed his camera. "HOLD IT RIGHT THERE! YOU PRODUCERS! YOU ASSHOLES! IF YOU WANT US TO CHANGE ROOMS TWICE A DAY, COME DOWN HERE AND DO IT WITH US. MAKE ANDERSON CHANGE ROOMS, WHY DON'T YOU?! YOU F*@@ING JERKS! WE'RE TIRED OF BEING JACKED AROUND, AND AREN'T GOING TO TAKE IT ANY MORE. YOU CAN TAKE THIS SHOW AND SHOVE IT! I QUIT!" (Quit? The stinking Mole can't quit! I figured that if the others believed I was serious this would cement the fact that I was not the Mole, and I think I was right for a while.)

There was a stunned silence as all the players and the remaining camera and sound crews rushed down the hall toward me. The poor cameraman whose camera I had claimed tried to back away, but I held on tightly and continued my tirade. Other guests in the hotel started opening their doors and looking out. The other players gathered around me and started trying to calm me down.

Reflections of The Mole

Bribs grabbed me, "Buddy, everything is OK. This is just part of the game. We don't mind. Calm down! Relax! It's OK!"

I continued to stomp around, then went up to the loft to get my bag. Once there I collapsed, laughing silently, on my bed. I composed myself, looked over the railing at the bed below, and saw that while the bed was surrounded by players, cameras, and boom mikes, the bed was clear. I launched my bag at the bed with another screaming fit, and the crew who were gathered around the bed shrank as far away as possible, expecting me to plummet after it, I suppose.

I concluded the evening by going on to my assigned room, leaving a confused and very wide awake assemblage of players and crew behind me. I slept like a baby, content in my machinations.

The next morning I was approached by Clay, in full view of everyone else. Clay shooed the cameras away and turned off my mike, then asked, "Bill, is anything wrong?"

I smiled. "Not a thing."

He was still concerned. "I saw some footage from last night; it certainly didn't look like everything was OK then…"

I laughed. "Clay, I was just tired of the players acting like pussycats. Everyone was just too accepting and depressed. I just thought I would give them something else to think about…and cement my image as not a company man!"

He grinned. "Keep up the good work." He walked away, smiling.

Everyone was very, very nice to me all day. Solicitous, even. It's sometimes fun being a big, angry, Irish man! I need to try this more often.

There was another fallout from the previous day, unconnected to me. When Anderson was asking for volunteers for the various tasks we had to do in the "Think or Swim" game, Al had volunteered to take the spot Katie had wound up in.

Darwin had protested, arguing that Al was the first to volunteer to take the choice roles, and someone else should be given the opportunity this time. So, Katie got the spot. For my purposes, I was thankful for that. I'm afraid Al would not have missed that "G" on the board! When we had returned to the hotel Darwin and Al had gotten into a shouting match. Al accused Darwin of trying to control things, and he, Al, was not one he could control! Darwin denied that, and the argument went back and forth with exceptional volume and vigor. Nice to watch. Two men, both quite definitive in their beliefs that they were right, standing nose to nose arguing vigorously. Both are nice guys, though, and soon calmed down and resolved their differences. As the Mole it was good to see a spirited fight. We needed some disagreement in this group! It was also nice to see two fellows, steadfastly believing themselves in the right, resolve their differences without resorting to name calling or other inappropriate statements; they just argued it out and came to an agreement. Still somewhat ticked at each other, but not terminally.

The game the next day involved breaking out of a jail cell, and the players were the three who had not participated in the previous day's game…Heather, Al, and Myra. There was a special bonus announced by Anderson. That night we were to get to talk to our "loved ones" back home via video phone. The three concluded their game successfully, with Heather being the one who first managed to break out of her cell. As she retrieved the key, Anderson stepped out and stopped her. Heather had complained quite vocally several times about never getting an exemption. She was now to get her chance.

"Heather, you have two options. If you will just walk away with me, right now, leaving Myra and Al in their cells, you will receive an exemption at the next execution. They will get out in the morning, but will not get to talk to their loved ones on video tonight. That's all you have to do." Anderson, smiling gleefully, extended his hand toward her and started trying to walk away with her in tow.

Heather dug her heels in and looked back and forth between Al, who was rolling his eyes and staring beseechingly upward, and Myra, who maintained her smile. Myra always smiles. I think this time it had to be forced, but, smile she did. Heather did not hesitate. "Nope, I'm letting them out."

As she started toward the cells, Anderson helpfully stopped her once again. "Think about it. This is an *exemption from execution*. If you accept this, you cannot be executed. Don't you want to reconsider? You have been quite vocal about this." As I said, Anderson was full of help.

Heather shrugged him off and opened the cells. Anderson smiled…as did Myra and Al.

That night, late, we got to talk to our 'loved ones.' Five minutes only, and we could say nothing about the game, the other players, where we were, and could not ask about any current events. Nor anything else substantive. Wow! Talk about a talk fest! Everyone seemed to enjoy it, however, as we all rehashed our conversations with each other the next day. My wife, Shirley, does not especially like to talk on the phone anyway, and as a very private person (unlike me), doing so on national television really stifled her ability to come up with anything meaningful to say. She smiled. I smiled. Then, for the first time since leaving the States several weeks before, she told me that my Mother was doing fine. I breathed a giant sigh of relief. That was the most meaningful statement she could ever have made at that time! A huge weight suddenly lifted off my shoulders. I knew Shirley would never lie to me. She expressed mild surprise (and for her, that was a major expression!) that I was still in the game. She had noted when I got on the show that my lack of attention to detail would surely get me executed early, and clearly was bemused to see me still in the running. As I explained earlier, she had no idea I was the Mole.

The games were over, and it was time for someone else to go home. When we congregated in the lobby of the hotel (we had moved again since our last execution), Rob and I stood talking. I commented on his spiky hair. He suggested that before the next execution he assist me in doing mine the same way. Sounded fine to me, so I agreed. He paused, then said, "Why don't I tell you how to do it in case I get executed tonight?"

Of course, I uttered the required response. "You!? Unlikely. It's much more likely that it will be me going home. If I do, I promise to get Shirley to do my hair like yours for one of the parties." He smiled, then told me how make my hair stand straight up without having to be scared to death as a precursor.

And, sure enough, Rob was executed. When executed we were supposed to leave immediately, without comment. Rob is an excellent impressionist, and one of his favorite people to imitate was Christopher Walken. As he rose to leave the execution, he uttered, "Damn!" in his best Christopher Walken voice. (One of the delightful ways we would spend time, especially at dinner, was listening to Rob do one of Anderson's spiels, word for word, but as a slightly deranged Walken.) We were going to miss him. Anderson was going to miss him as well. Rob was the first of his favorites to depart…but would not be the last!

One final word about Rob. I have had lots of folks ask me if the editors fully captured the essence of the personalities of the people on the show. I always answer that I am extremely impressed with the editing on all the reality shows. We do charity events around the country with folks from most of the other major reality shows several times a year, and the people are always like I expect them to be. The nice ones are…really nice, and the not-so-nice ones are…really that way as well.

Rob and Myra are the two people on our show (who managed to stay around more than a few minutes) whose personalities I do not think were fully revealed. Both are complex, funny, and delightful. Rob, especially, appeared very quiet and reserved on the shows, and not nearly the engaging, funny, talented individual he is in person. Rob really would be missed, by all of us……But, what the hell! One more gone!

What Was He Thinking?

Rob

Honestly I haven't thought about the mole in years. To me it was kind of just a cool experience in my past, but I doubt I could even give you an honest recollection of what was going through my mind, because I honestly don't know. Sorry to be one of the only ones left out, but I'm sure no one would remember I was on the show anyway, haha.

XVI

Too Much Ice Cream

We arose early the next day and caravanned over to a small, mountainous Italian village, where Anderson met with all of us in a square. There were no level spots in this village; why someone chose to build there, I know not. Perhaps the thieves in the Middle Ages were lazy and just would not rob a place they had to climb to and from.

"I need three people in the group who hate cooking." Immediately Myra, Katie, and I raised our hands. I knew the two games ongoing today, and this group was going to be in the less arduous of the games. If Dorothy had only known what she was going to be doing later, she would have claimed to be Julia Childs reincarnated.

Anderson grinned his little slightly malicious smile. "Haven't you all learned anything by now? When I ask for someone who hates to do something, hasn't it dawned on you yet that volunteering to be in that group guarantees that you will get to do just what you're trying to avoid?"

He laughed at us as he handed us an Italian dictionary and a list of 27 ingredients. "OK, here's your task. You have to go from home to home in this lovely little town, gathering only one ingredient from any house. Once you have all 27 ingredients, you have to then convince some nice homeowner to let you use her kitchen to cook *at least 3 pizzas!* That will be dinner this evening for the group. In fact, that will be *the only food* the group will see, so their stomachs are depending on your efforts. We will see you with your pizzas at exactly 7:00 PM up in the square next to the church on the hill. Good luck!" He laughed as he departed with Darwin, Bribs, Heather, Elavia, Dorothy, and Al.

Myra, Katie, and I looked at each other. It was only about 11:00 AM, and this did not look to be a very difficult task. So, we adjourned to a local restaurant to have lunch and sip some beer while discussing strategy. Our strategy was actually very simple: collect the ingredients and cook some pizza. No sense in trying to make this too complicated.

After a good lunch we began our rounds of town, with me pulling a heavy two wheeled cart containing the pizza boxes and our bags. My goal in this game was to help in whatever way I could, but to stay out of the lead. In addition, I was going to try to stir up a little suspicion, if possible. Unfortunately, neither Myra nor Katie were suspicious sorts where I was concerned, and had they caught me chatting privately with Clay, would likely have immediately dismissed it. It's tough to get respect for any devious behavior in this game, especially if you are older than anyone else present! I never would have thought the time would come when I thought the younger generation was too respectful. Several times while we were going from house to house I would disappear. I would walk quietly away from the others, and go around a corner where I would remain for a couple of minutes, then reappear. To absolutely no avail. Neither Myra nor Katie thought I was the Mole, and they weren't going to let little things like my wandering off out of their sight cloud their opinion. I was old. I was innocent. I was not the Mole. I just probably had a weak bladder. I finally gave up. I was not dealing with Sherlock Holmes and Dr. Watson here. Not even a curious cameraman followed me, though they surely noticed. Maybe they just thought I needed some privacy. Only a couple of weeks previously such behavior would have brought wild accusations from Patrick; I was starting to miss him. (I can't believe I said that!)

An immediate problem was that Katie was a Spanish teacher, and wanted to properly conjugate all the verbs before we asked questions...and this in a language she knew absolutely nothing about! Consequently, Myra wound up asking most of the questions--or begging for free food—whichever way you wanted to look at it. Myra actually was exceptionally good at this, being gregarious, friendly, and a cute blonde. However, in spite of all that we found progress toward our goal to be quite difficult. The language barrier was just too great. We had some limited success; we would knock on a door, and invariably a woman would stick her head out of a second floor window and say something in Italian. Myra would go into her gyrations, trying to explain what we wanted while using few words. She was so expressive that I am sure most of the people just assumed she was an Italian who had forgotten the old language; either that, or she had not taken her anti-seizure medications recently. The people could see the camera crews with us, so probably understood that this was another crazy American thing. Most just smiled and waved, closing their shutters behind them. A few understood, and invited us in while they rummaged about. One woman even took out a large hunk of cheese and grated it for us. None understood that we could accept only one ingredient from them, though to our good fortune a number of them chose to share their Chianti. We might not get any pizza cooked, but this was proving to be a fruitful afternoon vintage-wise!

An hour or two passed, and thus far we had barely enough basic cooking essentials to make a decent sandwich. We were still about 22 items short of a full load...an accusation I have had levied at me several times before. It was becoming rather clear that our initial optimism was outstandingly unfounded; this was not going to happen at this rate. Then, we came to a house where the door was answered by a delightful, and large, 15 year old Italian boy who was fluent in English! Roberto. What a find! He enjoyed playing to the cameras, even though he had no idea what we were really doing, and we could not tell him. As we left his house, one more ingredient in hand, he followed. We looked at each other as those little light bulbs lit up over our heads. You could actually see them as the glow illuminated our frustrated faces.

We asked if someone would contact the producer and find out if it was illegal for us to utilize this find. After all, we were just proposing to use what came naturally. After some discussion…and I'm sure part of the discussion was that we were the most inept communicators in all of Italy, and the only pizza likely to result from our efforts would be made exclusively with grated cheese and olives…we were told that if we were innovative enough to recruit a native speaker, so be it. Things all at once became much easier. More and more people invited us into their houses while our self-appointed 15 year old savior delighted in his role. He clearly knew everyone in the town, and was apparently well known and liked by all. The Italians, much to our delight, continued to ply us with wine and beer as they gave us free goodies. We eventually had only one ingredient to collect, the dried mushrooms, a very expensive item. We again knocked on a door, and a man stuck his head out of the window.

"What do you want?" Wow! An American accent! This should be easy!

We explained our quest, and the fact that we needed mushrooms to finish our ingredient list. "Do you know how expensive mushrooms are? Why should I give you any? Can you pay for them? Why are those cameras with you?" This was all delivered in a not totally friendly way.

We again explained that we were forbidden to tell what we were doing, exactly, and who the cameras represented, nor the name of the eventual show. Nor could we pay for anything.

The man was clearly unimpressed, and irritated. "I don't know why I'm talking with you! You won't tell me anything. Why don't you go somewhere else?"

We were prepared to do that by this point. The only irritating and irritated person we were to encounter was an American! Who would have thought it? I told him, "Never mind. We'll find someone else to help; I hope you don't mind being on national television!"

He suddenly relented. "OK, come on in." We got our mushrooms. I don't know if it was because he was going to be shown being a jerk on television, or just that he had given us enough grief to feel good about himself; probably the latter. We didn't care; it was only 3:00 PM, and we had our 27 ingredients.

Roberto, our 15 year old guide, then took us to another house, knocked on the door, and went on up the stairs. We soon had a delightful 32 year old woman (dressed only in a long T-shirt) come out and invite us to use her oven for our last task. She turned out to be Roberto's sister; he certainly knew who to approach. She explained to us in broken English that today was her 32nd birthday, and she was leaving later to go into a neighboring town and party. But for now, our house was hers!

Wonderful! She brought out the customary beer and wine, and our several camera crews assembled on the stairs out of the way. She quickly realized that none of us knew the foggiest thing about making a pizza, and instructed us in every step of the process. When we got the flour out, our hostess playfully tossed a handful of flour at one of us, and the inevitable fight broke out between us until we were fairly well covered with about half of our needed flour for the pizzas. We then began rolling dough out on her table and I took note of the bowl of goldfish next to us. I suggested that we add them to the mix, but she laughed and refused my request, watching somewhat nervously thereafter every time I ventured near the goldfish bowl. Family pets. I thought Bribs and Darwin would have appreciated some sushi in their pizza. When we finished rolling the dough on the table (which was covered by a green patterned vinyl tablecloth), I noted that our finished product contained hundreds of dark specks in it. We all were questioning what these were, when I realized that quite a bit of the green pattern on the table cloth was gone. In fact, it was becoming virtually color-free in many spots. I promptly shut up. It was unlikely that the green paint was too poisonous, anyway. Surely the Italians don't use lead in their tablecloth paint. Just added a little badly needed roughage. Besides that, Darwin, Bribs, and Al were likely going to eat most of the pizza, and they were young and strong and could probably withstand most anything. Anyway, we had no other ingredients so could not have made more pizzas if we trashed that batch. Myra and I looked at each other and shrugged. This fit right in with Myra's life philosophy. We couldn't do anything about it, so why worry!? Katie was still mulling over the proper conjugation of verbs, and didn't notice.

We made our pizzas, put them into boxes, hugged and kissed our benefactor and wished her Happy Birthday, and headed up the hill at about 6:45 PM, with Roberto tagging along with us to see what else might happen. We arrived in front of the 800 year old church to find a dinner table set up in the courtyard. We were right on time.

Soon Anderson showed up, followed shortly by the others, all dressed in biking clothes…very stylish…though looking somewhat weary. They carried two tired looking bicycles up the last flight of stairs just before their time limit ended. They had wound up dividing into two teams, and both teams had had to ride their bikes up some very steep hills, with chase vans behind them full of cameramen and whoever was not on the bikes at that moment. This was the contest that again showed beyond any definitive doubt (not that any of us had any doubt at this point) that Dorothy was not a physical person. She could not reach the pedals and probably couldn't have ridden it had she been able to do so, and consequently was not too much of a contributor to her team's effort. The task of both teams was to get to the top of a steep mountain road and secure some bottles of "Mole" wine, which they then brought to dinner. They were all worn out by the time we saw them. They had had a long day. Even Dorothy looked tired; sympathetic fatigue, I suspect.

They had had a couple of interesting evolutions in their effort. When Anderson first showed them the two bikes they were to use and began explaining the rules they had to follow to make their money for the pot, he clearly stated, "Don't touch the bikes until I tell you to do so." Heather promptly reached out and stroked a fender of one of the bikes. I don't know why she did so, and I suspect she wasn't even aware of it. It was there and she was there. That's all the reasoning a young woman in love needs, I suppose.

Anderson suddenly shouted, "WHAT IS THERE ABOUT THE WORDS, 'DON'T TOUCH THE BIKES' THAT YOU DO NOT UNDERSTAND!?" Heather levitated some distance in the air and jerked her hand back, unhappily. When you are as pretty as Heather, I suspect few people yell so sharply at you. Heather was convinced for the rest of the filming that Anderson did not like her. I seriously doubt that. Anderson has an exceptional ability to create an image, and did so in this case with some vigor. I expect he really does like Heather. Maybe. Actually, I'm not sure. Maybe he doesn't. He could be the only male in Europe to not like Heather...but I doubt it.

Heather also managed to ride her bike down an abyss off the road, but no major injuries resulted. The cameramen even had an adventure. They were in one of the vans with a sliding door on the side, leaning out filming the bike and rider ahead of them. The driver got a little close to the railings of a bridge they were crossing, and the door was...torn off the van. Snagged by the railing, it ripped off and went flying down the slope. Knowing the cameramen, I am sure none flinched nor stopped their filming. If one of them had happened to have been slung down the slope with the door, they would have finished the shoot before going to his aid. He would have been disappointed if they had broken off from their assigned task! Very dedicated individuals; to their jobs, and to having fun.

Back at the church, we all sat down for this most delicious of meals, prepared by master chefs. Anderson again noted, "This is your dinner. This is all you get to eat tonight. It's too bad the cooks didn't cook more than the minimum number of pizzas." He loved to stir everyone up. Shoot, we were lucky we didn't have to order take-out.

We cut the pizzas up and distributed them. Several people asked about the black specks in the dough. We mentioned paprika, or perhaps black pepper. That paint was pretty tasteless, anyway, so it didn't much matter. The pizzas and wine were consumed rapidly and we all headed back down to the bottom of the village and our vans. We three cooks had been able to consume enough wine, beer, olives, bread, and cheese during the day that we did not think we should deprive the others of our pizza. Shoot, if it hadn't been for the volume added by the paint, we might have just managed only two pizzas out of those makings! Nah, we knew what was in it; we didn't eat. If only we had managed to include those goldfish.....

When we arrived at the vans several folks mentioned they had to find a bathroom. There was a little café/store next to the parking lot, so we all headed over there to use their facilities. While wandering about the store, I noticed Darwin looking somewhat longingly at a case full of ice cream bars.

"D., let's get an ice cream cone."

"What do we do for money?"

"Ah, not to worry; I have a pocket full of lira." (I was always in the mode of being helpful, inasmuch as I'm really a nice guy.)

"Great!"

We both picked out our ice cream and I paid for it. I rapidly ate my ice cream as we headed back up the hill to the vans. By the time we got there, I carried only a bare stick. Darwin was still sampling the first bits of his cone. When he got in the van, Bribs said, "D! Where did you get that?"

"Bill bought it for me."

"That Bill; he's really a nice guy." (I had already noted that.)

"Yeah, he is."

About that time Luis, the Associate Producer, walked by their van, reached in, jerked the ice cream bar out of Darwin's hand, and threw it on the ground.

Luis yelled, "WHAT DO YOU THINK YOU'RE DOING? DIDN'T YOU HEAR ANDERSON TELL YOU THE PIZZA WAS ALL YOU WERE TO GET TO EAT?!"

Darwin reacted angrily, denying that Anderson had told us we could not buy something else. Luis stalked away, shaking his head. Darwin later apologized to me for losing that ice cream I bought him to Luis. He was still quite angry. I felt bad…not.

We were later fined $10,000 for multiple infractions, the most notable being Heather fondling the bike fender, and Darwin eating forbidden fruits. I *was* managing to do my job! I don't know how it was that I managed to get Heather to try to become familiar with a bicycle fender, but claimed credit for it. I needed a victory, wherever it came from!

Every time we would finish a game there would be multiple analyses going on about who might have been trying to sabotage the game, therefore revealing themselves as the Mole. As noted, my attempts at suspicious behavior had gone unnoticed, so our side had nothing to report, other than the fact that Katie was hopeless at begging in a foreign language. And, by this point none of the players had any suspicion of Katie. She was just too transparent. On the bike side, Dorothy's total inability to ride her bike was kind of suspicious…except that all of us could see that she had had a deprived childhood, devoid of any of the normal playthings that allow all of us to develop confidence in our physical abilities. Heck, Dorothy probably only had crossword puzzles, Scrabble games, and dictionaries as playthings, and was probably carried about on her Dad's back. Not her fault. Heather's attempt at taking a shortcut cross country on her bike could be construed as an attempt to delay the game, if it hadn't been straight downhill. Not too smart there; a dedicated Mole should have been smarter than that. Of course, she *had* developed that relationship with a bicycle fender, costing $10,000, along with suspicious-looking Darwin's ice cream cone. But, all in all, not a lot of suspicion could be cast from this day.

We left there and had another afternoon off the next day. We moved to Lucca, Italy, and en route got to stop for a couple of hours at an Italian beach, with the ever present cameras recording our every move. Mostly they concentrated on a bikini clad Heather, showing the infinite wisdom of the camera crew. At one point Katie got exasperated with the attention being showered on Heather, and heatedly demanded, "What am I? Chopped liver?" To no avail.

These were not really relaxing affairs, by and large. We were never allowed to just go off on our own, nor to get away from the pack at all. Cameras and mikes were a constant. Most of us found that the cameramen and boom mikes were not fond of water, so spent a good hour or so playing Frisbie in the edge of the ocean. Of course, the cameras also delighted in Heather jumping about. Regardless, I think we were all ready to return to the game.

As I have noted, Elavia was everyone's suspect. She continued to evade attempts at conversations, and only shared information sparingly. I expect virtually everyone in the game except me was putting her information down on every quiz. Thus, all were 100% wrong, all tied for last, and the slowest was executed each week. Unfortunately for the rest, the fact that they were still in the game after entering only Elavia's information week after week strongly reinforced the idea that Elavia was the evil one of the cast.

Anderson came up with a new mini-game. We were taken on a tour of the city the next day, and eventually came to another old church. Anderson told us all to wait out in the square, and began taking us into the church, one at a time. The rest of us occupied our time while waiting by confusing the locals and the occasional tourist. The local city buses ran frequently, and had printed on their side the name of the bus company, "CLAP." So, we did so. For each bus that came by, we clapped politely but vigorously. The locals kept looking wildly about trying to find some form of entertainer, and never did understand what we were doing. That's OK; we were unsure as well. I *have* mentioned boredom, haven't I?

Inside the church Anderson had us list all the players, starting with our favorite and ending with our least favorite. I really thought there was a good chance I would be least favorite, inasmuch as I was definitely the odd person out. No chance. Elavia, the "Mole" in everyone's eyes, came out as the least popular. Not because *she* was unpopular, you understand, but because...the Mole was the least popular. Myra was the most popular, by the way, which didn't help her in the least. Anderson then called us all back into the church.

"Let me share with you the results of today's survey. The least favorite player, as voted by all of you, is....Elavia!"

This was a little embarrassing. None of us disliked Elavia, but she didn't know that. As it later turned out, she was totally unaware that she was the object of everyone's suspicions. She was just playing her own little game, completely oblivious to how extremely effective she was being. She was hurt at being the least liked in the group. Anderson called her up to the front of the church.

Reflections of The Mole

"Elavia, because you were voted least favorite, you get an exemption for the next execution. Now, would you give up your exemption if I added $10,000 to the pot?"

Elavia didn't pause long. "No." She was still hurt, and would not look anyone in the eye. She was probably ticked, as well.

"$20,000?"

"No."

Anderson looked at her for a moment. "OK, my last offer. I'll put $30,000 into the pot if you will give up that exemption."

Elavia squirmed some with that, and various opinions were offered from the floor. The prevailing opinion was that an exemption was worth way more than that! So, Elavia took the exemption. Following that, there was considerable discussion from the group about how much would have to be offered before you would be tempted. For most, it seemed to be about $50,000. I think that was Myra's position. I think she felt it was too bad that the person *most* liked wasn't offered something! Shoot, I'm easy. I would give up an exemption for a couple of cold German beers!

The next execution came along. For the last 3 weeks, Myra and I had been in the last 3 or 4 people whose names were called by Anderson. At dinner that night Myra pointed that out to Anderson. "You're going to give me a nervous breakdown if you keep putting me off until almost last!" Anderson laughed and told her he would try to do better.

Did Anderson know who was going to be executed? I don't know. All I know for sure is that he did not know who the Mole was.

When we convened in the lobby of the hotel to wait for the vans to arrive, I carried a can of hair spray. I approached Heather.

"Heather, can you 'Rob' my hair?"

She laughed. "Really?"

"Yep. Rob was going to do it for me this week as a surprise. Now, I want to do it in Rob's honor."

She smiled. "Sit down." And, she went to work, turning my hair into a spiky work of art. The others looked on, laughing.

"Darwin, you're next!"

He grinned as he rubbed his bald head. "Sure! Hit me with that hair spray!" Bribs grinned as well as he rubbed his hand over his ¼ inch stubble. Al, on the other hand, had hair! He looked a little nonplussed, but then sat down and Dorothy went to work on his hair. Unfortunately, it wasn't really long enough to be noticeable.

An oddity that we all had noted was that of the 14 of us, 6 had listed blue as their favorite color. 5 of those 6 were the first 5 folks executed, and Myra was the last blue lover in the group…so to speak. We had all kidded Myra about that during the week, and I think she was a little more nervous than usual this execution.

We sat in our two rows facing Anderson, with Myra and me next to each other. We always held hands during executions for moral support. I had worked up another inappropriate sweat, and Myra was appropriately somewhat hyperventilating.

Anderson stood in front and looked at us, then started laughing. "Bill, what happened to your hair?"

I smiled and said, "Anderson, this is in honor of Rob. We were all sorry to see him go, and he had promised to do my hair for me this week. Heather substituted for him." Anderson just grinned, gave his customary spiel, then sat down at the computer. He looked out at us, suddenly unsmiling. "Myra." The first one this time!

He typed in her name, hit Enter, and waited. Beside me, Myra squeezed my hand, looked at me, and shrugged resignedly. The screen turned red. And, she was gone.

Myra told me later that she just knew she was going that night. I don't know who she had guessed as the Mole. I do know that I was truly distressed to see her go. If I could have given a hint to any player to save them, it would have been her. As I have noted before, I really felt isolated in the group. It was not only that I was the Mole, but the age difference, experience difference, the whole lot. Myra was the only one I could really communicate with on all levels, and the others knew that.

Following her execution the others commiserated with me; they knew that Myra and I had talked a lot, and she was sort of a lifeline to me. They were very kind. Of course, they could easily afford to be, inasmuch as none of them suspected me as the Mole! This game wasn't all that easy under the best of circumstances. With Myra gone, it was going to get much harder for me mentally. Of course, much later Myra chastised me. "You idiot; I would have been happy to have stuck around. All you had to do was hint a little!" I laughed at her. "Myra, you had more clues than anyone else, and refused to believe them. I don't think you would have believed me no matter what I did!" She denied that, of course. On the other hand, I don't know what it would have taken to have convinced her!

What Was She Thinking?

Myra

I AM SELECTED

I couldn't believe I had been chosen as a player for Mole 2. Mole 1 was my favorite reality show. Not a big Survivor fan, I loved the intrigue, the intellectual mind games and locations of Mole 1. I also liked how the players had to work together to fill the pot with moola, all the while not trusting anyone. No one "booted off" for personality issues. My sister, Carol, and I talked frequently about who was the Mole on Mole 1. Katherine really threw me when she really fainted during the knife throwing. I thought it was Steve.

On a whim, I auditioned for Mole 2. What? I was chosen? You are kidding me. Now, I had to get time off from my civilian and military jobs. Not easy but I got it. What do I tell family and friends? I told my airline buddies and family that I was working for the military and vice versa. All bases now covered. Only two near and dear people knew what I was doing. Plane tickets and secrecy instructions arrived. Now what to pack? How will I play the game?

Finally off to Europe. Under stealth of darkness and secrecy, I made my way to Zurich.

A young German man picked me up in Zurich and drove 240 kph on the autobahn in one of those cool new Audis to our mountain destination. "Youh ah eh pilot, youh ah naht afraid, yah?" he says as he gracefully negotiated the road at the speed of sound. "No", I replied in a faint squeak.

Undaunted by the highway closure due to heavy snow near the mountain summit (in June), my trusty chauffeur drives our car onto a rail car and we continue our journey.

Three days later, after being sequestered in a beautiful mountain top chalet, we finally assembled with blindfolds on to begin the games of Mole 2. Pinch me, this is surreal; like jumping into my TV set. I hear the unmistakable voice of Anderson Cooper. This is real!!! He tells us to take off our blindfolds. Game on.

I immediately look at all the players. All are looking around at each other, like I am, except for two: Bribs and Elavia. Both look straight ahead. My focus is now on Bribs.

We go through the introductions and immediately begin to play. Nothing suspicious. Yet.

As we go through the games, I watch Bribs like a hawk.

SEQUESTRATION

Reflections of The Mole

We are sequestered in our hotel rooms constantly, either alone or with a roomie, when we weren't playing the game. No TV, phone, internet, paper, magazine or camera. I spend most of my time in the room drawing the exquisite sceneries I saw out my window. We were constantly watched by "player wranglers" to make sure we did not leave our rooms unless told to do so. One time, I needed toilet paper and I could see the maid through the peephole right across the hall. Rather than bother the wrangler, I opened the door to ask the maid for more TP. Immediately, a wrangler was in my doorway admonishing me for what I had done and reiterating that I should contact them for any requests. Oops.

I also tried to get to know each of my roomies but not divulge any info to them. I think they did the same. Each and every one of my roomies was awesome. We had some great times. I spent the most time with Katy who I just adore. She is just like you saw her on the telly – a great spirit.

Sleep deprivation was a given. We played the games from early in the day until the wee hours of the morning. Cameras, settings, sound, etc., had to be just right. We played until we were done. The producers also plied us with LOTS of alcohol. None of us complained. Then off to bed with a few hours sleep and back at it in the morning.

SHARING INFORMATION

I gave very little in the way of information to anyone, including the producers. I have 22 years in the military working with top secret documents, secrets, etc. Our training is to keep discussions brief and pertinent, not to give up too much information. That's exactly what I did during the Mole. Didn't give up too much info to anyone, players or producers. Told them only what I wanted them to know and no more.

I came off as quiet and under the radar (which actually caused a bit of suspicion towards me). Unfortunately, this carried over to my interviews.

Bill McDaniel, MD

WHY I GOT SO LITTLE CAMERA TIME *(the excuses in my head, anyway)*

My interviews were brief as I thought I knew the identity of the mole and only talked about that person. So when asked, "Do you think Dorothy is the Mole?" my answer was no. "Do you think Al is the mole?" No. "Do you think Katie is the Mole?" No. Etc. I was sure of my choice so why would I talk about the others or offer up any more info.

When we weren't playing the game, we were doing the brief interviews that you saw. The interview process usually took all day long, especially when we had a lot of people to be interviewed. You were sequestered in your room until they came to get you for your interview. Yeah! You got to get out of the room. You were delivered to the location, some beautiful palace or villa overlooking some spectacular view. Everything was in place, the cameras, the lighting, the sound guys. One of the producers would conduct the interview. Mine always went something like this:

Producer (P), Me (M):

P: Ok, let's start (small chit chat) Cameraman: Myra's face is too shiny. (powder applied)
P: Ok, let's start again. So, Myra, how did you feel while playing the Get the Key Game where you were locked in the cell and had to get out or not talk to your loved one?
M: (very animated) I absolutely loved it! I -
P: Sorry, Myra, could someone please get the jackhammer in the background to stop?
P: Ok, let's try it again, and, this time, Myra, use the question in the answer
M: (still animated) Oh yeah, ok, uh, ...during the Get the Key Game-
P: Cut! Plane overhead...everyone wait...(pause)... ok, try again

185

M: Well, during the get the key-
P: Stop, could someone please kill that barking dog?....(pause)...ok, try again
M: (animation dwindling) Well, during the Get the -
P: Ok, stop, sorry, Myra, there seems to be a children's choir just starting to practice in the background. Could someone please go talk to them……ok....thank you....try again
M: During the-
P: So sorry, we have to stop, that dog is still barking...(pause) ....(sometime later)...ok, again
Cameraman: Myra's face is shiny again
P: Can someone please fix that? Thank you... ok, once again, how did you feel while playing the Get the Key Game?
M: (animation continuing to dwindle) Well, -
Soundman: We need to fix her mike...
P: Ok, ready, Myra? Go ahead.
(now, about 20 min later)
M: (in a monotone voice) I-enjoyed-the-get-the-key-game-very-much.

I am not making this up. Would you use my response on national TV? I think not.

BACK TO THE GAME

Bill became my bud. We bonded on day three of the game when he mentioned to me that he was having trouble mixing with the young kids and that he would be relieved to go home soon. No way this guy is the Mole. So we started hanging out together. We were the "elders" of the group plus we had similar military and medical backgrounds.

On the night of the "Bag Burning", after watching all our belongings go up in flames, I said to Bill, I wonder what we are doing next. He said, we're going to do this and that. I spun *around, looked him straight in the eye and asked him how he knew this. He said so-and-so told him. A few minutes later, so-and-so came around the corner and said the exact same thing. OK, that's how he knew. No worries.*

Later, after the show ended, Bill told me he had spilled the beans to me, realized what he had done, and was absolutely red-faced (which I could not see in the dark). Had I seen him in daylight, things might have turned out differently. Maybe...maybe not.

My focus was still on Bribs. Everything he did was suspect to me. I kept it all in my journal, which I kept in code in case my journal fell into someone else's hands, which it did later when we were forced to swap journals. Bribs stopped for a beer with Ali in the "Clothesline Game" while we all waited at the train station and missed our train (later we found out who had the dinero for the beers – Bill). Bribs vanished inexplicably into the hotel during the Tire Change episode. I was sure he was meeting with the producers. As he ran into the hotel, he passed by me and said, "you are all too paranoid". Every room he stayed in ended in the lucky number 7 (remember, Katherine the Mole 1 stayed nearest the front desk so producers could find her). One night, Bribs was the only one of us that did not change rooms. Are you with me on this? Everything he did was suspect.

A lot of players hedged their bets by playing 2 or 3 different people as their Mole choice. I did not.

One day, Patrick and I looked at each other and sort of nodded. We were now partners in the game and solidified this alliance away from the others. He saw the same things I saw regarding Bribs and reinforced my belief that Bribs was the Mole. We figured two heads could work better than one.

We arrived in Italy very early in the morning after a seven-hour bus journey. Patrick had gained a reputation for looking for clues anywhere and everywhere and he took a lot of grief for it. Upon our arrival in Italy, we were handed the telegram. Patrick was sure there was a clue in it, but after most players gave him grief about his constant clue searching, and as it was so early in the morning, he abandoned his clue-finding search. Had he continued, he may have decoded the telegram and found the identity of the Mole.

Back to the journals. We had been forced to swap them during a previous game so all your thoughts and ideas were in the hands of someone else. Patrick wanted some revealing pages back from his journal. I was with him when he asked a producer about getting some pages back. The producer told him to "do what he had to do". Patrick got his hands on his original journal and tore out the revealing pages. Not that it mattered much in hindsight. But he was in trouble for doing so. Patrick left in Episode 4. Although I was sorry to see my pal leave as we were working as a team, I thought his departure was now a good thing. I could continue on by myself and not have to worry about Patrick at the end of the game – just collect the million dollars all by myself.

EXECUTIONS

Each execution was traumatic. Bill would ask to hold my hand during each execution and would sweat like a pig on the way to the bacon factory! How could he possibly be the Mole if he is that nervous during every execution? No one can make themselves do that. Or could they? (After the show, Bill told me he was able to actually work himself into a sweat during those executions by thinking about being found out. I really think he put a hot pack down his britches).

On Episode #6, I know I hesitated for a few seconds during one of the computer questions. Yikes. I still answered all my questions focused towards Bribs. Computer questions done, on to Execution #6.

Anderson types my name in first. I feel a sigh of relief. All right, I'm still in!!! No one <u>ever</u> goes home on the first or even the fifth type-in. I watch the screen for the green. What?!!? A red thumbprint??!!? How could that be? Truly a surreal moment. Can't believe I'm going home. Anderson escorts me from the players to a waiting car with the sad music playing in the background (I hear it in my head). Wow. It's over as fast as it began.

Turns out, Bribs and I scored the lowest scores that night and he aced me out by a nano-second. Had Bribs gone home that night, I would have been blown away and have to refigure who the Mole was. Would I have figured it was Bill? I really don't know. Lots of people who watched the show said they knew it was Bill. It is much easier to figure it out from your living room especially with clues on the show and the internet boards. Much harder to do while you're actually playing the game. Remember, Dorothy would have been eliminated if Elavia would not have taken the $50K and left the game. But Dorothy won.

My sister, Carol, my confidante, had been contacted by the producers to come to Italy to be a part of the game. After spending two days of clothes shopping and dreaming of flying off to Europe to be a part of Mole 2, she was notified in the middle of the night that she was no longer required to go to Italy. Aargh. I will never hear the end of this.

FINAL THOUGHTS

This was the most awesome experience of my life. I will treasure the adventures we had and all the memories we made. This "Fifteen Minutes of Fame" has been a trip. And, Anderson Cooper, well, he is one of the most fascinating people I have ever met. Most of all, I will treasure the lifelong friendships I have made with these players forever. I just wish I could have seen Bill's red face in the darkness of those woods that telltale night...

XVII

A Whole New Ball Game!

This game was getting a little tighter. With almost half the competitors gone, I knew everyone was going to start watching everyone else a lot closer now, and the odds increased that someone would start picking up on my many clues. They couldn't stay blind forever. Could they? Even with Elavia established as the most likely to be the villainous Mole in everyone's mind, someone was still going to be executed each week. Therefore, for everyone else, staying was in the details you thought you knew…and the speed you utilized on the tests. In my case, while leaving was not a possibility, I had to continue to be the clumsy innocent able to sabotage upcoming games without appearing unduly suspicious. So, I decided to quit drinking my beer and wine. Having to monitor every thing I said and did was getting tougher and tougher, and I had already slipped just after the last round of quizzes. I felt that even one beer might affect me, so chose to abstain for the time being. As I sat at dinner the next evening with a full wine glass in front of me, taking tiny sips, I happened to be sitting next to Dorothy.

Dorothy leaned over and whispered, "Bill, I see that you're not drinking. Any reason?"

I saw no reason not to be truthful with her…to a point. "Ah, as I get older, I have noticed that my ability to drink any at all and remain unaffected has been really diminished. We're getting tight here! If I can stop drinking…and keep encouraging everyone else to drink…I might have an edge. It's worth a try."

This was all talking very quietly during dinner. The others were all doing as we did nightly, answering Anderson's questions while he tried to find juicy tidbits that the producers would add to the final edited show. Dorothy grinned and said, "Me, too. I like to act a little silly at times, and if not drinking can give me an advantage, I'm going to take it!"

We smiled at each other, having happily shared a very small secret. No coalition was proposed, but we achieved a tiny one on this note, nevertheless. The possibility that I was the Mole was...for the moment...outside the sphere of suspicion for Dorothy, so I think she felt comfortable. She *knew* who the Mole was...Elavia.

At that same dinner Anderson ambushed me with a question that came back to cause me a little discomfort when the show was aired. "Bill, how did you meet your wife?" He had been asking this question to everyone about their significant other.

I reacted without thinking, which I had promised myself that I would not do. "Oh, one day many years ago I was out by a swimming pool and saw this beautiful woman in a bikini. She had such a great ass that I *knew* she must be intelligent! That was Shirley." I said this to get a laugh from the group, although it was actually true. It never dawned on me that they would use that vignette in the final edited show. We were at a large party in Washington, DC, hosted by the Deputy Surgeon General of the Navy when this show was aired. When that statement boomed out of the television, Shirley immediately ducked for cover, and I had a lot of explaining to do! ("But...Shirley! All I said was that you were beautiful, intelligent, and well built. Is that so bad?" Shirley: "I can't believe they used that word on national television! I'm going to wear a coat until everyone has forgotten all about this show.")

The next game was to provide fun for the next few weeks, especially to Anderson, Clay, and me. We had two games to play in one day in Lucca, and the producers told me to try to get into the Gnome Home game and sabotage it in some way. Three of us were going to run a sort of relay race, and I was told to try to get the second leg, which looked to be the easiest to sabotage. The other two who chose to play the game were Elavia and Heather. Anderson met us in a large field out near the old medieval wall of the city and showed us two different garden gnomes, one quite large and one about 2 feet tall. Without elaborating, he told us we were going to have to carry one of these in a relay race, and we were told to choose one. We chose the smaller of the two, naturally. He then asked us in which order we were going to do the relay?

I spoke up. "Why don't I take the second leg. That way, if whoever takes the first leg is a little slow, I might be able to make up time so we can finish in the time limit and win the money." Elavia and Heather had no reason to disagree with that strategy. Heather chose to go first, and Elavia last. We had 30 minutes to finish the race.

Anderson then pulled the cover off a tub of grease and told Heather that she had to thoroughly grease up her gnome, but "you can only grease your own gnome, not someone else's." Elavia and I then were taken away to our selected starting points while Heather sat the gnome in the vat of grease and started slicking that gnome down. We looked back at her and started laughing. She became coated with the grease quickly, and as we disappeared from view already had very slick, shiny hands and arms, and had mistakenly wiped some sweat from her forehead and had a thick sheen of grease there as well.

Heather's leg of the race was about a mile or so long, during which time she had to climb up a ladder over the old city wall, and get strangers to take her picture with the gnome near one of the stone lions guarding the wall. As I waited for her at the beginning of my leg of the race, I walked my 400 yard course out. I was to receive the gnome from Heather, run over to a local soccer field and kick soccer balls until I managed to make a goal around a determined goal keeper, have my picture taken with the goalkeeper by some passing stranger, then get on a bicycle and ride through an obstacle course until I reached Elavia. Elavia was to put the gnome in a baby carriage and run through town to the finish line.

The wait began. Eventually, a very, *very* greasy Heather hove into view. She was dripping grease and sweat as she walked/jogged toward me; it had taken her about 20 minutes or so to cover the mile, and that greasy gnome was becoming harder and harder to hold on to. In her attempts to keep it from falling and breaking, she had managed to rub all the gnome grease off on herself, and was quite…fetching looking, I suppose. She looked like she had been to a Crisco party. I started laughing as soon as I could see her, along with the camera crews gathered around me. Anderson was standing there making wry comments for our benefit and cracking us up even more.

Heather was oblivious to all of this. She was hot, tired, and greasy, and just wanted to hand the damned thing off! Forgetting Anderson's initial admonition, when she came up to me she immediately plopped the gnome down in a vat of grease sitting there and began slathering more grease on it from head to foot. We all started laughing harder. This was funny, and not a little suggestive. Anderson was laughing harder than anyone, but finally managed to blurt out, "**You can grease your own gnome, but aren't supposed to grease anyone else's gnome!**" With that he again doubled over in laughter, as we all did. He couldn't get serious.

Heather, seeing no humor at all in the situation, picked up the greasy gnome and handed it off to me. I ran over and after several tries managed to kick a soccer ball into the net, but only after kicking a ball *hard* into the midsection of the girl goal tender. (I was to find out later she was a member of our crew, and managed to apologize to her.) I forgot to have my picture taken, and had to return to do that. 23 minutes had elapsed. Then, I hopped on to the bike, where *at Heather's suggestion* I propped the gnome up in the basket on the handlebar. I had already decided exactly where I was going to have my accident and break the gnome, depriving us of $30,000. I had to ride over a modified teeter-totter which had a 4 inch bump to get up on the board, and had decided that was a great place to lose my balance. However, the first time over it I felt my efforts were not realistic enough, so when I fell off the side of the board I caught my balance and went around to try again…or, rather, to definitely *not* get across it, but to do it with fervor! I was determined to break the gnome and even cut myself if necessary; I was acting like a member of the elder generation unable to remember the simple mechanics of riding a bike, after all, and wanted to make it good! The second try was good enough. I fell, broke the gnome, lost the money, and was awarded an exemption for the effort, inasmuch as there was an exemption slip inside the gnome, to be awarded only to the person who managed to break it.

Heather watched with exasperation. I don't think she was too distressed that I had broken the gnome, inasmuch as the money wasn't really real to us. She *was* irritated that she had not gone ahead and broken the gnome herself, so that *she* would have received an exemption. From clues given in our introduction by Anderson, she had an idea that breaking the gnome might result in such. She verbally kicked herself several times over the next day or two for not taking advantage of that probability.

Elavia walked back to join us, and a greasy Heather, still ticked somewhat at Anderson and convinced he didn't like her, decided to have a little fun with him. Anderson was still laughing at her greasy state, which was quite complete and somewhat remarkable. She suddenly grabbed him and hugged him as he attempted a hasty retreat. Too late. I joined in and rubbed a handful of grease in his hair. He's too young to have that much gray hair, anyway. If a little grease would do him good, a lot of grease would be that much better. I did lament loudly, though, about my clumsiness, and told Anderson that getting the exemption was bitter sweet, inasmuch as I had lost the money. Gosh darn. I felt...fine.

Over the next couple of weeks, and even months later when we were in LA filming the finale, neither Clay nor Anderson could talk about this game without breaking out laughing. Heather was just too classic, covered in grease. Someone would say, "You can grease your own gnome..." and the group would dissolve in laughter. Ah, well. Maybe you had to be there.

We three went back to the hotel and started attempting to get the grease out of our clothes. I have not mentioned this aspect; we really could not use the laundry service of any of the hotels we stayed at. No one was sure when they might be executed, or when we might be moving. So, for almost 7 weeks we all washed our clothes out in the sink when we had to get rid of a layer or two of dirt. It's lucky television does not include smell. Both Heather and I had a heck of a time getting the impregnated grease out. For several days I felt well lubricated.

Meanwhile, Bribs, Darwin, Katie, Al, and Dorothy were having a ball dressing in medieval warrior costumes and having sword fights down in the city square while tourists and locals cheered the strange spectacle loudly, undoubtedly thinking it was just part of an annual summer show. At the end of the effort, which was against other "warriors" (who were also members of the crew), Bribs had an opportunity to double cross all of his fellows and win an exemption for himself by betrayal, though losing all the money by doing so. He steadfastly refused the offer; the group had loved the game and was riding high emotionally. Bribs just could not betray them. Clay told me later he wished I had chosen that game instead of the gnome game, so I could have carried out the evil act denied by Bribs. I was awfully glad I had not played it. I managed to carry out my role the entire time without doing something I would have felt bad about doing. I suspect I would have really felt like a traitor to…something…if I had done that. I would have carried out his bidding if asked - I had signed on to be the Mole - but am glad I did not have to do so.

At dinner that night we were asked to go, one by one, upstairs where we met with Anderson. He gave each of us a dollar bill, and again asked us to write down the other player's names, from favorite to least favorite, on the bill. I had actually put down Katie's name as my least favorite several days before, inasmuch as she required so much emotional support. However, two people had put down my name that first time, and I didn't want to find out what might happen were I to be listed as the least favorite. On this occasion I decided to substitute Elavia for Katie; after all, Elavia *was* the Mole! And, I just wanted to make sure that she continued to maintain the honor as "least favorite." I had no idea what was going to come of this, and again just wanted to maintain a low profile. As events happened, it might have been very interesting if I had been named the least favorite!

The next execution came. We had taken the quiz, and were gathered outside in a great setting; it was the place where in medieval days the executioner had beheaded miscreants! What a place for *our* execution!

Anderson stood in front of us. "Before I get to the execution, Elavia, would you come up here, please?" Everyone looked at each other. Almost all were thinking the same thing: "What did Anderson want with the Mole?"

Elavia went forward and Anderson pulled out a briefcase. He opened it, and piled inside were stacks of money. Anderson said, "Elavia, you were for the second time voted the least favorite player. So, I'm going to offer you a deal. You can choose to leave *right now*! If you do, I will give you this briefcase, filled with $50,000."

Elavia looked shocked as we all looked at each other, smiling. No way! The Mole couldn't leave, so it was going to be entertaining seeing what kind of excuse she would come up with to stay. Elavia looked at the group, and then looked searchingly at Darwin, who was perhaps the closest to her in the group.

Darwin noted, "Elavia! Take the money! It's 50,000 dollars! That's more than you would get if you took second." Darwin felt totally comfortable giving that advice; he knew she could not leave.

Elavia wavered, looked at us one by one, gave a weak wave and said, "Thanks for not liking me..." She then took the briefcase and walked off into the dark, leaving shock and disbelief in her wake. We all looked at each other. Everyone was stunned, even me. I had no idea this was coming. What if my name had shown up as the least favorite? Shoot, I might have just taken the money and left! Talk about a wrench in the works!

Someone threw their journal up in the air, letting it fall to the ground. "That's worthless now!" Someone else chimed in, "Well, it's a whole new game."

Anderson returned from walking Elavia out. (Elavia was very upset that she had been listed again as the least favorite, and only learned the truth at the filming of the finale 4 months later.) Anderson looked solemnly at the group of speechless players. He suddenly turned and sat down at the computer. "Now for the execution." The group gasped in unison. Two gone in one night?

Anderson suddenly jumped up, did a little dance, and started laughing as he noted, "I love this game!" He then explained that because Elavia had chosen to take the bribe and leave, there would be no execution this night. He then started quizzing the group on their reactions to Elavia's departure. As you might expect, the reactions were many and all bordered on outright shock. (At the finale we were told who would have been executed that night had Elavia chosen to stay. It would have changed everything!)

A bewildered cast of players returned to the hotel, all rapidly renewing old suspicions and making new lists of possible

Mole suspects. This was going to be such fun! What a great twist to this complex plot of a simple game!

What Was She Thinking?

Elavia

From day 1 I picked out 4 people who would make good moles. Bill, Heather, Bribs, and Dorothy. I quickly eliminated Heather and Bribs by week 2, and concentrated on Dorothy and Bill. Dorothy and I had an alliance, but I always thought Dorothy might be the Mole.

Bill was always my top pick; from the cabin on. The reason for the top 4 was those who might be interesting for the long term, and might hold the audience's interest for the long term. If I spread my vote I didn't think I would get anywhere. I played all the games with either Dorothy or Bill as the only suspect. What would have happened if I had stayed around? I might have won, but the game was getting so hard physically and mentally. I was told that I had the highest score the night I left.

The game was so challenging I'm not sure if I could have won. It was getting a lot harder mentally and physically, but I think I might have made the final 4 or so. However, my strongest personal connection was with Dorothy, and the game would have been much harder for me if she had left that night.

When I left I had no idea people thought I was the Mole. Darwin was the only one that I was aware of who thought I might be the Mole. At that point the game was really, really hard, and I felt that I would just take the money and go. I had lost 10 pounds by that time. I also broke out in hives; it was very difficult and very stressful to act really 'moleish' all the time.

I really felt badly that people 'didn't like me.' The two votes against me were very troubling. I think the way I played the game (by giving as little information as I could in answering questions) might have alienated me from the rest of the players, and those two votes where I was the 'least popular' player were hard to take!

I signed up to play the game because I wanted to travel; I did not especially want to be on TV, but the travel was fun. I would never do anything like that again. I took all my marketing background and used that to determine in my mind who could hold the interest of the public for 10 weeks. I knew they were not going to pick another lawyer.

Since the show...I am a regional marketing manager for Pepsico, traveling and promoting. There has been no show business or spin-offs. I never pursued anything. I did not like what fame I got; I like being anonymous :)

XVIII

20/20 Vision

We were getting down to fewer and fewer players. With only seven remaining, it was time for everyone to re-evaluate, especially since Elavia was gone and the others had to totally regroup anyway.

At this point I don't think anyone considered Katie or Al as possible moles. Katie was just too emotional, and no one believed she could have carried the role off in her constant teary state. As noted, if she were an actress of that merit, she should definitely be in movies. Al was just too honest, too much a stickler for the rules, and too driven to win the money. While I certainly think he was smart enough to carry out that role, his actions just were such that no one believed in that possibility. Bribs worked his butt off on every game, and had turned down an exemption in the Gladiator game in circumstances that would have begged for the Mole to surface. He was extremely unlikely. However, he had one of the greatest mole expressions ever seen; when he wore it, he *looked* like a mole! Darwin worked equally hard, but was a lawyer and somewhat devious. He was suspicious enough acting to be a mole candidate, but had not really been involved in much sabotage. The remaining three had done enough sabotage, either inadvertently or on purpose, that all should have been high in everyone's consideration…whether or not we were. Dorothy, Heather, and me. Of course, it's really easy for me to sit and analyze the various players, inasmuch as I really didn't have to guess who the Mole was! On the other hand, I was constantly analyzing, both to try to put myself in the place of the other players and to be able to answer the interview questions convincingly.

I played the next two games straight. Our "loved ones" were coming on the scene, and it was time to just let the game roll along for a while.

The next game was the Eyes game. Our loved ones had been flown in and were all in a crowded square in the center of Lucca, surrounded by locals and tourists. Each of the loved ones was in a minor disguise, such as wearing a hat when they ordinarily did not wear one. Each of the players had to pick one of the other players to act as their eyes, and had only seconds to describe the loved ones to their selectee before he or she went to a second story window and had a minute or two to try to identify the appropriate person in the crowd below. A tough task. Dorothy and Katie picked Heather as their "eyes," not realizing that Heather was very nearsighted and did not have her glasses with her. Therefore, their loved ones were not selected.

My "loved one" was not my wife, which caused me some distress. My wife's brother, Blair, was in the courtyard, and I managed to describe him well enough to Darwin that he was selected. I tried to get Anderson several times to refer to Blair as my...ah, friend, or something, but he just smiled and continued to refer to him as the "loved one." Darn it! I noted quietly that if Blair came around the corner from the square and tried to kiss me, I would slug him. In good humor, of course. (Of interest to me was that when the show was airing, I got considerable criticism on the chat boards for that. "Why doesn't Bill like his brother-in-law?" That wasn't the issue; we are good friends. I was just disappointed that my wife was not there. As it turns out, she could not find her passport, which suited her just fine. (She was afraid she might have to eat bugs or something equally distasteful; too much reality TV.)

Katie was quite emotional in not getting to be with her father, as expected. Dorothy expressed little emotion about not seeing her mother, again as expected.

Reflections of The Mole

We all went out to dinner later with our visiting relatives. It was fun, and Blair, whose degree is in philosophy, explained "The Mole II" to everyone as a "circular conundrum," and proceeded to explain what that meant. We all listened open-mouthed. Darwin finally said, "I'm not sure what you said, but that is the best description of this show I have ever heard!" Heather and her boyfriend, Nathan, went off to a private seating…as private as you can get with cameras and boom mikes, of course. Nathan proposed to her and presented her with an engagement ring, an event several of us used as ammunition with which to accuse Heather of possibly being the Mole. I played this up to the others, and it was actually a pretty good argument. How would Nathan know that Heather was going to be still around, inasmuch as he had to order the ring several weeks in advance? And, how did the producers know this was going to happen and plan accordingly? Ah, it's easy to point fingers. Almost anything can be utilized as a suspicious act, building logical sequences after the fact that sound irrefutable. It makes one wonder about the "string of evidence" that lawyers pile together to convict someone of a criminal act. It's just too easy to compile evidence in retrospect, evidence that has absolutely no relevancy, but which sounds wonderful! (Heather, now married…to Tim, not Nathan…watched this episode the next summer with…Tim, who did not appreciate the show at all! Heather can smile about it all now, but rather weakly.)

We all returned to our rooms with our loved ones for several hours of relaxation. Blair decided he was going to help me figure out who the Mole was, and spent 3 or 4 hours assembling all the evidence for and against all the players. He was remarkably analytical; I was very impressed with the method he used to evaluate each of the remaining players. He came to the conclusion that Dorothy had to be the Mole. In fact, when questioned by the producer on camera, he stated with absolute conviction that there was no way I could be the Mole. "The Mole is the essence of evil, etc., etc." He was most emphatic, and months later when I was revealed as the Mole, I really think Blair felt betrayed! He was disappointed in me. On the other hand, maybe he just wanted me to win the money.... But, man, could he analyze! I really think he would been a wonderful contestant; probably far more successfully than I would have been...if I weren't the Mole.

The next day the loved ones were taken away and we all prepared to play our next game. As our vans entered a large area of open land outside the city, a 200+ foot construction crane was sitting in the middle of the field. We had been ribbing Al again about the possibility of having to tandem sky dive with our loved ones, managing to make him look rather white and pasty at times, and green and sickly other times. It was a fun game, and one that Bribs, Darwin, and I thoroughly enjoyed engaging in. We needed some entertainment and weren't getting it in the normal course of the day. When the crane appeared Al brightened momentarily, then realized how high it was, and glumly returned to his pasty green appearance.

We were later to hear from the loved ones—who had arrived well before us—that when they drove in Heather's brand new fiancé almost passed out. "I hope they don't expect us to jump off of that! I can't take heights!"

Blair asked, "How about Heather? Would she do it?"

"Sure, Heather will. But I won't!" Blair later told me that he was not "deserving" of Heather. Fortuitous, I suppose. Eventually, she apparently came to the same conclusion!

Anderson gathered all the players in the middle of the field, looking up at the tower and making remarks about how high it seemed, and that the bungee cords looked a little worse for wear. Anderson enjoyed making us feel secure.

"We have asked your loved ones if you will jump from the platform at the top of the crane, using an old and worn bungee cord. Each of you will be given the opportunity to predict what your loved one said. If you predict correctly, and do as they said you would do, you will add $5000.00 to the pot. If you do not predict correctly, no money will be added. In addition, if you correctly predict what your loved one will say, you will get to spend another day with them." Dorothy and Katie immediately brightened up. We could see Katie's Dad and Dorothy's Mom over at the edge of the field, watching solemnly.

We all lined up as the bungee cord experts (How does one become an expert in bungee cords? Is it the one still living after so many jumps?) went through the procedure with us. They explained that the reason we had had to put down our weight on the questionnaires we had filled out was that they adjusted the tension on the bungee cords accordingly.

Katie spoke up suddenly. "What if, say, you weigh...oh, quite a bit more than indicated on your forms?"

The bungee man explained, "Quite a bit? You'll hit the ground, I suppose."

Katie immediately revised her weight estimate upward, making sure the bungee instructor changed the number on her card. She didn't get to be a teacher by being stupid!

We each approached the platform in turn, donned our harness, got strapped into an old looking bungee apparatus, was hoisted almost 200 feet into the air, and stepped off into space. It sounds simple. It didn't feel simple.

I have always wanted to bungee jump, but felt that at 240 pounds and nearing 60 years old, it was unlikely to happen. It did. I didn't mind the jumping part; that was over with quickly, and the worst that could happen was a sudden and relatively painless death. It was going up 200 feet into the air that I did not truly appreciate. I was about the 5th one to jump, and Anderson pulled me off to one side before the act.

"Bill, try to yell something printable when you jump off, if you will. We have nothing but a string of bleeps at this point!" So, I determined to watch my language, and managed to do so. I reverted back to my college days, screaming the Oklahoma State University "YEEE---HAH!" as I jumped.

The only casualty from the jump was the newly engaged Heather. Instead of falling straight down from the tower she jumped out a little, and wound up doing a complete 360 degree flip when she hit the end of the stretch point of the bungee cords. That's not good. She was abruptly slammed head down again, sustaining a minor whiplash of her neck. She walked stiffly and somewhat painfully for the next week or two, and this, combined with her new engagement and the subsequent plans she was busily formulating, explained some of her actions over the next 3 weeks. Those actions would ultimately cost her. An expensive engagement to someone you're not going to marry anyway! We tried to tell her; she wasn't in a listening mode. Those engagement rings do tend to affect your hearing.

The only person to not correctly predict her loved one's answer as to whether or not she would jump was Dorothy. Dorothy did not jump because she said her mother knew she was afraid of heights. She was given about 2 minutes to hug her Mom, who was then driven back to Rome and a long plane ride home. Dorothy remained stoic throughout, showing no emotion. She just accepted this as another opportunity to sew some seeds of suspicion in everyone's mind as to whether or not she was the Mole, and was quite successful in the attempt. This might have kept her in the game, so was undoubtedly worthwhile in the end.

After another day with our loved ones, it was again execution time. The loved ones came to execution with us and were interviewed after the quiz and before the execution. Again, Blair stoutly maintained that I could not be the Mole. Not a problem. Finally, Katie's red thumbprint showed up, and for her sake it came at a good time. Her Dad, a delightful gentleman, was there with her to soften the blow and carry her home. It couldn't have happened better, especially since Myra had had the bad grace to depart and leave Katie's emotional support to the rest of us. Myra was the mother, not us!

While Katie's favorite color was not blue, she was the only remaining player with blue eyes. Does this have meaning? Most likely not, but if I were a good lawyer I could file some sort of class action suit about it, I'll bet!

Following this execution and the departure of our loved ones, Heather and I were talking when I made only the second real slip of the tongue that I was aware of. We had had a question on the quiz about where the Mole was sitting in relation to Anderson at one of the meals, and Heather was despairing. "I wish we had assigned seating for every meal; that way we wouldn't have to keep writing down our seating arrangement in our journals. That is so aggravating, especially when you don't know who the Mole is to begin with."

I replied with little thought, "That's the reason I always try to sit in the same seat every time, because"...(at that point I realized I was about to say 'because that way I don't have to think about it when I put down the answer'...i.e, *I'm the Mole!)* "because at least that way I know where *I* am." Now, this didn't make any sense at all. None. Heather was preoccupied with the problem and barely noted what I said. She replied with something like, "That's a good idea." (On the other hand, Heather was the earliest one to pick up on me as the most likely Mole. Who am I to say that she did not notice my slip of the tongue?)

After the conclusion of the airing of our show, though Heather denied taking any notice of this slip, she did say that she had had a coalition with Katie at that point. She only had two people left on her list as Mole suspects, Dorothy and me. Both she and Katie had agreed that Dorothy was the most likely Mole, and both resolved to put all of the answers to the quiz down with her information. The two of them had compared finishing times for the quiz, and Heather had been only a couple of seconds faster. When Katie was executed, Heather quickly realized that they had to be wrong in their assumption that Dorothy was the Mole, and the only reason she had survived the execution was that her fingers were just a tad faster than Katie's. After some consideration and a studied process of elimination, she started to believe that I had to be the Mole. She wasn't totally convinced yet, but was getting there. No one else had even begun to come to that conclusion yet. Heather had the money in the bank, if she could just keep her act together and not lose faith in her reasoning. (On the other hand, if frogs had wings, they wouldn't bump their butts so much! Ah, the vagaries of life!)

What Was She Thinking?

Katie

Honestly, I went into The Mole with this preconceived plan that I would sit back quietly and observe and not be my true self. That lasted about 5 minutes. When we got up to Anderson's chalet in the alps and there was so much alcohol provided for us, I think I was the loudest I had ever been in my life... I wanted to have an air of mystery and that was completely thrown by the wayside.

I didn't pack well for the show. One outfit for executions, and only a few pairs of pants, one razor and one pack of cigarettes... I was hoping I would make it past the first execution, because I didn't want to be that NH girl that was the first off of a reality show, like the girl from Milan, NH on Survivor.

The first night I had it pegged that Elavia was the Mole... She was just shady and my "red flag" went up when she was asked what her favorite food is and she said EDIBLE... So, that first night Heather and I became a coalition as I definitely needed someone to throw ideas off of... So, that was my strategy... I never once thought Bill was the Mole... It went Elavia, then Dorothy, then Bill - Bill reminded me too much of my dad to be

Reflections of The Mole

the Mole... And after Elavia took her bribe, both Heather and I thought Dorothy was the next possible candidate. When we took that quiz, Heather and I had all the same answers, she just took the test faster... So, after my execution, she was able to deduce that our assumption was wrong.

Never in my wildest dreams did I think I would last 8 weeks on a reality TV show, but it was the most amazing experience, to date, in my life.

XIX

Mechanics, Wine, and Tether Ball

In my brief following the interview, Clay told me we had three (or 4) games coming up the next day. I was going to be involved in all but one. This was a lot of information to pass along to me in a 5 minute conversation in full view of everyone, especially since I had to continually correct the answers my wife had submitted on my application. I'm sure that whoever was making up the quiz (Kathryn, Mole I, as it turned out) was driven to scratching her head vigorously and repeatedly looking up the answers again after my corrections. While life isn't supposed to be perfect, it should be a little more predictable than this!

The next morning we all went to breakfast where we found one of those enigmatic clues that dastardly Mole was prone to leave for us. It was a message, and we all analyzed it at length. In fact, I remained behind while everyone else slowly tired of the analysis and headed up the stairs to their rooms. I was really trying to figure out that clue that "I" had left. (Actually, I had been told to be the last to leave the breakfast table, without being told why. As a good Mole should, I followed orders.)

> "Four more losers
> Which will you be
> I'm counting down
> Dwindling numbers are key."

What did all this mean? Shoot, don't ask me; I'm just the Mole. No one ever tells me anything!

Reflections of The Mole

I went back to my room and stretched out; we had been told to stand by, and they would come and get us for our next round of games...eventually. We did a lot of this, sitting and waiting; then, going somewhere else, and again sitting and waiting. This was not the glamorous part of the game; in fact, we were still awaiting that part!

There was a knock at my door and Anderson came in, replete with camera crews.

"Bill, you've been selected for this next part," as he handed me several small green thumbprints with glue on one side. "You must select one of the other players and manage to stick one of these thumbprints into their journal, unseen. You can't tell anyone you are doing this, or that you were the one who did it if you succeed. Whoever you select will be ineligible for an exemption for the next execution. If you don't manage to do this, **you** will be ineligible for an exemption."

He paused. "Are there any questions?"

"How did I get the honor of screwing one of my fellow players? If I'm caught, they might think I'm the Mole! Not that that's bad, but...why me?"

Anderson grinned his grin, little blue eyes twinkling. "That's the penalty you pay for being a slow eater. You were the last one up from the table this morning, so you get the dirty duty!" Anderson *did* love this game.

I could do nothing else, so agreed. Now, this was fun! I was going to get to do an obviously molish act in front of the cameras and crew, as well as the viewing public. However, it was to be done with the perfect cover. Anderson made me do it!

We were called out and teams selected. Bribs, Darwin, Dorothy, and I were to be mechanics; Heather and Al wound up being wine experts, of sorts! We were all then driven out to a large vineyard, and Al and Heather departed in one direction as we walked off in another. We arrived at a greenhouse whose door was open about 3 feet, and which was quite immobile when we attempted to open it any more. In front of the greenhouse was a large collection of all kinds of tools, jacks, yardsticks, and other instruments of the trade…whatever the trade was to be. Then, down the road came a very old Citroen auto, which pulled up in front of the not-so-sliding door to the greenhouse. Anderson climbed out, smiling as usual.

"You have 3 hours to get this car through that door into the greenhouse. I will return at that time and attempt to start it. If it starts, you get $30,000. Good luck! Try to stay clean, please. There is an expert here who will not let you do anything dangerous, and you must obey him when he tells you something." Anderson turned and walked away.

We surveyed the car. Nice little car, but there was no way it was going to go through that 3 foot opening in the doorway. Dorothy looked somewhat apprehensive; if we were going to do heavy work, her best role was going to be cheerleader and water carrier.

Helpful as always, I said, "Well, we have lots of work to do before we can get this through that door! Let's do it!" I removed my green shoulder bag, in which my journal was concealed, and laid it down on the far side of the tools, a location that happened to be *out of line of sight of the door*, hoping the others would follow my lead. They did follow suit, laying their bags (and journals) down next to mine. If that step hadn't worked, there would have never been a chance of placing that stamp in someone's journal.

I busily approached the car, grabbed the yard stick, carefully measured the opening in the door, then took multiple measurements of the car itself.

"This car will never make through that door this way. We need to make it a lot smaller!" Note that in an attempt to be honest…somewhat…I did not claim that once it was separated into multiple pieces it would make it through. I just said it would not make it in its current condition. On the other hand, if any of the others had picked up the yardstick and done any measuring at all, or just stopped and looked carefully at the whole set up, it would have very obvious that without a cutting torch, that car could not be moved through a 3 foot space. It just wasn't physically possible. It wasn't a matter of believing me; I just had an idea before they did, so they acted. All that white hair. It gave me an illusion of wisdom and experience.

We all looked around the greenhouse some, then started dismantling the car. After a brief time, I noted, "The tires have to come off, obviously!" Before anyone could register an objection, I grabbed the back end of the car and lifted the wheels off the ground. "Get those off, fast! This thing is heavy!" Darwin and Bribs hopped to the task while Dorothy looked helplessly on…for a while. Dorothy did put on a pair of heavy work gloves…sort of an oxymoronic kind of thing. Her work was not going to be physical.

After we got the tires off, I suggested that someone take seats out. (Why? Why did the seats coming out have anything to do with getting the car through the door? Darned if I know.) I then vigorously attacked the top of the car; I'm not sure it was intended to be removed, but it had screws in it, and it *was* theoretically possible. Bribs and Darwin were busily removing the seats while I stayed near the front of the car. We had quickly been able to remove the doors, but the seats and the top were a little more stubborn. I managed to keep anyone from working near the instrument console, especially the odometer, because the mileage indicated on the odometer held an important clue.

Dorothy, meanwhile, in an attempt to follow Anderson's plea to stay clean, walked around looking at the greenhouse and thinking. Dorothy might have proven to be unable to walk far in a coordinated manner, but she had demonstrated several times already that she had a formidable brain.

Meanwhile, we had removed about everything we could get off except the engine, and I had the hood up contemplating that. Bribs, Darwin, and I felt the time had come to try to get our foreshortened car into the greenhouse; after all, almost half our allotted time had expired, and we had to get that damned thing back together again! I was filthy, and loving it. I was just as busy as I could be obscuring the real problem, and having great fun tearing a car to pieces!

We brought up a dolly on wheels and tilted the car up on its side in preparation for an attempt to roll it through the space. The mechanical expert stopped us. We couldn't put it all the way up on its side, so tried tilting it and balancing it on the dolly. Not a chance in the world that was going to work. The mechanic again stopped us, and indicated that we had to put the car back flat on the ground. We did so, and I opened the hood.

"The engine's got to come out!" Man, I was hoping these guys were going to get smarter soon. This was turning into work! And, taking the engine out wasn't really going to accomplish anything, unless we could get it in by itself, hook it up to the battery, and let Anderson try to start it outside of the car. I doubted that they would buy that. The only way that car was going through that 3 foot space was by benefit of a blow torch.

Darwin was dubious. "It'll take us hours to get that engine out." I noted that everything we had to do had been done by the crew, so it obviously had to be possible to do in the time limit...assuming, of course, the crew was dumb enough to try to remove it. Some of those motor mount bolts hadn't been turned since Hitler rode in that thing. (I realize Citroen is a French car, but it's not unlikely Hitler managed to snag a ride; he liked things French.)

Dorothy suddenly yelled, "Here's a combination lock on the greenhouse door!" Everyone rushed over to look, except me. I kept contemplating another part to remove off the car. By this time both Darwin and Bribs were becoming somewhat disgruntled with our efforts.

Dorothy continued to contemplate the lock, trying to figure out what the logical combination might be...as indicated on the odometer, which I had carefully kept screened from everyone's view. The clues had been given in the note from the Mole at breakfast as duplicated earlier, and she was busy applying varying degrees of logic to them. Meanwhile, Darwin, Bribs, and I continued to survey the dissembled auto, with them trying to figure out what else we could do. No one else ever bothered to measure, luckily.

Dorothy yelled, "Got it!" She removed the lock, and the greenhouse door suddenly rolled fully open. We looked at each other, somewhat confused by the sudden change of events. Darn! There had been no need to take that car apart! Ah, that's life. Sometimes you can't fry an egg without breaking it...and sometimes you can. (Please don't look for the origin of this philosophy in a learned text; I made it up only moments ago.)

We immediately began reconstructing the car. As I was putting the driver's side door back on, I decided to just twist the knife a little.

"Look at this! Dorothy, what did you say the combination was?" She repeated it. "Look at the odometer!"

Bribs and Darwin looked closely at it. "Damn! It was right there in front of us all the time! How could we have missed that?!" Hmm. Let me guess how... (Actually, the odometer said something like 65432...i.e., "dwindling numbers." In true moley fashion, the actual combination was the reverse of that; sort of dwindling backwards. Not a lick beyond Dorothy's imagination, however!)

We worked hard at the task; our completion time was rapidly coming nigh. Anderson would be sliding into the car to try to start it, and it would be nice to have the seats in for him to sit on. All of us pitched in. I worked just as hard putting the car back together as I had worked tearing it apart; if they could win the money in spite of my mechanical ineptness, so be it.

We were nearing completion of the task with only minutes to go; I stepped out to get a drink...and immediately grabbed Dorothy's green bag, out of sight of the other intrepid mechanics in the greenhouse. Dorothy had managed to get 3 exemptions already, and neither Darwin nor Bribs had received one. Just seemed fair, somehow. Besides that, it was the first one I picked up. Hastily, in full view of all the crew filming, I grabbed her journal and opened it at random. My hands were so greasy and dirty that I was afraid of leaving obvious signs of having been there. I grabbed a green thumbprint out of my pocket and licked it, sticking it quickly onto a page near the back of the book. I then returned to the greenhouse to assist in the final moments.

The car looked great. Everything was back where it belonged. However, Dorothy approached me frantically. "Bill, I have all these screws left! Where do they go?!"

"Dorothy, see that dark corner over there? Throw them away!"

She seemed upset. "Throw them away? What if the car falls apart on the freeway?"

"Dorothy, this car is not *made* to go on the freeway! If someone is dumb enough to take this antique out on the freeway, it *should* fall apart under them! That's called Darwinian selection!" I grabbed the screws from her...and there were definitely some healthy looking screws there, looking like they should be holding something on...and tossed them away, just as Anderson entered with a smile.

"Time! Let's see if this thing will start." He hopped in the somewhat wobbly front seat and started grinding the starter. We all looked at each other. There was always the possibility that this particular car had not been designed to sit up on its side, and something vital might have shifted...like gasoline. Soon, however, gravity reasserted itself on the gasoline we had displaced somewhere it should not have been, and the engine suddenly started purring...or, more accurately, started sounding like a moderate-sized lawnmower. It wasn't a big car. With the seats in I don't think I could fit in it.

(I heard of several wrecks causing lots of chaos on the highways of Italy in the next few weeks, and always wondered a little if that car had been one of the causes, spewing bolts and screws and loose parts in the path of oncoming traffic...)

We all headed down to the main winery. The 4 of us noted that Anderson seemed unusually chatty, and while he didn't normally walk in a straight line, preferring to amble about as he strolled, on our hike back he was most definitely weaving a wide track. Surely he couldn't have been drinking...without us? Besides that, his eyes, suspect always, at times appeared to actually cross a little.

We arrived at the winery where we met Heather and Al for dinner. Both were most definitely tipsy! Shoot, they went off with Anderson and had a lot more fun than we had! I had enough grease and dirt on me that it was going to take a long while to get it off; I had only managed to get all the grease out of my hair from the Gnome Home game within the last few days. Just wasn't destined to be clean on this trip, I guess.

As it turned out, they had played a fun game. Heather and Al had taken turns stomping barefooted on a vat of grapes, slowly eliciting grape juice. Al was an ideal physical specimen for this task; he wore size 14 shoes. Shoot, they probably had to get a bigger vat just to accommodate his feet!

Anderson had opened several bottles of the local winery's product during the process, and between the 3 of them they must have consumed 3 or 4 bottles, at least. They all were still feeling the effects at dinner. They had managed to collect 3 bottles of foot-mashed grape juice, or toe wine; and, while it had only had an hour or so to ferment, they called it wine and corked it. At the end of their ordeal, in which they had managed to make $10,000, Anderson offered them a challenge. If they could pour 3 glasses of wine without spilling a drop, they would add another $10,000 to the pot. Under the right circumstances drunks will accept most any challenge; this was to be no exception to that rule. They promptly lost all the money they had almost collected. Al then issued the same challenge to Anderson; as I have noted, he was clearly under the influence, and lost the bet as quickly as they had. However, he didn't lose any money.

We looked at the three of them with some suspicion. "You thought that being drunk had somehow improved your coordination?" Darwin had a way with words.

They grinned silly grins. All three of them. It was a hoot. Al then started begging us to have a drink of his wine, the toe wine. If only they had stuck with drinking their own, they might have won the pouring contest! Of course, they might have gotten sick to their stomachs as well, so perhaps they were wise in their choice of wines.

The four of us looked at each other. Suspicion was heavy in the air. Darwin, Dorothy, and Bribs all suspected that if they drank some of the wine, Heather and Al might get an exemption. Dorothy protested that she never drank wine under any circumstances. Darwin pointed out to us that if two more exemptions were given, the odds would go to about 1 in 3 or 4, depending on who the Mole was, for one of us to get executed. In spite of all the debate, I finally turned up a glass of the toe muck and drank. What the hell! I didn't care if they got an exemption! The others finally followed suit, whereupon Al announced that we had just added another $10,000 to the pot, and no exemptions were given in that game. We had trouble understanding Al when he announced that, you understand, because those several bottles of wine had really started to take hold!

At the conclusion of dinner Anderson suddenly announced, "I want everyone to pass me your journals." I think that's what he said; his wine intake was starting to show as well.

Reflections of The Mole

We did so, and Anderson started flipping through the pages. After going through all the journals, he reached over and picked up Dorothy's journal again, and asked, "Whose is this?"

Dorothy was looking a little worried. "Mine."

Anderson opened one of the back pages and showed the green thumbprint to all of us. "How did you get this thumb print in your journal?"

Dorothy was dumbstruck. "I don't know! I'm never apart from my journal! It hasn't left me at any time, I swear!"

Anderson grinned. "Too bad. This thumbprint means that one of your fellow players has guaranteed that you cannot receive an exemption in the next execution. Who did you irritate? Someone must really have it in for you!" As I said, Anderson was properly sympathetic and played things down, always.

Everyone looked at each other. I had trouble meeting everyone's eye; mine were full of tears from the toe wine. This incident did generate lots of conversation on the way back to the hotel. Darwin said, "Come on! Someone 'fess up! It's already done, anyway." This was followed with a silence that said, *Are you out of your mind?* No one was going to reveal that! Only the crew knew that I had been forced to do this terrible thing! And, all the viewing public. (Of interest, Dorothy later told me there was one white hair stuck under the edge of the thumbprint. She chose not to point this out to anyone, and noted that there were only two people with white hair in the cast: Anderson and me. She did not suspect Anderson had done it.)

Back to the hotel. Everyone was tired. It had been a long day and everyone just wanted to eat dinner and go to bed. I was the only one who realized that our day had only begun, but I couldn't remember what the devil Clay had told me to do at the night game! All that toe wine, I suspect. I thought about it for a while, then wrote a brief note to Clay and stuck it in my pocket. Maybe, just maybe, I might get a chance to be alone with him at some point. Of course, it hadn't happened in about eight shows, but there was always a chance...

We headed to dinner, a buffet style affair. The food line was along one wall, and we had all chosen to sit around the corner in a somewhat private area away from the buffet. We got enough curious looks from the other guests, so isolated ourselves a little whenever possible. Clay and the crew sat across from us in the main portion of the room. As we were eating I saw Clay get up from his table with his plate and head back to the buffet line. For a little guy he could pound down the food! I grabbed my plate and fell in behind him. I glanced back, and sure enough, could not see my fellow players. However, I figured that several were sure to follow soon; those were growing boys back there. I tapped Clay on the arm away from the other diners and slipped my note in his hand. He carried on surveying the food and slowly scooping up portions as he quickly glanced down and read the question. I just needed to know a number. He never looked back at me, but quietly said, "Three." And, headed back to his table. As did I, meeting Darwin and Al as they headed over for more food. If anyone had seen me slip Clay that note...they would undoubtedly have been smart enough to not say a word, and would have had me in their sights for the rest of the game. It didn't happen, and I'm sure both Darwin and Al wish they had just been a little hungrier a little sooner!

Back to our rooms, and to bed, perchance to sleep. Or, not. About 11:30 our den mothers started knocking on our doors, and we were herded in our pajamas down to the basement of the hotel. There stood Anderson, looking somewhat under the weather...though not so much as Al, who was definitely suffering. In the middle of a large empty banquet room a tetherball hung from a hook on the ceiling, with cushions scattered out on the floor.

"Here's the game. Arrange yourselves in a circle and start hitting the ball, keeping it moving in a circle. Each of you has to hit in turn, and if anyone hits out of turn, or misses a turn, the game is over. If you manage to keep the ball going until morning, about 8 hours, you will add another $40,000 to the pot. Make yourselves as comfortable as you want to and start....now!"

We started. What a stupid game! Al and Heather were hung over, Darwin, Bribs and Dorothy appeared determined, and I tried to just look resigned. I grabbed my back and slowly eased myself into a sitting position against a pole. The ball went around and around; no one was convinced that we were going to be able to keep this up, and Al was very vocal about it. He was hung over and wanted to go to bed!

After about an hour Anderson walked back in. He looked like he had had a nice nap, and appeared far more rested than we did. After watching a few minutes, he asked, "Who's tired? Someone can leave right now and go to bed, if you want to."

Al was up and moving before anyone could react. "Good night, everyone!" We all laughed. It was just as well; he had almost missed the ball several times, and was clearly hurting. I don't think Al drinks much wine. Or, maybe he should have had some of his toe wine. It was keeping me wide awake, though I was having recurrent nightmares about Dr. Scholl's Foot Powder.

Forty-five or so minutes later Anderson reappeared, and someone asked me if I was OK. I responded that I was fine. Heather departed.

Immediately after her departure I started doing back exercises between efforts at hitting the ball. I managed to hit it out of its normal circle several times, somewhat to the aggravation of the others. I apologized and resumed my exercises between times. No complaints. I'm a plucky fellow, and complaining is...unplucky.

Anderson reappeared. "Who's next?"

Immediately Bribs replied, "Bill!" He was echoed by both Darwin and Dorothy.

Anderson asked, "Bill, are you ready?"

"I guess."

Anderson grinned, then offered me an exemption if I would hit the ball out of turn and stop the game, costing us the $40,000.

I contemplated, and asked the others, "Listen, if you all think you can last until 8:00 AM, tell me! I don't think you can, and sure don't want to miss out on an exemption! Help me here! What do you think?" I waited a few seconds, curious if one of them was going to be smart enough to hit out of turn, inasmuch as that ball was still going as we were talking. The last thing anyone wanted was for there to be an exemption for someone other than them. I suddenly hit the ball out of turn. "Let's go to bed!"

There was silence on the way back up stairs. Everyone there knew they would have done the same, but quitting in the middle of a challenge just went against everything we were used to.

The next morning Bribs came up to me, apologetically. "Bill, I have a confession to make. I hit the ball out of order right after Anderson made his announcement, and told him about it after you left. I'm sorry. I cost you an exemption." He looked really sorry, and I'm sure he was. But, he had proven to be an outstanding player! That was a good move. I acted chagrined, however.

"Gee, Bribs, I'm sorry you did that! Shoot! I guess I should not have waited, but...I just didn't want to cost us all that money, especially after everyone was working so hard for it!" Ah, rub a little salt in that wound, will you? Bribs hung his head and again apologized. He knew he would do it again, but....

At breakfast Anderson brought out a video player. "Let me show you something." It turns out that Darwin had actually urged Dorothy to hit the ball an hour or so earlier, when in fact it was Darwin's turn. We could have been in bed by midnight! We all turned on Darwin; what a great move for the Mole to make!

Darwin immediately became defensive. "I didn't know I did that! Honest! Really! Why would I stay down there for another couple of hours if I had deliberately sabotaged the game? Think about it!"

Bribs replied, "Because you're the Mole!" Darwin caught a lot of crap for the rest of the meal, and the day.

We had a nice time the next day; 24 hours of fun and games before we had to face the next execution. We all got to spend the day at a public swimming pool with various games around it. The day evolved into a major ping pong tournament. Darwin emerged from the players as the winner, only to face a determined psychologist, Geoff White. Geoff did not look like the average ping pong player. With his white hair and mustache, I'm sure Darwin saw another victory coming. Not to happen. I now know what Geoff did in those lonely nights on call for psychology service. He was a darned good ping pong player.

The next execution came, and there were no exemptions to be had. Darwin bit the dust, much to his obvious disgust. It was only justice, however. Of the 8 or so coalitions he had formed, all his partners had been executed except Bribs…and me. I'm glad Darwin is in corporate law and not a deductive arm of the profession. A lot of his clients would probably be behind bars!

My last known (to me) misspeak came after the quiz that night. Al and I were sitting outside on a bench trying to come up with the 10 questions we had been asked and recording them in our journals. He asked me what answer I had put on one of them, and, again violating my rule, answered without giving it some thought. Then came a sudden realization of what I had done. Before Al could react, I exclaimed, "Damn! That's **my** information! I answered that question as if I were the Mole! I don't believe it; I'm probably gone." Al sympathized with me, reassuring me that somehow I had managed to hang in this far, and perhaps I had an idea who the Mole was. Maybe that one question wouldn't affect things.

He was right, of course; he just didn't realize how right. That one question didn't affect things, but it could have…if Al had given it a little more thought, and just had been a little more suspicious and a little less of a friend!

What The Hell Was I Thinking?

By Darwin Conner

At the beginning, I had no strategy. I swear. When the producers asked me what my strategy would be, I told them I would figure it out as I went along. And I only did it that way because I had no idea what I was doing. Why do you need this information? Well, because in order to judge my eventual strategy, you need to know the foundation from which it started. And no shakier foundation could exist.

From the moment the blindfolds came off, I was lost. And what made matters worse was the fact that I was paired with The Mole for the very first challenge. Here I was, spending all day with The Mole. I gathered information on Bill, but he just didn't strike me as very moley (whatever that means), so instead I stewed in my frustration at missing out on gathering information on everyone else. How unfair!

I took the first quiz painfully slowly. I read each question twice and was careful with my answers – a horrible strategy when you have not an inkling of what any of the answers should be. For the first quiz, you should answer as quickly as possible, trying to cover as many people as possible in each answer. If the question is a long one, don't even read it. Just pick an answer. Since there's a good chance you get none of the answers right, you might as well beat out everyone else on time, just in case you tie.

Reflections of The Mole

But I survived the first round, which turned out to be a good and bad thing. It was good because it set up my strategy for the rest of the game. It was bad because it set up my strategy for the rest of the game. You see, I figured that I was definitely the slowest to finish the quiz. So, if I had answered the fewest number of questions correctly, and anyone who tied me, I would have been gone.* Because of that, I could assume I had at least one correct answer. Since I wrote down each question after the quiz, I could go through the questions and my answers to the first quiz and determine who I could eliminate. Since the quiz is set up to ask questions about who The Mole is and what they've done, eat, said, etc., surely I could eliminate anyone who didn't appear in any of my answers. And guess what? Bill didn't appear in any of my answers to the first quiz. Bingo, baby! Game. Set. Match. I already eliminated one person. No one could stop me now. I've got this game figured out, man.

But I still don't know who The Mole is. So, while I try to figure that out, I answer every question I can so that I can include as many players in each answer as possible, yet always trying to avoid groups in which Bill is one of the answers. Let me give you an example:

> *As you know, we are given journals to help us keep track of game play and to take notes so we can be prepared for each quiz. In these journals we wrote down every detail of what the other players did from morning 'til night. We wrote down, for example, each player's favorite colors, what color clothes they were wearing, what they*

---

* *And there is the fatal flaw in my strategy. Bob (the first player to be eliminated) had to have taken longer to take the quiz because if he hadn't, I would have been eliminated first. I just didn't think it was possible that anyone took more time taking the quiz.*

ate or drank, what games they were involved in. Everything. And then we tried to anticipate what the questions on the quiz would be. So, if at dinner they served wine, we would write down who had red, who had white, who had none, etc. If asked on the quiz a question like, "Who had red wine with dinner?" I already knew what my answer would be because in my room, before the quiz, I had already figured out that 6 people had red, 5 people had white and 3 people had none. If Bill was in the group of people that had red, I would pick the group that had white. If he wasn't, "Red" was the obvious answer since more people had red and therefore I would have a better chance of including The Mole in my answer. I tried to do this for every answer. Simple test-taking strategy. But combined with my other strategy, it wasn't so great.

Actually, that part of my strategy wasn't so bad. In fact, it's what kept me on the show for nine episodes. I would recommend it to anyone because it is what kept me in the game for as long as it did. Until you get a real feeling for who The Mole is, you want to keep your bases covered and I think that's the best way.

So, what were my other mistakes? Let me give you a list:

1. <u>Not trying to be suspicious</u>. Since it is in everyone's best interests to make everyone else think they are The Mole so that the other players answer quiz questions incorrectly, it makes sense to act "moley." I didn't do this because I was so set on figuring things out that I didn't care if others didn't suspect me. Bad move. The best players were suspicious and did suspicious things. Not in an over-the-top way, that would be too obvious. They would do little things that would make you think twice why they would do something like that.

Reflections of The Mole

Elavia was just naturally shady. It's just how she carries herself (which isn't to say she's a bad person, she's great. She just naturally seems suspect). The producers did a great job picking her because everyone thought she was The Mole at some point. But, for me, the person who pulled off being suspicious the best was Dorothy. Looking back on it, she did everything right. She was smart and got exemptions from elimination when she could, sufficiently suspicious, sometimes doing things that seemed to make no sense, and a little bit lucky.

2. <u>Not listening to other people</u>. Look, the game is set up so that you can't trust anyone. But you're isolated. You can't talk to anyone but other players or the producers, so everyone wants to, or even needs to, trust and confide in someone. And most players let you know in subtle ways that they are not The Mole. It's weird, but when someone is accused of being The Mole or doing something purposefully to sabotage a game, the automatic reaction is to fight against that accusation. You should try to cultivate those suspicions, not fight them. Also, people need to talk about their strategies and suspicions. I had a thousand coalitions because I wanted to gather information and then confirm that the information I got was true by getting it from multiple sources. But what I should have been doing was listening to what other people thought. But I just knew my plan was bullet proof, so I ignored everyone else's opinions. Especially the ones who told me that they were sure Bill was The Mole. In fact, I managed to convince others (like Bribbage) that they were wrong, based on my flawed quiz evidence.

3. <u>Thinking I was at least as smart as the producers</u>. I tried to pick up clues from the producers all the time.

After executions, the producers would ask us questions about things and I would try to see who they were favoring (or more importantly, trying not to favor). One of the producers (Clay Newbill, a great guy) always wanted someone to answer this one specific question and no one would give him the answer he wanted. One time, Heather volunteered to answer the question out of the blue! I was convinced he had instructed her, as The Mole, in their private meeting to answer the question on her own (everyone meets privately with the producers at least once before the quiz for interviews and decompression time (and for The Mole, to receive instructions and information!)). But the fact is, the producers are professionals. They know what they're doing, are very smart and aren't going to give anything away. Because if they do, the show is pretty much over and it becomes about who can answer the questions on the quiz fastest.

If I had been paying the right kind of attention to people, I would have noticed that Bill wasn't really taking very many notes, at least not like the rest of us. But I was too convinced I had it right in eliminating him as a suspect. Plus, the guy's a surgeon, so I figured he had a great memory and might not need the notes. And because of the nature of the game, when he did intentionally sabotage a game, it looked like he was just another player trying to draw attention to himself (I mean, come on, the guy's a Rear Admiral in the Navy and he can't tread water for more than 2 minutes? I don't think so). But even though I wanted to be The Mole very badly, Bill was the best choice. Very few people suspected him and he had me bamboozled. And as it turns out, that was one of his best accomplishments, because I managed to convince other people he wasn't The Mole either.

Anderson called me the King of Coalitions during our reunion episode. But maybe he should have called me The Unintentional

Reflections of The Mole

Mole. I like to think of myself as a Jason Bourne, without the brains, skills, strategy or looks.

But I have no regrets. It was a great time. A once in a lifetime opportunity to do some things and see some places I otherwise would never have a chance to see or experience. Plus, I met some great people. I wouldn't trade my experience for anything (except maybe Dorothy's experience). It was a blast.

<u>*Fast Forward*</u>*:*

So, what am I doing now? Applying my analytical skills to transactional law, same as I was before I went on the show. I have a daughter who will turn six in December (and she's absolutely perfect as far as I'm concerned). That's about it, people. Nothing too exciting.

XX

Heather Loses Confidence

Things were starting to get tighter. As we were all sitting around after Darwin left, Al asked if anyone else was thinking about the money. We all denied it, for various reasons, the main one being that it didn't seem real yet. Al was dubious.

"Come on! You mean you can sit there and tell me the money doesn't come into your mind now? I don't believe that! There are only 4 of us left competing for it. One chance in four! How can you not think about it?" (When you read this, please try to read in Al's Long Island accent to get the best effect. Al was great at expressing disbelief, sort of "in your face, you're lying to me!")

Again everyone denied thinking about the possibility of winning. I know I didn't. Al remained highly skeptical about our truthfulness.

We had moved out of Lucca, and were now in Southern Italy in the little town of L'Aquila, about 60 miles or so from Rome. The drive down was as usual…harrowing. Man, there might be theoretical speed limits on those roads, but we never saw any one who was remotely honoring them. As we were leaving Lucca, we passed a large, newly opened McDonalds. After living on pasta and wine for the last month or so, we were all ready for a change of food…not necessarily drink, but definitely food. At this point our entourage included about 50 crew, a bus, and several vans, plus 5 players. As the signs for the upcoming McDonald's grand opening started showing up on the roadside, the call went out on the walkie-talkies. "Clay, can we all stop at McDonalds?"

The answer came back from Luis. "No, let's keep going."

Reflections of The Mole

Did he sound serious? Nah, none of us thought so, so we stopped, along with several hundred hungry Italians. The lines moved quickly, however; the workers there were afraid of summary justice and a quick lynching if they did not get the fast food out immediately! How good was that! Wow, McDonalds truly has never tasted so…not like pasta.

We arrived in L'Aquila, a moderate sized town and moved into a fairly nice hotel. Inasmuch as it was again going to take a good day to set up the next games, we adjourned via van to Rome, and the Vatican, the Spanish Steps, Trevi "Three Coins in a Fountain," and tattoo parlors. What a super day! When we entered Rome our first stop was at a classic auto warehouse ABC maintained on the outskirts of town. Absolutely incredible! There were vintage autos and motorcycles from the 20's and later, beautifully maintained. All the fellows had a ball wandering around looking at these magnificent Mercedes, Rolls Royces, Packards, and the like. We were hoping to be allowed to ride in one, or drive one, or something. Alas, it was not to be. We finally reboarded the van and went initially to the Vatican. Al, a Catholic, was visibly very moved by the beauty there; we all were, actually, but he was especially.

From there we went sightseeing to all the popular spots in town, including throwing coins in Trevi Fountain while the photographers snapped pictures. One thing I have not mentioned was that we were forbidden to take any pictures of our own, nor were we allowed to buy anything expecting to get to take it home with us. The show was not due to start for about 2½ months after we got home, and no one was to know where it was shot until the episodes were aired. So, all we have of those places are memories. We had hoped that perhaps ABC might allow the photographer to put together albums commemorating our stay there, and either give them to us or allow us to purchase them. Not a chance! Basically, as best I can understand from talking to the contestants on the other reality shows on the other networks, they felt like we did. While the producers took good care of us, we were truly simply there to make a show. Period. Extras like photos were not part of the deal. Our job was to get in, get executed, and get out, hopefully adding some excitement in the process. But once out, you were gone and forgotten. It's hard to complain much about it, however; we had a chance to do something few other people ever got to do, and many thousands would have liked to do what we were doing. We all agreed then, and I think now, the experience was incredible and we were honored to be allowed to be part of it.

At one point Al, Bribs, and I were sitting on the Spanish Steps, and I brought out the remaining Cuban El Cohiba cigars which I had purchased in a cigar shop. We all sat contentedly watching the throngs of people swarm about us, puffing away, as relaxed as one can get playing a game like we were doing. We didn't quiz each other any that day, nor accuse each other of being The Mole! At that time no one (except me) was sure about the identity of the Mole, though Heather had suspected me since Katie left. However, she was emotionally exhausted, full of plans about her upcoming wedding, and wanted nothing more than to get home to her fiancé, some good Mexican food, and a cold margarita. Not necessarily in that order.

Eventually, we wound up next to a large dirt square filled with amateur magicians, tattoo artists, and other vendors. We ate at an outdoor restaurant, and someone mentioned getting a tattoo. Now, while I spent 30+ years in the Navy, getting a tattoo was never at the top of my wish list, and I didn't want to start now! However, we all settled on henna tattoos, whose stain waned and disappeared by about 6 weeks post tattoo. We all got them in various spots; mine was a barbed wire around my biceps. I hoped it was still going to look recent when I got home; however, if it had been, there is a good chance that my wife would have carved it from my arm while I slept. She's not partial to tattoos.

Reflections of The Mole

We returned to the games the next day. The two girls were sent out into a local marketplace with some money and bought all kinds of goods, everything from farm implements to food to kitchen utensils. Bribs, Al, and I stood on the roof of a building and watched them; we had no idea what they were up to, and tried to track them through the maze of shops and vendors. Who knew what we were going to be asked to do? Retrace their steps? Sell the items back to the correct vendor? We confabulated multiple scenarios and discussed them, but didn't have a clue. We idly speculated about which of them might be the Mole, though all of us were careful to not let on what we actually thought. This was not a team sport, after all.

The girls returned, without their goods. Anderson gathered us together and told us that our job was to sell all the goods the girls had bought, utilizing a stand in the same market, and make money while doing it. Do this simple task, and we add $30,000 to the pot. Sounded easy. Heather and Dorothy looked at each other and rolled their eyes. They had driven the hardest bargains they could, and it turns out that the only things the vendors would bargain on were those items that no one wanted. So, they got lots of good deals…and lots of relieved vendors. Some of those items dated back a number of years, only because they had never, ever been purchased. Not them nor anything that looked like them.

So, we tried. I was going to sabotage this game, but Dorothy and Heather did far too good a job sabotaging it on their own. There was absolutely no chance of selling that stuff. We enlisted the aid of some very pretty young Italian women who were equally unsuccessful; we probably destroyed their self-confidence for several months, or until the next guy hit on them, which would only be a few minutes. Al tried to sell kisses; predictably (to Bribs and me), only one 80+ year old woman was interested in taking him up on it, and she didn't want to pay much. Just wanted to savor the experience; it had been a long time, after all. Al and Bribs managed to sell their own virtually brand new Ecco shoes worth about $200/pair for about $14.00. Really sharp salesmen. After that they were barefooted. I mostly just stood around and yelled in bad Italian and laughed. Was I really going to get to count this as sabotage? Needless to say, we did not add money to the pot, other than $10,000 we were graciously given by the producers for returning some money to a shill for the producers, who was assigned to test our honesty. He might have gotten a different result regarding that storied honesty if he had left enough money to have made a difference in the outcome!

Meanwhile, unbeknownst to us, Dorothy and Heather had established a coalition with each other. Heather, who strongly suspected that I was the Mole, approached Dorothy…who, unknown to Heather, strongly suspected Heather…and proposed that they work together to get two male players executed. Dorothy feared a set-up, and voiced that. Heather replied, "I swear on my family Bible that I'm not the Mole!" Game, set, and match. Dorothy believed her; Heather did set a lot of store in that Bible, and it was highly unlikely she would swear on it falsely. While Heather did not confide in her who her candidate for the Mole might be, Dorothy was a smart woman. She knew it wasn't Al. We all knew it wasn't Al. People who didn't even watch the show knew it wasn't Al! So, it was Bribs or me. If Heather had not been so exhausted, if she had not lost her confidence….who knows?

This was followed the next day by the Evader game, one of the most fun games we played the entire time…except to Heather. An entire small Italian walled village was wired for sound and lights. The village was beautiful. There were no streets big enough for cars, and the residents made do with walking or bicycle riding on the small brick throughways in the village, many of which went under centuries-old houses. In the center of the village was a tall stone watch tower, and Bribs,

Dorothy, and I were atop it with one walkie-talkie between us. Al and Heather were at the entrance to the village where we could not see them. Heather, who had never yet received an exemption, left the starting area and was tasked with finding and retrieving five of nine or so large green thumbprints scattered around town, left on steps, walls, in doorways, etc. She had to remain hidden as she did so, and if successful in securing 5 of these thumbprints before Al caught her, received an exemption. If Al caught her, we added $50,000 to the pot. Our job was to act as Al's spotters, reporting to him on his walkie-talkie where she was, once we saw her. He could not start until we initially spied her. To make a long story much shorter, we saw her, and he caught her, ending her chances for an exemption. Al, however, in addition to adding $50,000 to the pot, got an exemption. Suddenly, the odds were 1 in 3 that one of the others was going home at execution.

It was in this game that Al did the only suspicious thing he had done. I had the walkie-talkie on the tower, and Al was impatiently waiting for us to tell him we had spotted Heather, whereupon he could start running to try to catch her. We saw her and I yelled into the mike, "Go, Al, go!" Al didn't move, though we were unaware of it, inasmuch as we couldn't see the starting point. After a couple of more minutes Al suddenly said, "Did someone say something?"

I looked at my mike. "Aren't you moving yet?! I told you to go several minutes ago!" Whereupon he launched.

This should have been a much more fun game than it turned out to be. Heather was seen quickly, and caught almost as quickly. She was depressed, and the cameramen around the village were feeling somewhat abused, I expect. They had not gotten to do anything!

Anderson looked us over, all atop the tower. "Heather, would you like to try again?"

Heather looked up, teary-eyed. "Are you serious?"

"It depends on your fellow players. Are you all interested in another game, with a different chaser? We will add another $50,000 to the pot if the chaser catches Heather a second time."

Dorothy spoke up. "If Heather is successful, would that mean she would get an exemption?"

"Yes."

Dorothy immediately objected. "That's too many exemptions! Al already has one, and if Heather gets one, there might be a 1 in 2 chance to be executed! I vote No!"

I looked at Bribs. He loved these games, and always played as hard as he could. Besides that, both Bribs and Heather were from Texas; I figured he was used to chasing Texas girls…successfully. "Bribs, do you want to be the chaser?"

Bribs smiled. "You bet! I'll do it. I vote Yes!"

I voted yes also. Anderson asked Al how he voted. Al initially demurred. "There's already a majority voting to play the game; you don't need my vote." Al didn't want to give anything away, not even how he might be thinking. He was playing this game to win. Anderson pressed him, and finally Al grudgingly agreed that he would vote yes. Dorothy was really worried, however. She did not want Heather to get an exemption at this point. She suspected both Bribs and me, and in fact was probably about 90% sure it was one of us, and she did not want to be reduced to a 50% chance of making the next round of games. However, she was out-voted.

The game started anew. Heather had learned from the first game, and remained out of our view for a long, long time. Al was running around the top of the tower trying to cover all bases; he really felt that he could not afford to trust either Dorothy or me to reliably report it if we saw Heather, and at one point demanded that we all switch places. OK, we'll do it!

We finally spied Heather, for a brief moment only, and Bribs came running. We could see him, but not Heather. (Anderson later revealed that they had given Heather a walkie-talkie also so she could hear the instructions we were shouting to Bribs.) Heather would not be there, but suddenly a green thumbprint would be gone. We counted four thumbprints that had disappeared, and knew she was nearing the fifth one and an exemption. Dorothy was frantically looking at this point; she could see the odds of her remaining a player getting slimmer and slimmer.

We had lost sight of Bribs as he disappeared down a street, and could see Heather dashing down the walkway toward a 5th green thumbprint as we shouted vainly for him to save the day. Dorothy was about to jump off the tower and tackle Heather herself! Where was he? Suddenly, out of nowhere, Bribs appeared and snatched the flag off the back of Heather's pack signifying that she had been caught. She was literally within a foot of grabbing the last green thumbprint when he caught her. She immediately broke down and started crying, and Bribs almost did as well. In spite of the fact that four of the five of us did not want two exemptions in play with only 5 players remaining, we all felt sorry for Heather. She was exhausted, and might have walked away at that moment if she could have. The ride back to the hotel was long, slow, and very, very quiet. The only really happy person there was Al, but he understood Heather's depression. Al knew he was through to the round of four!

The next night we all took our test, and afterwards Bribs and I were sitting outside chatting. He was very pensive, and finally said, "Bill, if you're the Mole, I'm a dead man." I am not sure who he was going for, but I think it was Dorothy. Whoever it was, it wasn't me. He should have never listened to Darwin! Here Darwin was gone, and he was *still* getting his coalition partners executed!

I was truly sorry to see Bribs leave. He was an intense competitor, yet thoroughly enjoyed every aspect of the game.

While I'm sure the money was something he wanted badly, I think the entire experience was one that he savored to the max.

What Was He Thinking?

Bribs

I had no idea what I was thinking when I began the game. Honestly, I was completely along for the ride and I truly believed that "the ride" would be enough for me, regardless of my final placement amongst the contestants. I knew that my natural friendly demeanor would be suspect in such a setting, so I went in acting completely like myself, with no reservations or hidden agendas. Turns out, that suited me pretty well....for the most part.

My initial plan was to play the odds on answering the questions, throwing my answers to the majority. In other words, if asked whether or not the mole had red or white wine with dinner, I'd respond with whatever the majority of the contestants drank. This plan lasted for exactly one quiz, as I had already suspected one individual as the mole, only 3 days into the game:

Bill McDaniel. There was no particular reason as to why I zeroed in on Bill, other than my gut. And I should have followed my gut instead of mathematical reasoning. Basically, Darwin and I formed a coalition early in the game and since I didn't suspect him of being the mole, I threw a little more trust his way. It further helped my cause when we switched journals and I received his, where I saw that he had kept track of all of his answers to the quizzes, just like I did. When I looked at his answers for one of the early quizzes, he had absolutely NO answers thrown towards Bill. Since he admitted to taking an exceptionally long time to take the quiz, and since he had ZERO answers correct (assuming that Bill was the mole)....deductive reasoning tells you that he would've been the one to leave. As it turns out, Darwin marked down one of his answers incorrectly in

Reflections of The Mole

the journal, thereby giving Bill one question thrown his way and keeping Darwin in the game. From that point on, I was just hanging on by a thread and riding the "Elavia is the mole" wave that was rippling through us all.

I will never regret my decision to alter my initial focus because quite frankly...........I absolutely LOVED the game that I played and I appreciated every single memory that it provided me. I truly believe Dorothy played the best game amongst us all and deserved the last woman standing.

Since the mole ended, I participated in multiple fund raisers, donating various items from the show to raise money for a plethora of charitable organizations. Other than that, my ties to the show have diminished with each passing year, other than staying in touch with various cast members and occasionally getting to see them in person. Now, the mole resides in my memory and on the VERY seldom random night when a new friend wants to pop in
the DVD's for a few laughs.

I have settled back into my life in Austin, Texas along with my amazingly beautiful and talented girlfriend of over 4 years, Roxy. We spent the entire year of 2006 traveling around the Country in a travel trailer, covering the majority of the western half of the United States. (www.ourtrek.us) I guess you can say I will always remain an avid traveler, in search of the next great adventure!"

XXI

Anderson's Playhouse

The four of us returned to our hotel. While all prior executed victims had returned to the States, Bribs was taken to a hotel a few miles away, assigned a keeper, and remained in Italy until the filming was all done. He told us later that he got to go sight-seeing, have good meals, drink a lot of beer, and generally enjoy himself until it was time to go home. He wasn't allowed to call home, of course; the reason he remained in Europe was on the extreme off chance someone was trying to monitor the making of the show, keeping tabs on who was coming back early. This way there would be 5 of us returning at the same time.

We were all really tired by this point. Tired of the game, tired of eating pasta, tired of not talking with anyone other than each other, and tired of being completely cut out of knowing what was going on in daily life. If only it had been an election year, we might have appreciated the lack of knowledge of current events! We were ready to go home. And, Al, bless his soul, was about to go crazy with nerves. He was so fidgety and bound up following his many successful pre-execution procedural tics that we were ready to tie him down!

The four of us were allowed to wander about the town at length. Clearly, no one knew us, and we were not going to tell anyone what we were doing at this point, so the producers allowed us some slack. We went down town for lunch, and Kathryn, the Mole from the previous season, suddenly walked in the door, all dressed up and looking to party! Or something. She had never talked with any of us during the preceding weeks, though we had progressed to the point that she would smile at us when she saw us. We understood, of course, inasmuch as the producers had hammered us with the idea that if we tried to talk with any of the crew they would be fired. It was still a shock to see her walk into the restaurant.

She smiled. "Hello! I come bearing gifts!" Right. She set a neatly wrapped box down on the table, shared some small talk with us for a few minutes, and departed.

Al started unwrapping the box, and suddenly yelled, "What the Hell?!" and jumped back from the table, followed closely by all of us. We didn't know exactly what had caused Al's reaction, but were smart enough to decide to investigate it from a safe distance away. The box was filled with...live inchworms. I actually don't remember my reaction, but worms have never been a particular hang-up of mine; in fact, I like them...when fishing.

Al recovered quickly; the worms didn't scare him. He was usually in full control of his actions, and proceeded very deliberately. A box full of worms at your table is not in the normal controllable events you anticipate, however! We all gathered around looking somewhat gingerly into the box.

"Al, check in the box and see if there is a clue in the bottom." Dorothy was full of helpful advice, and Al wasn't buying it. He grinned.

"That's OK; you go ahead; I'll watch." He handed the box off toward Dorothy, who quickly backed again out of range. I grabbed the box and stirred the worms about with a knife, but no other clue was evident.

We then tried to figure out what this clue meant. I don't know why we tried; we had never figured out what any clue meant yet! As I have noted before, the producers did not give me any more information than was absolutely necessary, for 2 reasons. First, it was very difficult to communicate with me without someone noticing, and that was most definitely not a desired outcome. (The others would disagree with that statement, I expect.) Second, and most importantly, the more I did not know about the upcoming games and clues, the less I could give away. And, the more natural I would act when presented with something like a box full of worms. However, in this case it was somewhat fun to speculate. The most obvious conclusion was that we might be placed in the position of having to eat something like this to make more money. None of us expressed a lot of enthusiasm for that prospect!

"If I had wanted to eat bugs, I would have tried out for 'Survivor!" My comments were echoed by the others. One of the great things we all had enjoyed about being on this show was that we were truly treated well. Too well! I had gained way too much weight during this production already.

Never to fear. This was too classy a show to make us stoop to that level! (We hoped.)

That night we were picked up and taken an hour or so away, with the van pulling up in front of a magnificent old villa, built sometime in the Crusades. We sat around downstairs; it turned out to be someone's private home! The folks were nice, but communicated little with us. We only got to see them when we asked to use the bathroom. This house was filled with every kind of odd old farming implement and other devices of unknown use, as well as paintings of every conceivable item, plus some not conceivable. You could spend hours walking around trying to figure out what the articles laying about were. It was really a unique place, and looked like it could have been a museum, except that none of the materials were identified, and none were catalogued in any kind of rational manner!

Finally we were called upstairs. There sat Anderson at a table, surrounded by dolls of every size. On a bench next to him were some dressed up dolls about the size of 3-year-olds, all arranged so that they appeared to be looking at Anderson. He sat there with a wild look on his face, and proclaimed, "Welcome to Anderson's Fun House! Please don't offend my friends here; in fact, you should be nice to them.....," giggling as he looked over at the hair-brained bunch. He continued on this theme for a while, creating a thoroughly spooky ambiance in this surreal setting, then got down to business.

"We're going to play some cards, and the winner gets a *special treat*." Right. In the past when he said something like that, the winner got a treat all right—the winner was treated to something they did not aspire to, every time.

He started dealing. The game was simple. In order to get the maximum number of dollars added to the pot, we all understood how we needed to play. Each of us had one $25,000 chit in front of us. Whoever got the high card on each deal could either direct that someone else place their chit in the pot, or, if desired, could kick one of the others out of the game. However, if you kicked someone out before they donated their chit, that money would not be available for the pot. So, the sensible thing was to direct that all the chits be put in the middle before you started eliminating people. We discussed this before play started, and it was assumed (by Al and me, at least) that no matter who got high card each time, they would add the other's chits to the pot until no more chits were out. It sounds complicated; it wasn't. It was simple, and the first 3 people who won did the expected; they had someone else throw their chits in the middle of the table. Then, it was Dorothy's time to win, and Al had the only chit left; she did not immediately tell him to give up his chit, but instead just smiled and looked at him. She would have been perfectly within the rules to kick him out of the game. He was incredulous.

"What are you doing? What do you think you're up to? Come on! We need to get the maximum money in this pot! Why are you hesitating?" Al was really getting worked up. What he didn't realize…and I did not know at that point…was that Heather and Dorothy had conspired to deliberately make themselves look as suspicious as possible, trying to get Al executed at the next opportunity. They were quite effective! Dorothy finally added his chit to the pot.

The game proceeded, and the last two left standing were Heather and me. I drew an Ace, so was the winner. As I left, the three of them were preparing for a long, long night.

In spite of Anderson's promises, I really did not get to do anything spectacular. (Anderson was not noted for giving good things away; in fact, he had not done so yet!) What had actually been planned was for me to get a massage in a luxurious setting while the others were undergoing their deprivations back in Anderson's Fun House. I'm sure the camera would have switched back and forth, from me lying with a cold beer and a beautiful massage therapist working on me, to something like Heather in a room with a big snake. Ah, but Anderson had, as usual, delivered a promise he had no intention of keeping!

What actually happened was that one of the local helpers had gone out to secure a massage therapist for this endeavor, and wound up hiring the services of a…woman who used massage as an entry point, so to speak. Her forte was most definitely not massage. I suspect Luis, the Associate Producer on the scene, handled this. He grew up in Columbia, after all, and could not reliably be expected to be able to correctly identify a good Italian massage therapist! Actually, I would not put it past either Luis or Clay (the on scene Producer), to have done this deliberately just to see what the lucky person would have done when the massage strayed! They probably were rooting for one of the girls to win, just to see how confused an Italian woman of the night could get when one of them walked into the room. Not to mention the looks on Dorothy or Heather's face in that instance! Unfortunately Clay realized at some point before I got there that the girl might attempt to turn this show into one of the "X" rated variety, and called the event off. (Shoot, they could have at least *tried* to see if she could give a massage…) So, instead of a massage—which I would dearly have loved about then—I was

Reflections of The Mole

taken back the hotel. The only problem with this was that it was 1:30 AM when we left the villa, and almost 3:00 AM by the time I got to bed, only to be rousted out at 7:00 AM and taken back to see how the others were doing. And, I will say that as bad as my night had been, theirs had been far worse!

All three had to complete their tasks to add the $100,000 from the card game to the overall winnings of the ultimate winner of "The Mole II." Dorothy had to sit in a small cage for about half an hour while roaches were dropped more and more rapidly down on her. Moderately disgusting, but nothing she could not stand. Shoot, she lives in New York City and had probably eaten at the Taco Bell there featured on TV recently. Cockroaches were pet-like!

Heather had been placed in a small room with a large python, allowed to look somewhat askance at it for a moment, then the lights were turned off. She could hear the snake, and it was easy to imagine her fears about what might happen in the pitch darkness. However, she knew, as we all knew, that nothing *really* bad would happen. Regardless of rational thought—or perhaps *because* of rational thought!--she lasted only a couple of minutes before demanding to be let out, thus losing the game for all of them, no matter what Al did.

What Al did was to go into a room and be shown a bed with only bedsprings on it. No mattress. No box springs. Just springs. He was told that this was where he had to spend the night, and that *he could not leave the bed* if the money was to be won. (By the time of this explanation, of course, the money was already lost. If Anderson had been a nice man, he might have entered and told Al this, saving him from a tortuous, uncomfortable, and potentially embarrassing night. On the other hand, Anderson's persona in "The Mole" was not as a kindly stranger, but more like Tony Perkins in "Psycho.") Then, "Tiny Bubbles" started up. It played all night, loud, soft, backward and forward, in slow motion, speeded up; whatever variation could be done to a song was done to "Tiny Bubbles," which is not a very melodious song anyway.

Al actually lasted all night. In a scene certainly not aired, about 6:00 AM he began suffering severely from an overly-full bladder. He had not slept at all, and was just lying there, reviewing the orders given. Nothing had been said about bathroom breaks. He had to figure that if he got up to find a bathroom, of necessity leaving the bed, the money was lost. As I have noted before, Al was a player. He came to win, and wanted to win the maximum amount. A little thing like a full and painful bladder was not going to derail his plans. So, he finally just turned over on his side and prepared to initiate a relieving maneuver...so to speak...through the bare springs below him. This resulted in frantic action as Luis raced into the room, laughing. Al ceased his relieving action (with some difficulty, as you might imagine) and was allowed a potty break. Al is, or was, a *player*.

When I finally arrived back at Anderson's Funhouse, Al was in the upstairs room with both girls, who had slept on the floor in sleeping bags. I was not supposed to know anything about their night at this point. In fact, Clay had shown me brief videos of what each of them had done, and we had sat laughing at Al trying to sleep to Don Ho's crooning voice.

(An aside here. Months later, after all shows had been aired, Al was asked to be in a relative's wedding as one of the groomsmen. There was a live orchestra playing, and as Al started up the aisle, the orchestra quit playing the traditional song and struck up a lively rendition of..."Tiny Bubbles." Everyone seemed to enjoy it, Al said, except him. He said he had never heard of the song before that night, and developed no liking for it during his ordeal. Poor Don Ho.)

We then got to play a new game based on the night's events. I sat while each of the three came in one at a time and told me their version of what they had done during the night. I was supposed to pick out who was lying and who was telling the truth, and if unable to successfully identify them correctly, another $30,000 was to be added to the pot. If they had managed to win the $100,000, I would have correctly picked the liars out of the three. As it was, the Mole had to show some heart; the night had just been too tough…on Al. He deserved better! And, the pot was still far less than Season 1, which had 4 fewer players and was seen for four weeks less. So, I did not guess the liar, thus adding the money. Again, this worked out in Heather and Dorothy's favor. As it turned out, Heather had deliberately thrown her task in order to create more suspicion in Al's mind. Heather had shown a lot of grit, as a good Texas girl should, throughout the many preceding weeks, and Al rightly didn't really believe that she would be chased out of a room by a non-poisonous snake, even a big one. Shoot, we had seen Heather's fiancé greet her, and were aware that she could withstand a very, very tight clinch if she needed to. Then, by my adding more money to the pot when I had an excellent opportunity to correctly guess the liar and thus cost the pot money, more uncertainty had to be added to Al's mind about who the Mole really was.

That afternoon after some sleep we were taken out to some museum grounds and split up. Dorothy and Heather went one way, armed with a video camera, and Al and I another. We were to interview each other while videoing the interview. It was interesting. We were very used to cameras by this time, but the only times we spoke directly to cameras were in our formal interviews on execution day and at confession, after execution. We were used to really being frank in these interviews, revealing our strategy and who we suspected as the Mole, inasmuch as we knew none of the others would ever see any portion of the interviews until the show was aired. In my case, I had to carefully make up my suspicions, and had to work to keep my stories straight, inasmuch as the cameramen did not know who the Mole was, nor would the viewing public. That was probably the most true "acting" I had ever done. (My sincere apologies to all those wonderful actors out there for calling any of my efforts anything akin to theirs!) Almost everything I said in those interviews was for some effect, and was seldom the truth.

In this case, both Al and I found that speaking to the camera made us far more frank than we would have been if the camera had not been present. Obviously I still had to watch everything I said in order to not give myself away. It seemed clear to me that Al was really leaning toward Dorothy as the Mole. So, I leaned toward Heather. However, his reasoning was very sound in suspecting Dorothy; he was still upset that she had hesitated in the card game the night before. I supported him, though I think I definitely left him suspecting that I thought Heather might be the Mole. Confusion reigns! It was my kind of territory!

(An interesting sidelight here about cameras. We are all used to television, and by extension, cameras. A famous psychiatric institution has shown that for many patients receiving psychological counseling, person-to-person interactions with a psychiatrist are often far less effective than facing that same psychiatrist on a television screen. Tele-psychiatry is proving highly beneficial in some cases. Often we are far more comfortable interacting with a television...an object we see virtually all day, every day...than we are sitting face to face with a stranger in the same room with us. So, it is no wonder that the four of us found ourselves opening up more than we desired when faced with a camera, not another person's eyes. It's just...easier.)

Al received the dreaded red thumb print that night; he was clearly disgusted at that, and quite distressed. I think he split his answers between Dorothy and me. He really did not think I could be the Mole, but couldn't totally leave me out; the evidence amassed was just too much for that. On the other hand, by this time both Dorothy and Heather were pretty definite in their beliefs that I was their target. Poor Al; he played too hard for his own eventual good. If he had just managed to throw a game or two, deliberately, and had not been such a stickler for following the rules, he might have created doubt in our minds. As it was, no one had suspected him of being the Mole for a long, long time. Hard work and honesty are wonderful attributes to have, but won't win many reality games! I suppose, you might say, that that is why they are called…reality. (Not that I believe this. With the possible exception of politics, it still seems to me that Al's virtues…honesty, loyalty, and hard work…are the cornerstones to a successful and happy life. But in reality shows? Not a chance!)

What Was I Thinking?

Al

My strategy for the game, believe it or not, was to get by without having a coalition. I intended to win the game merely by asking the right questions of people, observing all the players moves and by paying attention to everything going on around me. After all, I had watched Mole 1 so I knew what to do, right? Well, obviously that didn't work out too well!

First of all, there is so much information to absorb that it's nearly impossible to keep your facts straight. Even when I wrote them in my journal I questioned their validity later on. Second, I fell victim to making friends with the other players, especially Bill! So a lot of what was done was forgiven as honest mistakes. (Yikes! What is ever honest in the Mole!)

Eventually, I felt I couldn't win this game on my own so I decided it was time for a coalition. So one night, the famous night that he and I were shown shirtless sharing a bed together, Darwin and I made an agreement to share info with one another. I asked him if he wanted to join forces and he readily agreed. His response was followed by a warm, manly embrace that only convicted felons would understand but that's another book...

This strategy did not work out well for me because the next day, while in Florence, I observed Bribs and Darwin sharing info the way we had agreed to do. This son of a b*&^h was already cheating on me! So I said the hell with that and although I never told him so, I decided at that moment that I was out of the coalition. Maybe that's why I out lasted him? Nobody else he paired up with stayed in the game long after being drawn into his venomous web.

I decided to stay with my original plan and as it turned out, my plan was fatally flawed because two eyes are never as good as four in this game. So because I had no clear read on who the Mole was, I was forced to gamble and I split my answers on my final quiz between Dorothy and Bill. Since Dorothy and Heather had already figured out the Mole was Bill, the end of my game was assured.

Unfortunately, I have received no fame, no vast wealth or notoriety from my participation in The Mole 2. Life continues as it was before the game. Granted, I had a fleeting moment of fame during its airing and shortly thereafter but I gained something more. I saw and did things I never dreamed I would do and I gained many new friends along the way. Friends with whom I will always share a special bond with because the Mole was a truly unique experience.
Except Andersen Cooper. He doesn't return my calls or e-mails anymore....
bastard....

XXII

Two Against One

Al's gone. Bribs, Darwin, Myra. All of the others, and all left indelible impressions behind. I don't know who might dare to handicap reality shows in trying to determine who might come out the winner; probably the same folks who try to predict which leaf is going to fall from a tree next. You might get it, but let's face it; it was a lucky guess! Just too many imponderables. Look at the beginnings of all reality shows; are you ever right in your predictions? One might think that this game, "The Mole," would be a little easier to peg as to the finalists—if one were delusional. After all, it is the "thinking man's (neutral gender noun, please) game." If it were only a game of intellect, and not one based on popularity, physical strength, or other perceived non-intellectual abilities, then it should be fairly easy to predict with some accuracy who *might* be standing at the end. The problem, though, is that *all* of the participants were selected in part for their intelligence. Not that we were in the genius range, but all had accomplished something, and the only non-college graduate, Al, was probably one of the brighter people in the field. So intelligence, which *should* be some harbinger of success, was almost a non-factor in this, generally. Luck certainly was a significant factor. Self-confidence should be a factor, you would think, except that the most confident person in the game was Darwin, and he was long gone. Analytical ability certainly seems like it should have a bearing, but the most analytical person in the group, Lisa, was one of the first gone; she just didn't have the time to develop her analysis. Analysis without lots of information is…guessing. The capability of paying attention to detail and retaining many little facts truly was a factor, and those who ignored those little details were very likely to depart quickly. However, the greatest detail maniac of the group, Patrick, left rather early in spite of the his capability of recording the smallest detail. Testmanship was certainly a key. We all know folks who can go into a test knowing little about a subject, yet consistently come out with far more right answers than they should be able to get. They know how to read the questions and pick up on the little clues that might indicate a correct answer. That ability was definitely a factor in this game. There were always a few questions on each test that everyone should be able to get, inasmuch as the answers could apply to a majority of players. You just could not afford to miss those answers.

More than intelligence, the ability to create doubt in other's minds about whether or not you might be the Mole was a factor in determining who reached the final three. And, as it turned out, the three people who sabotaged more games than anyone else—whether deliberately or accidentally—were the three left at this point.

So, all in all, regardless of my personal feelings about who it might have been most fun to play these last games with, I really believe that Heather and Dorothy played the game of deviousness best and managed to cast suspicion on themselves better than anyone else, and therefore most deserved to be two of the final three players. The only other person I think who might have replaced one of them was Elavia, and she had elected to bail out with a goodly sum of money. Al almost made it solely on playing every game as hard as he could, and sheer desire to be there in the end. His one major failing? He created no confusion in anyone's mind. Both Dorothy and Heather were able to totally rule him out in their considerations of which answer to click on in the quizzes, making their task a little simpler than his. Al did not have that luxury; he had to consider everyone, and therefore every answer. If he had been able to create conflict in everyone else's mind about whether or not he might be the Mole....?

Reflections of The Mole

Now that there were only three of us left, my life was really much less complex. There was no doubt in my mind that both Dorothy and Heather were...almost...100% convinced that I was the Mole. They had sworn to each other that neither was the Mole, and both were believers. While I certainly was not going to admit my molish shortcomings, I didn't have to consciously work at maintaining much of a subterfuge around them. I still had to play hard, and had to act like I was confident that I knew who the Mole was, of course. (Quite easy to do in my case.) The crew and Anderson still did not know who was who, and the viewing public might, or might not, know by the time the show aired. So, all I had to do was maintain...and have fun.

Because, somewhat ironically, regardless of how certain Dorothy and Heather were about my identity, they still did not know—*could* not know—for sure. I still had ample opportunity to mess with their minds, and I intended to do that to the max!

On the morning after Al's departure, we all knew our time in reality purgatory was almost done! We were really, really ready to go home, to not be in front of cameras constantly, to drink no more wine, to eat other foods, and to see our families. To be normal again. Here I was, a full grown Admiral (and perhaps even slightly *over*grown), playing kid's games! How sweet *that* was!

We left for another of several small villages an hour or so away from L'Aquila. There were so few of us that we got to ride in the new Audis reserved for the producers! Man, we were moving up! We were all in one of the two Audis, following a crew truck closely, driving down dirt roads like we were in a country race, trying to find a small country villa. *All* the vehicles were following each other closely; Italians do that. Everything is a Grand Prix preview, even when you are driving trucks loaded with equipment. The truck in front of us stopped suddenly, and we pulled up close behind it as Clay prepared to hop out and check out what was going on. You know those signs on the back of trucks that say, "If you can't see my mirrors, I can't see you!" Well, we couldn't see his mirrors, and the truth of that statement was borne out when he reversed and slammed backwards into our beautiful new Audi. We were really knocked around, and hopped out fearing the worse for our first ride in the luxury class. Nothing. I was amazed. The low hanging metal bar on the back of the truck had impacted directly on the license plate holder on the front of the car; I don't know what those things are made of, but I'll bet they use that holder as a lift point when they are preparing to pick the car up with a crane! No damage; no harm, no foul.

We finally arrived in a small village, and Anderson took the three of us for a walk. He turned to us.

"You three have been together now for almost 7 weeks. You probably know each other better than almost any strangers have *ever* known each other after that brief a time. It's time to let that knowledge make you money!"

He proceeded to give each of us 10 questions about the other two contestants. We took a few minutes coming up with the answers, and in my case, coming up with the exact opposite of what I thought the answers should be, in every case. No sense in going half way on this test! After several minutes we handed our answers back to Anderson, and with a grin he walked off to review them. Now, many of those questions are designed to create havoc and destroy friendships. I.e., "Which of the other two would be most likely to cheat on their significant other?" "Which would be less kind to little animals?" "Which would be more likely to pass a homeless person on the street and never give them a second thought?"

How do you answer questions like that? There is absolutely no way to do so without irritating someone severely, even with the most exhaustive of explanations as to why you chose a particular answer. Those questions were designed to test the best friendships, and certainly to provide some great fodder for severe consternation since we were more competitors than friends. I'm sure Anderson delighted in the answers and seeing how they caused severe angst among us. If that were his goal, he must have loved the answers I gave! Dorothy and Heather were beyond trying to fake anyone out; they wanted to add money to the pot, and answered accordingly; i.e., they used a logical approach to each answer, hoping the other two would see it the same way and we would all agree. In spite of both thinking I was the Mole, they still could not wrap their minds around the concept that I would deliberately give answers that were not logical. I don't know why not; they had done pretty good thus far. However, something in them just did not…*quite*…believe.

While the game was being set up based on those questions and answers, several of the crew, with Clay and the three of us went to a small coffee shop to sit and have breakfast. After breakfast Clay suggested that everyone go to the bathroom, inasmuch as the game might go on for a while. Sounded right, so we got up and got in line for the one facility. Clay hung back a little, politely letting Heather and Dorothy get in front of the line. He urged me to join them, and fell in place behind me. As I stood there I felt him poke me in the back. I held my hand slightly behind me, and in a very quick move felt a small piece of paper pressed into my palm. I casually put my hand in my pocket, depositing the paper therein.

Once in the bathroom I pulled the paper out and looked at it. There were all of Dorothy's and Heather's answers, which I quickly read over several times. Once I had a good idea of the answer each had put down to the 10 questions, I tore the paper up and flushed it, then exited the bathroom. "Too bad Italian bathrooms don't have reading materials in them; it would be great to get caught up on current events, even in Italian!" Heather and Dorothy agreed; it just so happened that I had suddenly become much more current than them, however.

Anderson came and picked us up, then took us into the middle of the village. There he explained the rules of the game.

"OK, kiddies. I have reviewed all your answers, and have picked out three questions of the 10 each of you answered. One at a time, each of you will be hidden inside one of the houses in this town, and the other two will try to predict which answer that person put down to three questions, in order. For each answer we will either turn right or left and proceed until I stop. If you are correct in predicting all three of the answers the absent person put down, we will wind up in front of a house, and when one of you knocks on the door of that house, the absent person will come out. In that case, you will add $10,000 to the pot. If you miss even one of the answers, however, we will have veered off in the wrong direction, and who knows what might lie behind the door you eventually knock on! What *won't* be there, however, will be more money for the pot. We will then let another person wait in a house, and the other two will try to predict his or her answers; we'll continue this until all three of you have had a chance to be found, with a possible $30,000 total being available to be added to the pot."

He smiled at us, expectantly. Did we have any questions? Well, yes. We didn't understand a thing he said! However, lack of understanding should never stand in the way of proceeding with the game, especially when my goal was to be flagrantly wrong on every count.

So, we started. It was fun. First Heather hid and Dorothy and I were tasked with predicting her answers. I let Dorothy answer first, and each time would take an opposing stance, but not too firmly. I tried to verbally explain to Dorothy the reasoning behind my thought processes for each answer, which proved to be a little difficult to do, because reason did not enter into my thinking. Luckily, Dorothy started out predicting one of Heather's answers that I knew to be wrong; I argued with her pretty vigorously, backing off only when she showed signs of wavering in her conviction. The rest of the answers were of no consequence; we were already off in the wrong direction. I argued just for confusion's sake. Needless to say, Heather was not in the house we wound up at after the third question. Once we found her, she gave her answers, whereupon I immediately pointed at Dorothy as being the cause of our moneyless state. In fact, it *had* been Dorothy. The result would have been the same regardless, however.

This was repeated with Dorothy in hiding, and this time I had to provide the wrong answer, inasmuch as Heather was correct with each one. However, even then I "tried" to switch back to the correct answer after Heather reluctantly conceded that I might be right. That way, I still managed to point the finger of guilt at her when Dorothy did not answer the door. A considerably weaker case, however, though Dorothy did not know that. Heather was just getting too tired to argue, and did not deny her apparent guilt.

Finally, I hid. Needless to say, they were totally wrong in predicting my answers. Once I was finally located, again with no money to be added, I had to give and justify my answers. With each carefully, and totally fallacious, explanation, Heather and Dorothy openly expressed disbelief at my answer. They just could not believe the gap between generations was *that* big! I would have thought they might have laughed and looked at each other, acknowledging tacitly to each other that I *must* be the Mole. No, they just looked irritated, forgetting, I suppose, the function of a Mole. A Mole is designed to screw with your mind and cost you money. They seemed to have overlooked that little fact.

When Anderson came to the last question, I knew I might be in for some grief. "Bill, which of these two, Dorothy or Heather, did you predict will be alone in five years?"

Heather spoke up. "That's obvious. I just got engaged 2 weeks ago, and Dorothy doesn't even date anyone. The answer has to be Dorothy!" She looked at me expectantly.

I replied, "Well, no, not really." Anderson's eyes got a little wider, and he backed up a step. "You see, statistically, more than 50% of all marriages will end in divorce within the first 3 years." Anderson rolled his eyes and backed off another step. Heather stared at me, stony faced, not seeming to catch the humor in the situation.

"Both you and your fiancé are very attractive, and he will be a young doctor in a residency. I figure the odds of Dorothy finding a boyfriend and sticking with him in 5 years are quite a bit better than your marriage surviving those five years. Statistically speaking, of course." I could see storm clouds gathering on Heather's face, and for the first time saw some semblance of alarm cross Anderson's. He stepped a little further back, just within hearing distance. Shoot, I was already dead, and making this stuff up as I went; might as well pull dirt in on myself. "And, Dorothy's Chinese. They are notoriously more faithful in their relationships than others." The dirt was getting high in my hole; I was trying to figure out how to pull the last little bit in on me, just to get out of the line of sight of Heather's eyes, which were truly pinning me back. I had *promised* myself when I started this show that I would carefully consider each answer I gave beforehand, and here I was blabbering. I was trying to think of something else I could say that might get one of the cameramen to swing a camera at my head; that's all I was missing.

"I can't *believe* you came to that conclusion just two weeks after I got engaged! I can't believe it!" Heather was almost inarticulate with rage. I suddenly decided to keep quiet. After all, I had been successful beyond my wildest expectations, and was wishing I had aimed a little lower, expectation-wise. Anderson was wisely maintaining silence, but I heard him mutter,

Reflections of The Mole

"Statistically?" He shook his head, envisioning a last game with only two players of sound and intact body.

Finally, the last game. We had moved to a beautiful small village at the base of a mountain. We were ready for this! Or, so we thought. I had no idea what the game was; Clay just told me to play it however I wanted to.

We ate lunch in a small café, and at the end of the meal Anderson walked in and handed us three "menus." We were to each pick a "dessert." Needless to say, there was nothing sweet about what we wound up with. We were then driven up a steep, winding, road to the top of a precipitous mountain, on the top of which perched another quaint little village. (It was an Italian village, lest you wonder.) The mountain sides plunged almost straight down to the valley below, maybe a mile from the top to the bottom. I don't know for sure how high the mountain was, but suspect it was 2500-3000 feet high. It was not one I would choose to climb for the pleasure of a picnic.

Anderson took us out to a viewpoint and collected our menus. Selecting Dorothy, he pointed down to a hayfield at the bottom of the mountain in which were several hundred of those large rolls of hay. (I used to buck hay for a living; I'm sure glad those days are long past! I would like to see the fellows they have to hire to buck *these* bales of hay.) He told her that there was a GPS receiver on the top of one of the hay rolls; all she had to do was find it, and it would direct her toward the final objective of the day. Heather had a somewhat similar task; however, she had to go off the back of the mountain to a lake, and there on a table would find her GPS receiver. My task was a little trickier. I was given a GPS receiver…momentarily…and told that 3 miles along the course of the arrow, *as the crow flies*, I would find a "leaning castle," and somewhere in that castle I would find my GPS receiver that would help me find our final objective of the evening. I sighted down the arrow as critically as possible, and determined that my objective would be a building across the valley and up on another ridge. Unfortunately, the needle tended to swing in a 30 degree arc, making my true destination somewhat ambiguous. Shoot, we were in the last game!

Our objective? A castle somewhere many miles away. The first one there would be able to add $100,000 to the pot...or not. Anderson actually handed the GPS back to me a second time and instructed me to take a careful reading, inasmuch as I would not have it with me. I read as well as one can...in the dark. And, I was there, indeed. As we prepared to depart, we were each given a backpack containing several bottles of water, some candy bars, and a headlight. (That last item was a bad sign!) It was about 4:00 PM, and darkness fell rather purposely about 7:30 PM or so. None of us wanted to use those lights.

Heather spoke up. "Can we catch a ride if we have a chance?" Hmm. Someone as attractive as Heather and Dorothy in Italy might get drivers to take them directly to our objective! I did not anticipate any possibility of enticing someone to give me a lift. What self-respecting Italian would stop to give a 58 year old, 240 pound man a ride? And, if someone were that confident, I probably would not want to ride with them! This could be a problem. For me.

Anderson answered Heather's question. "You can get a ride with someone if you are able; however, the only stipulation is that the car must be able to carry your cameramen along also. And, nothing illegal. You can't steal a car. Or a horse." He grinned at us, an always frightening event. Anderson seldom grinned unless he was thinking of something evil to do to us. And he grinned a lot.

We departed on our jaunts, each going separate ways. I am an avid hiker (recently completing the 2174 mile Appalachian Trail, I am quite tickled to say!), and felt that I knew my pace well enough to be able to fairly accurately predict when I had hiked 3 miles, which should in theory be in the vicinity of the

Reflections of The Mole

leaning castle and my GPS receiver. Heather and Dorothy left down the same mountain road we had come up. However, it did not go nearly as straight toward my object building on the opposite ridge as I desired, so I eyeballed the mountain side carefully. It was mostly loose rock, with patches of trees and sticker thickets scattered across it. I looked across at my building and headed straight for it. None of this pussyfooting around! I loped in 15-20 foot long bounds down the rocky slope, sliding several feet every time my feet hit, followed closely by two cameramen carrying large cameras, shooting as they went. I was glad I wasn't those camera folk.

 I ran down that mountain. About half way down I heard some crashing and banging behind me, and glanced over my shoulder. One of the camera men had fallen, tumbling head over heels, but immediately was up and running again, covered with bleeding scratches. Tough fellows! We were not supposed to notice our cameramen, and certainly not acknowledge them, but we all got to know and admire them. They earned their money. Near the bottom of the mountain I entered a large thicket of huge stickery vines wrapped around the biggest stinging nettles I had ever seen! While I had vowed to not turn aside until I reached my designated building, I quickly chose to break that vow. Shoot, I really didn't mean it, anyway. As the stickers started grabbing my clothes, pulling me toward those killer stinging nettles, I abruptly turned around and almost ran over the two cameramen. They laughed and turned, following me, probably quite happy that I had applied a little discretion to my headlong rumble down the slope.

 I was then on the valley floor, looking over at the hay field to see if my shortcut had enabled me to beat Dorothy down. Ah, she wasn't tall enough to be seen, anyway. Besides that, if her earlier physical stamina was repeated here today, she was dry heaving somewhere on the mountain road at the moment. Unfortunately, she might also already be in a car, sipping a cold beer as she directed her handsome young Italian friend toward the distant castle. Nothing I could do about that; all I was capable of was doing the best I could, and I really, really wanted to win this final game, just to throw another twist into the viewer's minds. In fact, this was the first game I was playing with the viewers in mind; I just wanted to confuse them a little.

I crossed the valley floor and went straight up the steep ridge on the opposite side. Little kids came out of houses along the way and watched this curious parade with wide eyes. I probably gave some of them nightmares for a long while afterwards. (In Italian: "Iffa you don be good and do your chores, a fat white-haired old man will come up out of the valley and eat you!") Reverberations through the years. That's how stories about the *Abdominal* Snowman got started. I finally reached my objective house and looked at my watch. An hour had passed, and I knew that I had been averaging about 20 minute miles. My leaning castle had to be near!

However, it certainly wasn't all that apparent. Could it be a tiny little castle hidden behind something? Maybe "castle" was a loose usage of the term; maybe this was an outhouse. They contain thrones, after all. I walked up and down all the side streets near my target building, but to no avail. Nothing looked like a castle, and every building I looked over appeared distressingly upright. Not a sag any where. I saw a rather large building that had burned out, with definite leaning walls. In I went. Nothing but dirt and more bramble bushes covered with stickers. My cameramen wisely stayed up on the street, filming with their long distance lenses.

Several people had come out to watch the fun. They had no idea what we were doing, and shouted several phrases I intuitively interpreted. "Hey, Crazy! Whatchu doin? Stay out of the old buildings, stupid person! We have trouble enough keeping our kids out of there, and here you come upsetting everything!" I'm not sure this is an exact rendition of what they were saying, but bet I'm close. I saw a man and (presumably) his wife in a back yard and practiced my few Italian words. "Donde esta una castilla declinato?" (Where is a leaning castle?)

"Castilla declinato? Declinato?" The fellow looked at me doubtfully. Then, he said in halting English, "Leaning castle?"

"That's it! A leaning castle! Do you know where one is?" I had almost outstripped his English. He turned to his wife and three little girls, all about 10 or 11, and discussed the issue with them. I guess. He might have been asking them if they wanted ice cream with dinner. Regardless, he finally turned back to me and indicated that I should head down the road toward the main part of town with the three girls as guides. Finally! Some help! I had been in that town for almost an hour, and was getting desperate! Dorothy and Heather had undoubtedly caught rides, had dinner in a fine restaurant, been to the castle and collected their money, and were en route back to L'Aquila!

The little girls ran on ahead as I hurried to keep up with them, with me glancing occasionally at my cameramen. I suspected strongly that the cameramen knew where we were supposed to be going. I was checking to see if they were going to just stop in some intersection and await my inevitable return. Nope, they stuck right with me. They were game. Maybe this was the right way!

About a mile down the road we came to the city municipal building, a large white building with decidedly straight walls. The little girls proudly gestured toward it. I walked around it, dejected. It was a large building, and I went around the entire thing, trying all the doors. No luck. It was most definitely not a leaning castle. Perhaps the man who directed me there didn't like the politics practiced in the building, and interpreted my "castilla declinato" as a euphemism for a building full of crooked politicians. Whatever! With the little girls in the lead, I headed back up the road to the point at which I had emerged from the valley, cameramen gamely following behind. Man, if I had been one of those cameramen, I might have been tempted to break a shoelace or something and just sit down and await my return! Nope. They were true professionals, and were not about to let my stupidity affect their demeanor. Maybe my interpretations of what the folks who had shouted at me were right.

I looked back along the way I had come almost 2 hours before, contemplating retracing my steps to see if I might find some tiny, hidden, leaning castle nestled down among some of the trees in the distance. I *knew* I had covered about 3 miles.

Suddenly someone yelled at me. I *guess* they were yelling at me. I looked over at the man who had directed me on my futile hour-long detour, and he was standing at a car window chatting with another fellow, beckoning me over. I approached the window, and was greeted in good English by the gentlemen inside the car. (I really didn't know if he was a gentlemen or not, but anyone with a car that had 3 empty seats was a gentleman to me at that point.) I asked him about a leaning castle. He said there was one about half a mile up on the mountainside above the village he lived in. In response to my further inquiry, he said we were 10 or 11 kilometers from his village. Damn! That had to be wrong; it was too far. What now?

As I turned away from the car, a sudden sobering thought struck me, and, I mean, *struck* me. Right between the eyes. I remembered Anderson's words, "three miles in that direction *as the crow flies!*" What an idiot! I had walked 3 miles or so, true. Straight down and straight up, with a mile or so flat in the middle. I eyed the darkening mountaintop back across the valley. As the crow flies, I'll bet it wasn't 2 miles away.

I turned back to the fellow in the car. "Is your village just a short way across these mountains in front of us? Is the reason you say 10 or 11 kilometers because the road winds about a lot?"

Reflections of The Mole

Yes, all that was true. I hit my forehead with my open palm in exasperation. By this time I should have had a flat spot there.

So, both cameramen and I hopped in and he took us for a winding ride across the mountains. When we got to his house, I could barely see the castle on the side of the mountain above us, and, yes, it was definitely leaning! That was my castle. "As the crow flies." A catchy phrase…if you can remember it! The kind gentlemen tried to get us to come in and drink a bottle of wine with him; however, after a hasty thanks, we left on a run up the mountain. It was almost dark and I didn't want to have to search the grounds for a cigarette-package sized GPS with only my headlight. We got there and immediately I spied the GPS unit. Picking it up, I sighted along the unwavering arrow, and could see a brightly lit building on a hilltop way off in the distance. The mileage indicator on the unit indicated 3.6 miles, but that building looked a lot further away than that. However, nothing was lit up in between. I headed off, by this time wearing my head lamp.

As we passed through the village again, there stood Anderson beside the road, eating an apple. He was always eating something. How did he stay so skinny? He greeted me.

"Bill, how are things?"

What could I say? Things suck? I'm an idiot? Crows fly crookedly in Oklahoma?

"Greetings, Anderson. Have Heather and Dorothy long since finished and gone to dinner?" By this time I was hoping they might have done just that. Surely they wouldn't leave me out here stumbling around in the dark! Anderson just grinned and walked off down the street. I picked up my pace.

I tried one time to get one of the townsmen to give me a ride, and pointed to the lit up building in the distance. Nah, he wasn't interested. It was dinner and a little vino time. At least for him! So, I decided to just get there.

Initially I was hopeful that there might be a road headed directly toward the distant building, but when I came to a highway, it ran off at 90 degrees from where I was going. I could flip a coin and turn either right or left, hoping to eventually find a road headed in the right direction. However, I was just as likely to not find such a road. So, I turned to my rather sweaty, and probably tired, cameramen, and apologized.

"Fellows, I'm sorry. I'm headed to that hilltop, and I'm going to go directly there, road or no road."

They looked at each other. They had obviously expected no less.

Away we went, crossing fields of grass (Are there snakes in Italy? I still don't know.), climbing fences, jumping almost invisible ditches, and rousing the ire of some mean-sounding country dogs. There was no moon out, and my headlight threw a pitiful beam, just sufficient to make out the ditch I had just fallen into. When we were suddenly surrounded by 4 or 5 violently barking dogs, sounding for all the world like we were their prime menu item after a long fast, one of the cameramen became nervous. We closed ranks, and I don't think any filming was being done at that moment. "Shouldn't we, maybe, retreat and go around?"

I answered with assurance. "Don't worry! They are just announcing their presence and showing us they don't like us here." Well, duh. The two cameramen seemed unimpressed by my doggy logic. "Seriously, guys. If they stop barking and get real silent, but you can hear their little doggy paws scrabbling in the grass, run like hell!" A somewhat useless recommendation, inasmuch as they had already come to that conclusion themselves. Soon, however, we left the dogs behind.

And came to a bar! We emerged from a field onto a dirt road, and there off to the side of the road was a little bar with an outside patio crowded with families laughing and drinking. I stopped and stared. Man, I was thirsty. I had water, but other than bathing, try never to actually consume any. I know it's recommended, but as long as there's good beer, why torture yourself? I paused a long minute and felt the lira in my pocket. I probably had…oh, enough to buy each of us 3 or 4 pitchers of good beer. And a hamburger. The temptation was just overwhelming. The cameramen had stopped just behind me, and the looks on their faces was just as revealing as the one on mine. All I would have to do was say, "I'll buy," and we would be seated comfortably, kids bouncing on our knees, sipping. After a long sigh, I turned away, almost losing my cameramen. They were convinced, so they told me later, that we were going to stop for a while. The only thing that prevented me from doing that was the thought that Heather and Dorothy just might not have gotten a ride. Even if they found their GPS units immediately, it was still a hard 6 or 7 miles or so from where they found them to the castle. And, if they had been as dumb as I had been, they might have covered 10 miles or more. If they hadn't managed to get a ride, I could still be in the lead, and would forever kick myself if I stopped for 30 minutes and just barely got beat. So, on we went.

The rest of the journey was sort of anti-climatic. There was a road leaving from the bar, passing by the bottom of the small mountain I was heading for. I hurried up the road, and watched the GPS as it counted down to 0.4 miles…then started rising again. At 0.46 miles I stopped. I was definitely headed away from the castle, and while there might be a road a short distance ahead that turned directly to it, it could well be on the other side of the hill. With another apology to the cameramen, I pointed up at the castle, which was barely visible through the trees (and brambles) on the mountainside.

"Fellows, I'm headed there."

With that, I turned up the mountain, immediately encountering a large ditch. I shouted a warning to the cameramen and jumped over, instantly entering a dense stand of trees and stickers. I ignored them and pushed through. By this time I was within 300 yards or so of the top of the mountain, and wasn't going to attempt to find an alternate route. I felt my shirt tear, and could feel what I thought was sweat dripping off my hands. I pushed harder. Glancing around, I realized that my cameramen were far behind me, and in fact seemed to have turned aside. Undoubtedly they knew where a road was, and just could not push through the undergrowth I was in with their cameras.

As I exited the trees on the top of the hill I was met by several new camera crews who gathered around me, cameras on and lights lighting the way; I later found out that my camera crew had called them on their cell phones and had given them a heads up. When I entered the main gates of the castle, the producers and crew were gathered in the courtyard. It was 10:30 PM, 6 ½ hours since I had left the mountain top.

Scott Stone, the senior Producer, absent since the first week of shooting, had come back to Italy for the last few days with his production partner, David Stanley. Scott came hurrying over, smiling, but as he approached me he suddenly lost his smile.

"What happened to you? SOMEONE GET THE MEDIC! HE'S BLEEDING!"

I looked down. Blood was dripping off both hands in a steady stream. Man, it looked neat! My forearms were covered with blood! Scott was horrified.

"Scott, Scott, I'm OK. This is really mostly sweat. I just have a bunch of superficial scratches on my arms, and the blood and sweat together look far worse than it really is."

He ignored me. The medic came running and started wiping my arm down. Suddenly Scott reached out and stopped him.

Reflections of The Mole

"He's right! He's not hurt! Leave that blood there; it looks great!" I had already said that; maybe *I* could be a producer!

He asked me if there was anything I wanted. I looked around.

"Where are the girls? Have they finished?"

"Nah, don't worry. They are a long ways from here. You win."

Well, in *that* case! "Does anyone have a cold beer?"

Scott yelled at one of the crew, who brought me over a beer. It wasn't cold, but it was wet, and if any beer drinker turns down hot beer, make 'em drink water. I took a long pull, then handed the bottle to Scott as I picked up my backpack, dropped while the medic was trying to do CPR on me.

Scott yelled, "This beer is hot! Someone run down to that little bar and get some cold beer!" Now, *this* was my kind of producer! Undoubtedly Clay and Luis, the on site producers, managed to prevent that hot bottle of beer from going to waste. They were frugal.

I headed on into the castle, winding through a candle-lit room and up candle-lit stairs, finally opening a door and seeing a smiling Anderson standing across the room. (I expect one reason Anderson was smiling was that he had to be as thankful as we were that the filming was almost over. It had been a long, long siege for all of us, and Anderson had had to be somewhat mean throughout. On the other hand…maybe he enjoyed it!)

I crossed the room and stuck out my bloody hand, with Anderson grabbing it and shaking hands with me, then looking down at his own bloody appendage. He casually wiped his hand on his jeans, never losing his grin. (I felt bad about this, and apologized to him the next day. With blood being a sign of stigma of sorts in today's society, deliberately getting your blood on someone else is downright rude. What I thought was funny when I stuck my hand out became…a crass move a moment later.

Anderson just laughed and told me it was no big deal. He is a gentleman.)

I was unaware that Anderson had inadvertently discovered that day that I was the Mole. He told us months later that he was leaning heavily toward Dorothy as the Mole, but was driven around the countryside that day so he could tweak each of us in turn, while eating his apple. When he hopped back in the car after he had seen me leaving the leaning castle, the two producers in the front seat were talking about my actions as the Mole. They suddenly turned and realized Anderson was in the car. Nothing to be done about it, but Anderson carried on like the exceptional professional he is. So, as I stood in front of him that night, he knew at long last that I was the Mole.

Anderson looked steadily at me. "Bill, congratulations! You are the first in, and can add $100,000 to the pot. However, I am going to make you an offer." He handed me a leather-bound dossier. "In this dossier is information on the Mole which might be critical to have when taking the final quiz. If you will give up the $100,000, not adding it to the pot, the dossier is yours to keep."

I looked at the dossier, turning it over in my hands a couple of times, contemplating. As the Mole, the only logical move would be to take the dossier and forfeit the money. As the Mole wanting to throw one final wrinkle into the game, however, and for one last time attempt to mislead the watching public, I had other plans. I handed the dossier back to Anderson.

"Got a cold beer?"

As I turned to leave, Anderson stopped me. "So you think you know who the Mole is?"

"Anderson, I've got a pretty good idea!" I left the room. I figured that adding that money to the pot might screw with the minds of some folks who thought I might be the Mole. One last effort to lead astray. And, frankly, I had worked my butt off. I had no desire to have done all of that, tearing my favorite OSU shirt, only to receive some worthless information on me that I didn't need. And, finally, I thought both Dorothy and Heather had played superb games, and deserved the money. So, I did my final molish act.

I went back outside where there were several liters of cold, cold beer waiting. Dorothy came into the courtyard shortly after I emerged from the castle. She had actually made good time, had never gotten lost, and was just ½ mile from the castle when I finished. One of the crew had gone out and picked her up. Amazing stamina for someone who had been unable to walk any distance at all in town without getting nauseated! Something to play up in my sessions in front of the cameras the next day. We sat for a while, and Heather...a totally exhausted Heather...slowly walked toward us. She was wearing one of the producer's $300 Goretex jackets against the chill of the evening, and could barely move.

"Heather, what's wrong?" Well, almost everything!

She described her day. She had gone down the mountain, all the long, long way to the lake at the bottom. She had found her GPS, and picked it up, sighting along the needle. It pointed straight back up the mountain! So, she climbed all the way back to the top, never stopping to think about the mileage indicated on the unit. If she had considered that, she would have realized that the needle was pointing *in the direction* she was supposed to go...about 7 miles. Like me, however, she didn't think enough, so wound up making her laborious way back to the top of the mountain, only to realize that the castle was still about as far away as it had been before...back down the mountain and across a bunch of others. Very discouraged, she once again headed down the mountain, deciding to catch a ride. And, she did catch rides. Several of them. All in the wrong direction. About dark she gave up and started walking along the indicated course of the GPS unit, and at that time was just as far away from the castle as she had been at 4:00 PM!

Exhausted physically and emotionally, keeping her left hand clinched to prevent possible loss of her engagement ring, she fought through almost impenetrable trees and vines along her course. She was crying, and finally sat down in despair, begging the cameramen to put their cameras down. How could they? This was drama!

As she sat there, crying, there was a loud snort and snarl in the bushes immediately adjacent to the clearing they were in. Cameras slung aside, as well as Heather's backpack, all three took off running. They finally called on their cell phone and were picked up, 4.7 miles away from the castle, at about 11:00 PM. She had had a bad day. And, it was to get a little worse.

As Heather related her tale to us, we were sitting on a wall inside the castle. Candles were burning behind us and off to the sides. Two cameramen were recording our conversation, though I would have thought they would have had enough by now. Heather let out a large sigh and leaned back, stretching her back.

"You're on fire, you're on fire!" The cameramen were shouting as they dropped their cameras and rushed toward us. Heather had leaned back into a candle, and Clay's nice new Goretex jacket was rapidly melting away. It repels rain, not fire. Dorothy and I grabbed each side of it and stripped in off of her. She was not burned at all, and stared stoically as the jacket melted into a puddle of yellow Goretex. She just shook her head. It's really too bad the cameramen went to her rescue; if they could have kept the cameras running, it would have been the perfect ending to one of the more memorable days of Heather's life! Well, actually, it was anyway; except that no one but us got to see it!

We were through. A long ride back to the hotel, sleeping late, and finally a long ride the next afternoon back to the same mountain top village we had departed from the day before. Very little was said. We left the van and all went into the village, where we had dinner with Anderson out on a beautiful view point. As a special last day treat dinner was a large platter of Big Macs; about 10 per person, I believe. Unfortunately, because of the long lead time in having to set up, the hamburgers had been there for an hour or two, and were cold. Not cool. Cold. That was OK; we ate anyway. Had they been hot we might have managed to finish the platter. Even Anderson seemed to enjoy them; of course, Anderson seemed to enjoy all food! He never stops eating.

Then we took our quiz, stationed at computers at some distance from each other atop the mountain, sited in very picturesque surroundings. The wind was blowing, torches lit, cameramen scattered about, and it grew dark as we finally sat down to the task. Due to the impending darkness we were afraid we might have to finish the next day, and we were ready to go home! Thank goodness for camera optics, however. We could barely see each other, but when viewed many months later, we all looked like we were in overcast, but very visible, daylight. We weren't.

The next day we were taken to the airport, where we were supposed to leave separately. We did, but in going through the lines I managed to see and talk with Al and Bribs. While they were still ticked at not making the finals, they seemed well rested and relatively pasta-free.

It was nice to arrive in New York City. I called my wife, who was quite excited to hear from me after 7 weeks. I called my Mother, daughters, and sisters, telling them of imaginary adventures in China. They were envious and all wanted to know if I had brought them anything. I told them all I had purchased some Chinese pasta. They didn't catch the joke. I flew into Denver, where I was to change planes. The Denver airport has great Mexican food, and I headed immediately into one of the restaurants for a burrito and a Dos Equis. Beside me I suddenly recognized another reality show contestant, Nick, a lawyer from

Seattle who had been on one of the first "Survivors." What a coincidence! We chatted a little, and he told me that other than getting a modeling contract in New York City, he had not enjoyed his stint on "Survivor," and would not do it again. He was distant; after all, while I had seen him for several weeks on television, he had never seen me. I knew him, but he didn't have the foggiest idea who I was, and didn't care. I was dying to tell him I had just completed filming "The Mole II," but the threat of a $10,000,000 penalty was sufficient for me to keep my mouth closed. I wonder if he watched the show, and if so, did he realize we had chatted? And, I started to realize that this was going to be happening to me. Strangers coming up to me, knowing me, wanting to talk, and my not having any idea who they were. I determined that if that did occur, I would treat them like any other old friend, and act accordingly. I was to wait a long, long time before I had a chance to find out how this experience would be, however.

XXIII

The Finale...sort of

Gee, that should do it. We've taken the final quiz and all returned home to our lives, attempting to explain our absence to anyone who might be interested, and to some who weren't.

We were not allowed, still, to tell anyone what we had been doing. Only when ABC decided to release a press announcement about the upcoming season of "The Mole II" were we allowed to even admit that we had been on the show. And that was all. Not where it took place, how anyone did, no details. All this under a threat of a major fine, of course, but more importantly, I think we all enjoyed making this so much that we certainly were not prone to tell anyone the results. Besides that, none of us really knew the results, so could not tell anyway.

We were under strict orders to not communicate with each other, again because of the fear that we might give something away inadvertently. Probably an apt fear. So, we didn't communicate... for a while.

Immediately after arriving home, I kissed my wife, walked over to my desk, and pulled her passport out and handed it to her. She smiled. I still don't know if it was really lost! However, I feel...almost certain...that she would have wanted to see me after so much time! Absolutely almost certain. After kissing her, I pondered a moment.

"Shirley, do you want to know anything about the show?"

"No, I want to watch it and be surprised like everyone else!"

I paused. How to do this? "Well, let me rephrase. If I had, say, a *special role* in the show, would you want to be aware of it?"

Shirley's eyes suddenly teared up as she saw a million dollars slipping into the dark night. She laughed.

"Yes, William, I suppose if you had a *special role* I should be aware of it. It would be more fun for me to know and share it with you as we watch the show." She knew suddenly, of course. With my noted eye for lack of detail, she had been convinced that I wouldn't last over a couple of weeks initially. There had to be an explanation, and she had just realized what it was.

"OK. I was the Mole. I have to do some work with the producers to aid their editing, and I don't think I could do it without alerting you to my role as I did so. So, now you know."

Shirley went back to her desk and starting scratching out ways one might spend a million dollars, sighing softly and smiling. (The truth was that she had never thought I had a chance at winning, anyway. However....)

I excused myself and sat down at my computer, where I proceeded to write up in great detail everything I did to sabotage and mess with people's minds during the preceding 7 weeks. Once that was done (24 pages of single-spaced sabotage), I fired it off to the producers so they could have it when they edited the show.

Think about this. We all had mikes on about 18 hours a day. We all had cameras on us 24 hours a day! Do the math. It works out that the producers had about 800 hours of material to screen for each two shows of 42 minutes each. Man, what an opportunity! They could make us look like...most anything. Good or bad, smart or dumb. Whatever. The power of the editor!

Finally, in mid-August ABC contacted us and told us we could start telling folks that, yes, we had lied with great vigor to all those we loved, as well as those we didn't. That's starting off on the right foot, I must say! ABC was getting ready to start advertising the show.

Reflections of The Mole

I called my daughters and parents to tell them. Few were really surprised; my sisters, especially, have lost the capability of being surprised by any actions I might be involved in. They just shrug, say "So what?" And go on with their lives. They don't believe most of it anyway.

I got my oldest daughter, Valerie, and granddaughter, Sasha, on the phone.

"Girls, you know that trip to China I went on?"

"Yeah, so what?"

"Well, I lied."

"You lied!? Why would you lie? That's not nice."

"Well, you know that show, "The Mole?"

At that point Sasha dropped the phone and started running around her house, screaming. I never did get to talk with her again that day. She did know "The Mole." (Well, come to think of it, she *did* know him.)

Everything went OK for a while. It was fun, and somewhat odd, to see my face come up on advertisements for the show on ABC. At this point we were all still in the dark as to who had won won and (other than me) who the Mole was. A few neighbors saw the bits as well, but not too much was made about them. The local paper seemed unaware; in fact, there did not seem to be any awareness in the print media. I finally went to the local paper and took the press release from ABC, which resulted in a tiny blurb in the paper. Gee, this was looking like a promising beginning!

The first season of "The Mole" had resulted in good ratings in the "critical" age group of 18-34. This season, ABC had decided to have the show at 8:00 PM on…Friday nights. Now, where do you think all those 18-34 year olds are on Friday nights? Well, I honestly don't know, either, but I suspect most of them are not at home glued to their television sets! We had all tried to point this out to Scott Stone when we met with him, and while acknowledging the truth of our statements, also noted that he had no control over when ABC decided to air their scheduled shows. We just had to live with it. What's new?

Finally, one Friday in September, 2001, our show aired. Few people were aware of it. The old Mole message boards were still asking when the show might be coming on? Man, somewhere here there was a major lack of communication! Things were not looking good. Even our families were unaware that we were rapidly becoming celebrities!

Then came 9/11/2001. More reality than anyone wanted to be exposed to. Shoot, I didn't want to watch our show, or any show. So, after three weeks of absentee watchers, we were cancelled for the indefinite future. The publicity agent for ABC called all of us and told us that, yes, the heavies at ABC did indeed truly, *truly* think our show was the greatest thing to light up the networks in many a season, but....maybe next year. Maybe never. However, we were all told to adhere to the contract we had signed and never, never reveal anything. Only in our wills, assuming we didn't die until well into the next decade. And, never talk to each other. Never. Under any circumstances. *We will be listening....*

There had been plans for us all to fly to Los Angeles in October to film the finale, and after some discussion the producers told us to come on in. The tickets were non-refundable, anyway. We did so, spending only 2 days to film that last 42 minutes of reality.

It was interesting that we were still subjected to the same level of secrecy that we had been subjected to when we first went to LA when we were striving to get on the show. We were blindfolded at the airport, where we had arrived separately. We were taken to a very nice hotel in Hollywood and told not to leave our rooms, under penalty of...what? Our show might be cancelled? We might be still kicked off the show? What could the penalty be? In our rooms were videos of the entire season, with the exception of the finale we were preparing to film. So, each of us settled down and started watching hour after hour after hour of the show. For most of the players, almost everything was new; they only knew what had happened up until the time they had been executed. I could hear Lisa laughing on one side and Myra on the other. I went to my patio doors and stepped outside, spying Myra and Bribs, waving. Someone on the crew saw us and asked us to please go back inside.

It was fascinating to all of us, I think, to see how they had edited us. What I found astonishing (which should not be interpreted as a vote of no confidence in the producers' editing skills), was that they really caught the essence of who we were...or at least who we projected we were. As I have noted before, many of the reality show contestants from all the networks get together several times a year for charity events, and I have come to know some of them pretty well. I have found that they are basically exactly as shown on their shows as well. Shoot, I'm getting more and more impressed with producers and editors! Michael Moore lulled me into complacency regarding their abilities! They *do* have talent and skill.

By the next day we had all watched all the episodes, and were ready for the big finale. Again, blindfolds and isolation. Finally, blindfolds off, and I found myself with Heather and Dorothy, which was the mix we had ended with several months before in Italy. Clay explained that we were to be placed behind three doors, and eventually we would hear Anderson talking with the other players. Once Anderson announced that the winner would be revealed, he would pass a key to each of us. We were to try our keys in the doors, and the key that worked would reveal the winner. Up to that point, none of the three of us knew who had won. Finding out would be a shock to the loser, I expect. Shoot, I was eager to try my key, and I *knew* it wouldn't fit! Maybe, just maybe, they had added a new twist to the show, one where the Mole got all the money! Wouldn't that be a surprise?

The Mole being the winner *and* the Mole? I like it! (Of course, I still put out cookies and milk for Santa at Christmas...)

All the players were polled by Anderson. Several picked Dorothy as the winner, others Heather, and Al, my friend, picked me. The keys were passed, the doors jiggled, and finally, out walked Dorothy to applause. I had almost broken my key off in my lock; heck, why can't they have a major surprise in some of the shows? Like me winning?

An interesting note on the final quiz. It was 20 questions instead of 10. Remember that Dorothy had thought Heather was probably the Mole instead of me until Heather convinced her otherwise. On that final quiz Dorothy scored only one more correct answer than Heather. Heather was that close. The only answer that Heather missed that Dorothy got correct? What was the number on the house in which I was waiting in that next to last game? This was a game of details, and of luck, and of confidence.

Dorothy stood for a few minutes while Anderson talked with her, then told folks it was time to find out who the Mole was. Only three (Rob, Bob, and Bribs) had picked me in the polling of a few minutes before. Again, the keys were passed, the middle door opened...ever so slowly. With a melodramatic creak. (Or perhaps that was my knees; I had been sitting in that little room for quite a while.) Finally, I stepped out, to general astonishment from the other players. (I had managed to dry my tears quickly when I found out that I was not the winner.) As I watched and listened to the others clap and express many thoughts, I saw Bribs turn to Darwin and indicate that Darwin was a dead man as soon as Bribs could see to it!

Finally, belatedly, Anderson had us let Heather out. Tears were still flowing; she had just realized only a couple of minutes before that she had not won the $636,000 dollars, and was also realizing that only if she had managed to keep her cool and not take Dorothy into her confidence...that money might have been hers.

What Was Heather Thinking?

When I first signed up for The Mole, I had NO idea how mentally, emotionally, and physically grueling it would be. I thought - how fun, I'll travel the world and possibly win some money - ha! While it was amazing fun, it was intense. I had no idea (and most viewers don't realize this) that all players would be cut off from the world - no communication with your family and friends, no TV, no magazines, no clocks in the rooms, no music - just your thoughts for six weeks. And there were really only a few hours out of the day we were filming - the rest of the time it was seclusion in hotel rooms. Talk about pressure!

I thought I had it nailed (as we all did apparently) right away - Elavia was The Mole - hands down! I was smart enough to narrow it down to a few backups at least and my list of suspects were:

1. Elavia
2. Dorothy
3. Bill

With the elimination of Elavia, and Katie's execution, I knew for sure it was Bill. Little did I know I was the only one remaining who had it figured it out. I was so convinced that everyone left knew it was Bill and that I needed help to ultimately win the game - thus, I confided in Dorothy and asked to work together.

Boy does that decision haunt me! If I had only had the confidence in myself to move forward on my own, I could be a whole lot richer.

As is with life, I suppose! In fact, that is the biggest lesson I took from The Mole. Believe in myself, trust in myself, and don't doubt my intuition in situations. I really surprised myself with how well I did, and how well I performed.

The Mole was one of the most amazing experiences of my life and I would do it again, and again! Of course, it would have been nice to win - but for whatever reason, that wasn't meant for me. And I'm ok with that!

I still keep in touch with just about all the players and they all hold a very special place in my heart. I truly think we will stay in touch forever.

What Was Dorothy Thinking?

Coming into the game, I thought I would employ a multitude of strategies. First and foremost: behave suspiciously. I thought I'd try to throw a few games on purpose and appear slightly evasive amidst the questioning that would happen throughout the game. Additionally, I knew I wanted to identify one or more other players with whom I could trade information -- whether or not as formal coalition partners. The game would be too big to try to take note of with just one set of eyes.

As it turned out, my natural klutziness (and non-athleticism that would become a running joke) made it unnecessary to purposely sabotage many games. A few chance happenings made a few other players suspect I may have an inside track with the producers -- unwittingly claiming a second slice of blueberry cake resulted in a chance for an exemption, solving a puzzle at the last second during the brain teaser game.

The quizzes I decided to tackle as quickly as possible, spreading my answers out to cover a few suspects. Based on probability, I thought that through the early rounds of the game, it was very likely that many players would end up with the same number of correct answers, so a quick finish could be helpful. I tried to link executed players with who I thought they suspected in order to make my own deductions; however, it was difficult to tell who suspected what and when!

I wanted to try to keep a close hand as far as my suspect list and not let on too much of what I was thinking to other players.

The first round I thought Bob was suspicious -- seemingly cavalier about finding out information about other players (was he just laid back or was he the mole?). Of course, there was the time he appeared at dinner with flames on his sleeve following the Burn Your Bags game. My suspect list was all over the place during a greater part of the game. During my brief coalition with

Bill McDaniel, MD

Lisa, we'd discussed Bill as the obvious choice as the Mole and therefore dismissed him immediately! As the game progressed, I suspected Bribs at times and Heather became a focus. I had ruled her out during the first half off the game, after we'd roomed together in Switzerland, but then ruled her back in later on and became a prime suspect.

I constantly questioned myself and others through out the game; in the end, this allowed me to be flexible and switch suspects quickly and focus on Bill, as Heather removed herself from the suspect list after a rooftop conversation during the last rounds.

Playing the game was an amazing once-in-a-lifetime experience, the ultimate game blending exploration, intrigue and a test of your own stamina - one that I will always remember. Life since the show has been great.

I am still involved with music.

Chapter XXIV

A Long, Long Wait

That last show revealed all the clues, how each of us had sabotaged multiple games, and how Darwin led almost everyone astray. Elavia finally realized how good her deceptiveness had been, and probably was also sitting there thinking that if she had just hung in there, she might have been walking away with the big money. Finally, Anderson revealed that had Elavia not taken the bribe in that 7th week, Dorothy had scored lowest on the quiz and would have been executed. Talk about a turn about! (I still sort of wish I had had the opportunity to be offered that $50,000 by Anderson instead of Elavia. What a lot of fun I could have had with that!)

Finally on clues. Hidden clues. Did you get them if you watched? I watched carefully, and don't think I got one! In the first episode they electronically augmented the stars in the sky above the mountain cabin so that the Picses constellation was visible...if you were watching very, very carefully. In all of the episodes the opening screen with "The Mole" on it had rapidly appearing letters coming and going. In one of them, if you had stop action, "Admiral" appeared, and in another, "Bill is the mole," appeared. In one episode immediately preceding the execution, plaques of 2 astrological signs were shown, one of which was mine, a Picses. The only picture ever shown during a quiz was of a naval vessel, indicating my background. In Anderson's Fun House 3 different pictures of sailing vessels were shown, indicating the same. Anderson was eating an apple in at least two episodes...the state fruit of Washington State, where I live. We wrote on dollar "bills" to list our favorite to least favorite players in the episode where Elavia took her bribe. An incredibly obscure clue was revealed in the second episode, in which the statement (attributed to the Mole) admonished players to stop "shmoozing the ladies," indicating that the mole was likely a male. Two different episodes referred to William Shakespeare, supposedly indicating me because of my name. And, the episode where we had a platter of "Mickey D's" burgers...i.e., McD...me! Finally, the telegram received from the Mole in Episode 4 had a series of numbers at the bottom; when those were matched up with the letters on a phone dial pad, the message was, "Bill is the mole." Now, the only people that I am aware of who got these were those folks who recorded the episodes and did phenomenal frame-by-frame studies of them. However, for most of us...we were clueless.

Now the long wait began. ABC apparently had no idea when they might air the show. Rumors abounded on the Internet, and the chat rooms were filled with Mole fans, many of whom had not even realized the show had started briefly. When would it air? We were told maybe January, then in January, maybe March. Nothing. Meanwhile, we were expected to talk to no one? Nor to each other? Hmmm.

In January I had to be in Austin for a business meeting, and, quite by accident (almost assuredly) ran into Bribs and Heather in a small bar downtown. They, of course, had run into each other by accident, also. Accidents do occur, after all. We sat and talked for a long while. I had been recognized by many people in my home town of Oak Harbor, WA, many of whom had actually seen the initial three episodes. Bribs, likewise, had been recognized by a few people. Heather bemoaned a little that not a person had ever recognized her as being on the show. Soon, she got up to go to the bathroom. I grabbed a passing woman of about thirty-five, explained what was going on, and arranged for her to "recognize" Heather.

Maybe 20 minutes later we were sitting quietly talking. The blonde woman passed our table, did a classic double take and came to a sudden halt.

"Heather! Heather! Is that you?"

Heather looked startled and turned around. "Well, yes, my name is Heather."

"From 'The Mole?' Are you really Heather from 'The Mole?"

Heather smiled, "Yes! I'm that Heather!"

Meanwhile the woman had grabbed Heather's hand, and started proclaiming, "I really loved you on that show. I mean, *really* loved you!" She continued to cling to Heather's hand, gazing steadily into Heather's eyes. Heather became somewhat uncomfortable and starting trying to extract her hand, to no avail. The woman hung on rather desperately, repeating her affections.

Heather turned to Bribs and me. "These two were on the show, also!" The woman glanced dismissively at us, then turned her full attention back on Heather.

"But I love you!"

Heather was getting a little frantic, and again turned toward us. By this time Bribs and I were laughing so hard that we were falling off our seats, and in a flash Heather realized what had happened.

"You bastards! I can't believe you did this!"

The woman turned loose, laughing, and we congratulated her on a wonderful performance. She did promise to watch the show if it ever aired.

So, time passed. We all emailed each other about rumors heard, and repeated any communications we had had with the producers or ABC word for word. The Mole message boards started getting morose, and fewer and fewer people were chiming in. So several of us got different screen names and started stirring the pot again, getting people worked up to forward emails and letters to ABC. Only one time on a message board did someone think I might be a player, and I just quit replying. No sense in messing with that big threat of a fine!

Finally we got the word that the show would air in the summer, beginning May 28, 2002. We had a good time slot, Tuesdays, and the only show up against us was an unknown show on Fox, called "The American Idol." Shoot, hopefully no one would watch a show with a lame title like that!

I headed back to the East Coast and hiked 400 more miles of the Appalachian Trail in May, finishing on the morning of 28 May. While hiking, I detoured into a small town after three weeks on the trail to get a few large cheeseburgers. I had not shaved in 3 weeks, hadn't bathed in about as long, and was still wearing the salt-encrusted clothes that I had begun that portion of the hike in. My mother would have had difficulty recognizing me. As I sat in a bar/restaurant, far away from everyone else, I felt a peculiar sensation. I looked around, and spied a mother and her 12 year old daughter eating on the far side of the restaurant. The girl had a fixed stare…on me. She wouldn't look away. Somewhat nervously I stuffed another cheeseburger or two down, only to realize that the two females were walking across the floor toward me.

The mother apologized. "I'm sorry, but my daughter swears she recognizes you."

I looked at the little girl. "So you think you know me?"

"Yes."

"Who do you think I am?"

"I **know** who you are! You're that old man on 'The Mole!"

I laughed. "How many times have you watched those three episodes?"

Her mother replied, "Maybe 20 times or so. She has been so upset that the show went off the air."

I reassured the two that "The Mole II" would be back on the air on May 28th. They left. I don't think the little girl was particularly thrilled at meeting "that old man." She just apparently felt vindicated that I was indeed who she said I was. I

Reflections of The Mole

sat back, bemused. Really, other than a few folks in my home town and a couple of relatives, no one had realized I had had a brief foray on television. Even my mother was not really sure I had been on TV yet!

On the evening of 28 May a bunch of recent graduates from the Harvard MBA program whom I had run into on the AT threw a big party in Boston for my debut. However, when even some of the recently anointed MBA graduates could not grasp the concept of the show, I began to fear for our audience! Besides that, several of them kept wanting to switch over to watch this American Idol show. Darn! I hoped that would not be a common occurrence! Unfortunately for us, it was! Here we get a good night, and are up against the hit of the summer! Ah, well, our fans…few though they were…seemed to love us. (I suspect they watched Idol and Tivo'd us!)

Well, the show did air. My wife and I traveled all over the country having parties every Tuesday night with friends, all of whom were assuming that week was my last; I could neither deny nor confirm that. The last two weeks were spent back in Oak Harbor partying with several hundred of our friends at a large Mexican restaurant, Mi Pueblo, which devoted itself to our evening. I was finally revealed as the Mole, somewhat to my children's disappointment, I think; they could already taste the money! And, my brother-in-law, Blair, is still a little ticked. Mom kept asking when I was going to get voted off; I don't think she watched. I suspect she was an "Idol" fan!

Following the conclusion of the season, all the players except Al and Patrick met in Las Vegas for 3 fun days, arriving only 2 days following the last show. For the first time, I suspect, most of us felt that maybe there *were* a lot of folks that watched. We were recognized and giving autographs about every 5 minutes for all three of the days. Delightful! We even got to be the "Good Morning Las Vegas!" folks. Of course, at 5:30 in the morning, few people were aware of that fact.

Some of us have gotten together several times since the show for skiing in Colorado (Now, you've seen Dorothy walk; you should see her on skis! The ski patrol kept one person stationed with us at all times...waiting.), and at various charity events where we have had the pleasure of meeting many other reality show contestants. Many of you have shown up in Cincinnati for Tasha's diabetes benefits, or in Toronto for the multiple events Magee, Jessica, and Liam put on for various Project Cool charities there. (These are very remarkable, very young people who put these events on. We are constantly amazed at their courage in taking on what would be a daunting task for any business person, and with their desire to make the world a better place if they can.) And, we visit one another when we are in the area. Darwin, Elavia, Dorothy and I have harassed poor Anderson until he was forced to take us out to dinner in NYC. We did note that he took us to a very dark restaurant and sat at an adjoining table, but at least he paid! (He was a delightful friend and host, actually.) Bribs and Roxie have been out to the Pacific Northwest and have gone hiking in the Hoh Rain Forest with me, but I was unable to convince them that our part of the country is any more delightful than Austin. We have talked recently about all trying to get together again, but it's unlikely. Time does march on. I'm very proud of having a peer group of such young and delightful friends!

I suspect all shows have devoted fans; however, I can only speak for the incredible devotion Mole fans have shown. I continue to get emails from many of them, even today. I was in Toronto for my 3rd event with Project Cool in August, 2007, again meeting with rabid Mole fans who keep demanding to know when the show will air again! In the summer of 2003 I received a call from one of the Internet Mole groups; the woman, Carol, who had been the primary focus of the group had invited all of them to New York City for 5 nights at the Waldorf Astoria, Broadway plays, dinners, and just to get to know each other in person. She told me that she would extend the same offer to any of us who would show up and surprise the group. Seven of us went; Shirley and I had a delightful time with this devoted group of fans, many of whom we still correspond with today.

I would like to report that many of us received hefty contracts for commercials and speaking engagements. I would like to report that, but it would be another molish' fib. While there have been significant changes in some of our lives, the changes are of our choosing, not secondary to anything that happened on the show. Heather got married, but not to Nathan. Patrick has made a few commercials, but was working on that before he was on the show. He hasn't communicated with anyone since shortly after the show aired. Lisa still prosecutes folks in Chicago, though she recently quit her dream job as beer salesman in Comiskey Park. She runs in the Urban Challenge races...in which she beats all the men! Maybe I was lucky I didn't really engage her on that log! Heather and Elavia both worked for the same company for a while, and still get together occasionally. Bribs is still in Austin, has his own company and is still doing his art, and has a great girlfriend. Darwin continues as a corporate attorney, though I expect he still would rather be in show business. Katie quit teaching, and now has another job and proudly drives a new PT Cruiser convertible. (I suspect her students found out about her jelly phobia and made her life miserable!) Katie has lost a significant amount of weight; the next time on that bungee cord she will give her true weight immediately! Bob is still a financial counselor, and is still smiling. Rob has moved to LA and does professional videos. He swears he has given up magic; I hope not. Ali worked as a nurse some, took acting classes and tried some acting, but now is a television reporter, finally getting air time! She has the looks and personality to make it, I believe. And obviously I'm not prejudiced. Myra, dear Myra, still lives in San Diego, flying and laughing, recently getting married to her long-time boyfriend,

Vic, another Delta pilot. Shirley and I visit them occasionally. Al is still on Long Island working as a foreman in a warehouse. What a talented individual he is, and is truly one of the nicest people I know. And Dorothy still lives in New York City, playing in her band at various clubs, dreaming of a Top 10 CD.

So there we are.

Me? I was approached shortly after the season to see if I would do a show called "Street Smarts." While I initially said I would do so, Shirley and I watched it a couple of times and just decided it wasn't me. I received a couple of calls from agents who told me that living on an island barely within the continental United States was a detriment to a continuing show business career. If I would move to Los Angeles or New York City they *might* be able to oblige me with a commercial or two. Didn't seem like a sane thing to do.

So, I'm still in Washington State, still travel a lot, and finished the 2174 mile Appalachian Trail in October of 2004. I wrote the majority of this book around that time, and left in January 2005 for Banda Aceh, where I was hired by the US Navy to help with the tsunami aftermath. After 3 months living and helping there, I've given about 80 talks over the last 2 years on that most memorable experience. I can't think of anything more meaningful than that. In 2006 I helped two friends sail a 53' sailboat from Hawaii to San Diego...not a task for the weak of heart, nor the clumsy and slow of thought! You can find me this summer of 2007 hiking the Oregon portion of the Pacific Crest Trail.

Oh, yes! Anderson! Well, you all know where he is. What a great newscaster he is! I think he is the best on television, and claim to speak with no bias. We all love to watch him, and look him up when we are in New York City. He is always gracious, and swears he remembers us! Shoot, see! I told you we might be famous some day!

Reflections of The Mole

Bill McDaniel
Bill McDaniel
Rear Admiral/USN/retired
The MOLE II

Please check out the web site for additional insights, and for the audio version of this book.

www.TheMoleBook.com

Made in the USA
Monee, IL
16 January 2022